ATTACHMENT
AND
DEPENDENCY

ATTACHMENT AND DEPENDENCY

Edited by

Jacob L. Gewirtz
Chief, Section on Early Learning and Development
Laboratory of Psychology
National Institute of Mental Health

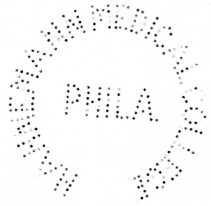

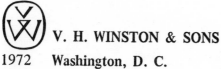

V. H. WINSTON & SONS
1972   Washington, D. C.

DISTRIBUTED BY THE HALSTED PRESS DIVISION OF

JOHN WILEY & SONS
New York   Toronto   London   Sydney

V. H. Winston & Sons, Inc., Publishers
1511 K Street, N.W., Washington, D.C. 20005

Distributed solely by Halsted Press Division, John Wiley & Sons, Inc., New York.

ISBN 0-470-29709-3

Library of Congress Catalog Card Number: 72-6913

Printed in the United States of America

CONTRIBUTORS

Mary D. S. Ainsworth
Robert B. Cairns
Jacob L. Gewirtz
Robert R. Sears
Leon J. Yarrow

CONTENTS

PREFACE

Some time ago, while surveying the field of object relations, I concluded that having a critical discussion of that topic would be of considerable value. Hence, I approached several theorist-researchers of human social development who have written extensively on object relations under the headings of *attachment* and/or *dependency* (dependence). Some of these theorists have also been involved in occasional exchanges in the literature. Through the years, the writings and reports of the theorists to whom I turned have done much to set the tone for the systematic research that has been carried out under one or both of these conceptions.

The envisioned discussion was to include a comprehensive treatment of attachment and dependency as conceptualized by each theorist, as well as a consideration of the utility of a distinction between those constructs. The objective was for each participant to define concepts and issues from his particular viewpoint, and to delineate clearly his or her conceptual posture. At the same time, the participants were asked to avoid arguments that might be based only on differences in style, in the tactics of research, or in the choice of a heuristic. This volume is the result.

The phenomena grouped under the terms attachment and dependency have come to provide a central focus in diverse approaches to social development. Yet those terms have often been used in divergent ways. While these two constructs share some of the same origins, they appear to have evolved in separate ways, partly insulated from each other. Thus, the work carried out under the attachment and dependency terms has often centered around different purposes and problems, species and age spans of subjects, research procedures, and behavior systems and criteria. Also, the terms have sometimes served as labels for: (*a*) a developmental *process* (or processes), (*b*) the *outcomes* or end points of that process (or processes), or (*c*) process *and* outcome simultaneously. Disagreements between theoretical approaches to these phenomena which may seem fundamental can often be traced to theorists' preferences for alternative paradigms. Hence, even when they are focused on the very same events, alternative conceptual approaches may on occasion seem aimed at organizing very different phenomena. For reasons such as these, and because the attachment and dependency terms have been employed in varied, often overlapping, ways to deal with a wide range of issues, the task set for the contributors to this volume seems timely.

In this framework, each contributor has outlined his or her approach to the phenomena and conceptions of attachment and dependency. The utility of a distinction between the concepts has also been considered. The theorists have approached their task by detailing the assumptions and factors each of them conceives to be most important and relevant, taking into account the history of thought and research in the object relations area, as well as in fields other than human development and socialization. The six chapters that follow can thus stand as working statements about attachment and dependency phenomena, couched in the heuristic terms each theorist prefers.

A final note about the procedure followed in preparing these chapters can provide additional perspective for the reader. The contributors had opportunities at one seminar and, less formally, at other times to discuss early drafts of each of their chapters. Moreover, while editing the chapters, I discussed successive chapter versions with each contributor. Hence, it was perhaps inevitable that the contributions have drawn together on some conceptual points. However, at the same time, some of the approaches to, and assumptions about, the issues that continue to separate the contributors have become better delineated. (A possible weakness of this process is that the editor's own chapters very likely required far more surgical editing than the editor could provide. *Caveat lector*!)

I think that the attempts that appear in this volume to organize diverse phenomena under the concepts of attachment and dependency constitute advances in the conceptualization of object relations. At the very least, they can serve as catalysts for theoretical and research developments pertaining to attachment and dependency.

Jacob L. Gewirtz*

*Dr. Gewirtz has edited and contributed to this volume in his private capacity. No official support or endorsement by the Public Health Service is intended, nor should such support or endorsement be inferred.

ATTACHMENT
AND
DEPENDENCY

ATTACHMENT, DEPENDENCY, AND FRUSTRATION[1]

Robert R. Sears

Stanford University

Introduction

In spite of the substantial research literature on both dependency and attachment which has developed within the last 20 years (cf. Maccoby & Masters, 1970), these two concepts are still tangled in definitional confusion. The reasons are historical, and a brief chronology of dependency theory may help in the untangling.

Influenced by some of Freud's incompletely developed notions concerning mother-infant relationships, Murray (1938) proposed a motivational construct, *n Succorance,* to account for a class of infant behaviors that included crying and pleading for nourishment, love, aid, and protection. Freud's emphasis on orality as an important element in the child's motivational system was clearly reflected in Murray's conception, at least with respect to early ontogenesis. Since Murray was also concerned with young adult behavior, *n* Succorance was by no means limited to oral strivings, but referred more broadly to a general need for support, nurturance, sympathy, love, and attention.

Following a somewhat similar line of reasoning, Whiting (1944) proposed a construct of *dependency* within the then-current Yale framework of learning theory (Miller & Dollard, 1941) and frustration or action theory (Dollard, Doob, Miller, Mowrer, & Sears, 1939). Dependency was viewed as an acquired drive for which the primary reinforcements came from feeding and other forms of infant

[1] Financial support was received from a Ford Foundation Grant for a study of child development, and from an NIH Fellowship taken at the Center for Advanced Study in the Behavioral Sciences.

caretaking. Whiting's main emphasis was on dependent behavior as a reaction to frustration. My own first theoretical statement (Sears, 1948) followed directly from Whiting's position, but with focus on the acquired drive as a determinant of learning and goal-directed action.

Clearly, the Freudian emphasis on infant orality influenced the development of dependency theory. To learning and action theorists, the infant's need for oral gratification offered a convenient hypothetical primary drive antecedent for the learning of help-seeking and other forms of child behavior for which the giving of aid, care, reassurance, comfort, and attention were the appropriate parental responses. With additional data, it was even a simple matter to reinterpret "oral need" itself as a "secondary oral drive" (cf. Davis, Sears, Miller, & Brodbeck, 1948; Sears & Wise, 1950), and hence ultimately to derive the hypothesized dependency drive from feeding reinforcements.

In retrospect, these views seem extraordinarily limited, even archaic. They did serve, however, to embed an important sector of little-examined behavior in the pervasive learning theory of the day (Hull, 1943; Dollard & Miller, 1950). The result of even a limited theory is to activate research. The secondary drive theory did this. In its successive elaborations it stimulated much naturalistic investigation of child-rearing antecedents (Sears, Whiting, Nowlis, & Sears, 1953; Sears, Maccoby, & Levin, 1957; Sears, Rau, & Alpert, 1965; and cf. Becker, 1964) and virtually all of the experimental study of satiation, deprivation, and arousal or anxiety as these relate to dependency (cf. Maccoby & Masters, 1970). Nevertheless, its heuristic value, for dependency, has disappeared along with the original form of the Hullian learning theory of which it was a part. One can only hope that the gradually emerging new theories of dependency and attachment will be equally fertile in spawning research.

In short, the elaborated dependency theory of 2 decades ago was developed in the context of an action and learning theory which was attempting to derive later social behavior and personality from a child's prior learning experiences. In the process various Freudian concepts were converted to behavioral analogues. Secondary drive was an inherent part of that theory, and the psychoanalytic emphasis on oral development made an easy juncture with the theoretical formulation of primary drive reinforcement, especially for a generation of developmental psychologists who were more accustomed to working with such concepts as hunger drive than with those more immediately related to the complex dyadic behavior of human infants. In this connection, it is worth noting that an actual study of the *learning* of smiling in infants did not appear until Brackbill (1958) published her paper on reinforcement and extinction, and even she did not relate her work to dependency theory at the time.

The key to the present controversy over dependency and attachment lies not so much in the outmoded secondary drive interpretation, however, as in the operations chosen by early investigators to define and measure dependency. Starting with the conception of the helpless infant's seeking food and other necessaries of life from the relatively omnipotent mother, they looked for examples of behavior which seemed to exemplify such striving. The theoretical concern was with the development of help-seeking and attention-seeking, not with the love relationship between mother and infant. Since the available research subjects for most early investigators were preschool-aged children (Baldwin, 1949; Sears et al., 1953; Heathers, 1955; Gewirtz, 1956; Kagan & Moss, 1962), the measurement operations sought, and adopted, were ones appropriate to help-seeking at that age and in the social context of the preschool. Even among researchers from different laboratories, there was considerable similarity in the categories of social behavior selected. These included seeking to be near, touching and holding, asking for help, comfort, or reassurance, and seeking attention by positive or negative means. Essentially, these observable behaviors were interpreted as representing the class of appropriate actions to secure help, aid, comfort, and attention from others. The *need* for—or the *drive* to obtain—such outcomes was the hypothesized antecedent to dependent action.

The occurrence of such behavior, even when directed toward other children rather than to an adult (teacher), was conceived as a response mediated by stimulus generalization from an original learning situation in which the mother was the primary reinforcer. The generalization operated with respect not only to the stimulus person but also to the particular needs for help in an instrumental sense. That is, the initial reinforcement was supposed to be provided by the mother, the need for help in getting food being the need for which instrumentation was required. Once formed, however, the hierarchy of dependency responses could be evoked for other needs as well—reaching something, moving a heavy object, tying a knot—and by other persons. Later, with the formation of attention-seeking itself, the same process of stimulus generalization was supposed to operate.

Useful as these categories may have been, however, they derived from a conception that seems less coherent today than it did 20 years ago. The validity of any such class, subsumed under a label like *dependency,* rests not only on its utility in leading to predictable research findings, but also on the empirical question of whether by some criterion the members of the class are systematically related to one another. The record has proved only moderately satisfactory. Empirical evidence has thrown doubt on the unitariness of the single construct supposedly represented by these operational definitions. While an obtained matrix of positive correlations among their frequencies is not the only validity criterion to be considered (Sears et al., 1965, pp. 68-71), it is an important one. On this the findings are painfully clear. For girls, there is only a very modest coherence (Kagan & Moss, 1962; Sears et al., 1965), and for boys there is none. What is also fairly clear is that for both sexes the frequencies of the two more general categories—proximity-seeking and attention-seeking—are quite unrelated to one another. So far there are no research data to test other possible criteria, e.g., substitutability of one category for another under conditions of constant stimulation.

The original choice of operational definitions—i.e., the particular categories—was more heavily influenced by the initial (vague) theory of the variables conditioning dependency's development than was apparent at the time. The initial hypotheses which seemed important to test were those which related the strength of the presumed drive to parental child-rearing attitudes and practices. The first studies were naturalistic ones designed to discover, by correlation, the relation between such practices and the amount of dependency behavior (inferred to be determined by the strength of the drive) shown by the children. In consequence, the validity of the concept itself rested heavily on expected confirmation of the specific antecedent-consequent hypotheses. Since none of the original orality hypotheses have been reliably confirmed (Sears et al., 1965, p. 70), the theoretical foundations of the operational definition of dependency were somewhat shaken.

As an historical footnote, it is wryly amusing to recall that in selecting Freud's emphasis on orality as a basis for hypotheses concerning antecedents, the early theorists ignored his more cogent concept of cathexis. Had this affectional concept been taken into account, no doubt attachment would have reared its head sooner among American behavioral theorists. Also, perhaps the distinction between proximity-seeking and attention-seeking would have been made a priori rather than as a result of exhaustive and exhausting empirical investigation. Another set of behaviors that was ignored was that relating to peer interactions. Because the early theoretical focus was on parental child-rearing, sheer social play and other reflections of peer friendship or affiliation were left out of the definitional statements about dependency. These, too, might have led sooner to attachment.

The two above-mentioned failures to find empirical support for the dependency construct—as defined in terms of the behavior categories heretofore used—require us to reexamine this area of behavior and search for new conceptualizations. Attachment has already proved very promising indeed; it has a special value here in that it subsumes the proximity-seeking categories formerly included in dependency. The relative coherence of attention-seeking behaviors suggests the possibility that they also may be considered as belonging to some higher level construct that can be introduced usefully into an antecedent-consequent model. Other candidates will be presented in a later section.

Part of the difficulty with any higher level construct derives from the fact of multidetermination of the actions which represent it. A given bit of behavior may serve to express more than one motive or be directed to securing more than one kind of reinforcement. Just as *negative attention-seeking* appears to be a fusion of aggressive action with a seeking for responsiveness from the other person, so certain of the observational categories of dependency seem to fuse attachment behavior with a similar seeking. In particular, this seems to be the case with *touching and holding, being near,* and *seeking comfort* or *reassurance.* To the extent that these behaviors are elicited (in part) by different internal instigational systems, to that extent they fail to serve usefully as indices of any one.

It must be added quickly, to avoid further confusion, that such a statement does not contain any lingering assumption of differentiable acquired drives serving as internal instigation, but simply that many different internal properties of the person—such as sets, cognitive maps, the outcome of reasoning, expectancies, frustration- or conflict-induced instigation, deprivation, physiological states, and special states of readiness-to-respond resulting from genetic bias—determine the *meaning* to him of the external instigators (including people) which impinge on him and serve to elicit a response. If there can be shown to be universality in the nature of some of these sources of internal instigation—e.g., expectancy of securing attention—it should be possible to define the ensuing behavior in such a way as to provide concepts at a higher level of abstraction than that of single responses.

The Utility of Higher Level Concepts

Such concepts as attachment and dependency (and many others, e.g., aggression, achievement, nurturance, etc.) have been widely used in both psychoanalytic and behavioral theories of personality. Little consideration seems to have been given to the reasons for their adoption. Recent developments in stimulus-response learning theory (Gewirtz, 1969), and critical examination of evidence concerning the clustering of such behaviors (Mischel, 1968), have raised a question as to whether such concepts are, indeed, even useful or justifiable. Since I will propose some modifications in the concept of dependency—but not its abolition—the utility and nature of such higher level concepts needs comment.

Gewirtz (1961, 1967, 1969) has described the process by which the child's repertoire of actions will be determined by the elaborate interplay of excitation, inhibition, discrimination, shaping, and fading to which he is subjected by all the environmental agencies of reinforcement and extinction that operate in his stimulus-response universe.

The child's action systems are therefore unique, and at first blush we seem left with but two alternatives. One is to use such principles for engineering children's behavior in response to external control. The other is to develop an idiographic psychological science, in which the only regularities to be discovered are those within the behavior of a single organism. Neither of these alternatives is appealing; the first limits the use of the theory to interventional purposes, and the second lacks sufficient generality to make it useful in any but an "understanding" context.

The engineering use of learning is suitable for large-scale teaching carried out by experts or preprogrammed machines. There is little hope that average parents could ever become sufficiently skilled—or be in sufficient control of their child's environment—to use a complex learning theory for rearing children. An exact and detailed learning theory is like the machine language of a computer; only the experts know it even exists. The great bulk of computer users work with

FORTRAN or PL/I or some other highly simplified language of entrance and control into the computer.

Hence, from the learning theory standpoint some consideration must be given to the chaining or patterning process by which small response units are combined into larger ones. No one seems to have examined in detail the conditions under which, for example, a winning smile, an outstretched arm, and a murmured vocal expression get combined into a single unit of behavior that constitutes a "pick me up and love me" action which, in turn, is a stimulus to a mother's reaction. Yet it is just such combinations of action that come to form the repertoire of a child's supplicative behavior.

This chaining of segments into wholes doubtless depends on a number of processes and conditions. Most obviously, the withholding of reinforcement until the child completes a particular sequence of actions will provide discriminative learning. Then labeling, after language has developed, can provide a representation of the total action as contrasted with its parts; the total supplicative action becomes chained with the labeling action. Expectancies of ultimate reinforcement can serve as constant internal instigation to accompany the continuously varying response-produced cues and external instigation that accompany the performance of the sequence.

Within such a total unit there is considerable substitutability of segments. The outstretched arms can outstretch from many different positions, and the vocalization is rarely the same twice. Response generalization is a commonly used term to refer to what must be a very complex process by which a hierarchy of alternative segments are connected with one another. Whatever the mechanism, the fact must be faced that almost all behavior is composed of large molar units that are never identical on successive elicitations. To pretend that, in any precise form, a given action can be reinforced even twice is to ignore this high variability.

In hypothesizing any general class of behavior, we are doing no more than specifying a larger chained action with larger numbers of substitutable segments. With respect to some subvariety of what was formerly called dependency, for example, "asking to be picked up" is but one of many chained actions that form a still larger unit that includes asking someone to "help me get the ball," "help me get my stroller unstuck from the carpet," "play with me," or "start that mobile swinging again." In the case of any one of these actions, the external stimulation, the internal sources of instigation, and the actual qualities of the available manipulanda determine which of many available segments will be called into play and unified into the action. To hypothesize a dependency class of behavior is simply to assert that the same principles hold true for the larger class (dependency), including, as segments, such a group of differentiable actions as those suggested above. A similar conception characterizes all the other higher level classes of behaviors, e.g., attachment, aggression, competition, achievement, and so on.

The principles Gewirtz has described (1969) seem quite able to account for the establishment not only of molecular actions but also of more molar actions, and the question arises as to how these larger conceptualized bundles of responses can be formed, bundles like dependency and attachment. Provisionally, an answer may be given by reference to the same conditions that chain simple movements into full-blown actions, namely, labeling and the formation of expectancies. But in place of the condition that specifies the delay of reinforcement to the end of the chain of movements, another must be hypothesized, namely, that there is an overriding consistency in the reinforcing behavior of the parent (or other agent) such that great classes of responses (e.g., exhibitionistic ones) are reinforced or ignored or punished. If this substitution is made, the explanatory mechanism is taken out of the range of the learning theory itself, of course, and is placed in the realm of the *conditions* of learning.

The suppositions either that the behavior of each child is unique, or that the pattern of reinforcements he receives has no consistency from one occasion to another, are not useful. The cognitive processes of adults—and even of quite young children—lead to generalizations about the outcome of past actions. Such conclusions then lead to decisions concerning the probable consequences of either (*a*) repeating the actions, or (*b*) changing them, on the outcomes expectable on future occasions. The language structures in all societies provide for more than molecular conceptualizations of the self's conduct, and hence lay the bases both for consistency and for the utilization of higher level constructs of behavior.

These comments are especially germane to the problem of *individual differences*, for which higher level constructs are required on the antecedent as well as the consequent side of the equation. So far, univariate analyses of the effects of warmth, punitiveness, and other such conceptualizations of parental behavior, have provided evidence for a few consistent (i.e., replicated) relationships with child behavior, but these are mainly of small size, in terms of amount of variance for which they account. Obviously, some new strategies are required if we are to get beyond the level of theoretical precision—and of behavioral prediction—represented by the level of $p \leqslant .01$ to $\leqslant .05$ common to correlational studies of child rearing and to experimental studies of modeling, satiation, frustration, separation, reunion, etc.

Two considerations must be kept in mind in searching for new strategies. One is that the specific stimulus conditions associated with a particular response must be included as part of the definition of the stimulus—response unit. While the trait concept cannot be altogether discarded, it has not so far proved as useful as one might wish for such large constructs as dependency, aggression, masculinity, achievement, or other personality qualities. With respect to the former concept of dependency, for example, such a higher level concept as "seeking positive attention" seems to have greater internal consistency as a descriptive term applying differentially to amounts of observed behavior in a nursery school than does the broader, more inclusive term (Heathers, 1955; Gewirtz, 1956; Sears et al., 1965). It seems not unlikely that due attention to the stimulus conditions, and to the reinforcement schedule related to each kind of action, would provide more precise predictions as to when, how often, and with what intensity a given action would occur. An example of close mother-child interaction analysis is the study by Bishop (1951), who recorded a running account of the mother's and child's behavior, and analyzed the child's behavior with respect to specific maternal stimulations.

The second consideration relates specifically to antecedent-consequent developmental research. Although there has been wide recognition of the dyadic character of children's development, relatively little research has employed methods that permit a study of the interactive influences between the child and his mother (or other reinforcers). As Bell (1968) has emphasized, children influence the parents' behavior by the same action and learning principles as the parents influence children's. Hence, to discover regularities in a child's personality development, it may be necessary to study the parents' development also. One recent example of the effort to measure maternal and child behavior simultaneously in a search for correspondences between maternal reinforcements (or other qualities of her behavior) and her child's behavior with respect to relevant actions is the mother-child interaction study by Hatfield, Ferguson, and Alpert (1967). Using a circumplex model, they compared the qualities of mothers and children displayed in the quadrants of the model. This procedure places emphasis on single variables, of course, and does not disclose the specific character of any one mother-child dyad.

To summarize: there is some clustering of certain dependency behaviors in young children. Given our current understanding of how the learning of such behavior occurs, a reasonable hypothesis is that the consistency of the *reinforcing agent* determines such clustering. If so, we have been on a too limited track in some of our research on child-rearing antecedents. Even studies of overt mother-child interaction, under controlled laboratory conditions, have tended to emphasize such variables as warmth, permissiveness, and other global attitudinal qualities that do not accurately reflect the really relevant variables, i.e., the contingencies of reinforcement and the precise behavior being reinforced. More detailed studies must be made of actual behavioral events in the mother-child interaction if we are to understand the complicated matter of dependency behavior structure, especially in the first 2 years. The use of higher level concepts will be essential, however, if we are not to be left with a purely idiographic science dealing only with the molecular actions of single children. The dyadic quality of the learning situation requires that careful consideration be given not only to the stimulus and reinforcement qualities of the parents, but also to the reciprocal influence of children on parents.

Dependency

In light of the above comments, further use of the term *dependency* as a higher level construct seems unwise. Its original operational definition included too many kinds of behavior. In the present context the word is used only as a convenient heading to indicate the general realm of behaviors under discussion, those involving a child's help-seeking and another person's help-giving. It refers to the setting in which secondary behavior systems can be developed. To the extent that it refers to a kind of behavior, what has been called instrumental dependency is the substance. Postulating any higher level construct is worthwhile if there is a quasi-theoretical reason for believing that some set of actions is ordinarily chained together, as common responses to some recurring stimulus situation, with an expectancy of some recurring reinforcer as an outcome from the dyadic partner. Whether such a postulate will prove useful can be determined only empirically.

The long period of helplessness in the human infant and child—in many respects lasting about one-sixth of the total life span—requires the development of an elaborate set of help-seeking behaviors. These are paralleled in the behavioral repertoire of the dyadic partners by help-giving reciprocals. Commonly the child's actions have been called *succorant* or *dependent,* and the partners' *nurturant.*

Since there is no certainty as to exactly what constitutes the initial catalogue of requirements for the human infant's comfort—no list of reinforcers that are universally sought—we can only hazard a guess (educated by naturalistic observation) about the kinds of supplicative actions that are established first. The clear persistence of hyperactivity and of crying in the absence of food's being given suggests that securing help in allaying hunger is an early form of dependent activity. Doubtless the other bodily needs are similarly influential. Equally prominent in the first few weeks of life are the seeming search for repetition of certain visual stimuli, and its opposite, the search for novelty. Infants who have had experience with tactile stimulation in the form of cuddling and snuggling appear to perform actions that reproduce such behavior by the caretaker, and within a very few months, or even weeks, evident efforts to secure help in overcoming obstacles to mastery of the immediate physical environment can be observed. In motivational language, the early months of life give indications of activity the outcome of which is to provide help from others in satisfying not only the various organic needs but also the less well-defined motives of mastery of the immediate physical environment, curiosity, body contact, and locomotion.

Associated with help-giving by the dyadic partner are various subsidiary behavioral characteristics. It is difficult to give help without orienting oneself toward the child, i.e., giving attention. And whatever may be the ontogenetics of smiling, human beings almost always smile (or frown) and usually talk when responding to supplications. These actions, whether necessary or not, inevitably become secondary reinforcers (if they are not already in some degree primary) and are part of the nurturant pattern of parental behavior sought by the child.

The postulate of dependency has been that the various supplicative actions are organized into a response hierarchy in which one can substitute for another in securing a wide range of responses from the partner that are perceived as similar and equivalent. The position of a given action in the hierarchy at any specific moment is a function of the appropriateness of external stimulation and of internal states (e.g., expectancies), and these in turn are a product of the whole history of scheduled reinforcements and nonreinforcements.

One of our major concerns with such behavior is the range of individual differences in style and strength, strength being understood to be measurable by frequency, intensity, duration, or resistance to extinction. While these measures are by no means perfectly correlated with one another, the differences between them probably being a product of differences in the learning history, they represent different facets of a quantitative aspect of behavior that is well recognized by any observer and is of great importance to any description of the differences among people. With young children, for example, there are moderately consistent differences in the frequency of positive attention-getting actions, some children showing a good many in the nursery school and others showing relatively few. Again, some children can be turned away rather easily if the mother indicates she is busy, while others persist indefinitely and with increasing irritability to demand help or attention. These are the types of variation in style and strength toward which the search for child-rearing antecedents is directed.

Exemplary assertions like the above have a certain face validity from the uncontrolled observations of daily experience, but hard data substantiating such consistent behavioral qualities are not easy to find. Maccoby and Masters (1970) have made an exhaustive review of the relevant literature, securing much of the original and unpublished data from several researchers to permit more cogent analyses. There are no more than a dozen studies that can be cited with reference to the issue of consistency. In general, the conclusions to be drawn from their review are: (*a*) there is a moderate consistency in frequency and/or intensity of certain categories of dependency behavior when these are measured on separate occasions in children of approximately the same developmental level; (*b*) the correlations are clearly higher the closer the measures are in time and the more precisely the stimulus conditions are limited; and (*c*) the correlations *among* certain of the self-consistent categories approach zero and in some cases are significantly negative, proximity-seeking and attention-seeking being two prime examples.

The first two conclusions support the position I have taken that there are clusters of actions, ones which are seemingly representative of a help- and attention-seeking higher level construct for which one may reasonably seek higher level antecedents in the reinforcements of child-rearing. The third conclusion supports my initial contention that the particular categories of action that we have commonly accepted as the operational measures of dependency do not, in fact, represent a useful delimitation of such a unitary concept. It seems clear that further detailed research is required to determine the exact nature of those actions to be studied under one or several labels.

Evidence so far in hand suggests that *attention*—i.e., a dyadic partner's noninstrumental interaction with and orientation toward the child—is one general kind of reinforcer that begins to be effective quite early in infancy, perhaps by the end of the third month. For convenience, let me call the child Alpha, and his dyadic partner (a parent, sibling, teacher, playmate, etc.) Beta. Developmentally, Beta's attention-giving to Alpha gradually changes in form and style as Alpha grows older, his new cognitive or intellective capacities requiring or permitting different behaviors which stimulate him. The simple smiles and murmured baby-talk that appeal to the 6-month-old are not likely to be appropriate for a vigorous 3-year-old. As Beta's style of attention-giving reinforcement changes, in response to Alpha's developing interests and capacities, so do Beta's expectations of behavioral maturity in Alpha. The kind of simple restlessness or crying or gurgling that elicits a parent's attention-giving when an infant is a few months old is insufficient to elicit the new kinds of attention appropriate as a reinforcer for the 3-year-old child. This is not to say that early forms of either supplication by Alpha or attention-giving by a particular Beta are relinquished in any magical fashion, or without some of the strain that goes with any developmental behavior change which results from shaping and fading processes. These processes are fundamentally based on reinforcement and nonreinforcement, and the latter inevitably produces some frustration. Nevertheless, the changes do occur—and provide a serious difficulty for the researcher who wishes to measure the consistency of attention-seeking behavior from one age to another (cf. Kagan & Moss, 1962).

The particular actions used by Alpha for gaining attention on any given occasion will be determined by the history of reinforcements for each of his hierarchy of responses, the nature of the stimulus situation at the moment, and the character of concurrent internal instigation. A number of studies have shown that various combinations of social deprivation and anxiety have facilitative or inhibitory effects on the frequency of bids for attention; and others have shown that a history of high positive reinforcement is associated with a high emission rate. Still others have shown that immediate delay of reinforcement—as in a "mother busy" situation—or a history of high frustration of attention-getting behavior, tends to produce negative attention-getting actions.

The changes in the specific behavioral content of the dyadic interaction relating to attention, however, do not seem to be as great as the changes involving actual help-seeking or help-giving. The latter interactions are strictly instrumental, their content depending on the type of accomplishment the child is striving for, the setting in which help-seeking occurs, the nature of the manipulanda involved, the parental resources for helping, and so on. There is a vast difference between the physical help provided in the bodily care of the infant and the problem-solving or informational help given the 5-year-old who has begun to ask questions and to reason about the movements of the sun and moon. The help given is appropriate to the help needed; what is asked for by the child is in style and content what will serve to evoke the needed help from the parent. For both Alpha and Beta these responses appear and disappear, some being kept in easily accessible storage and others being placed in such remote storage that only a situation producing severe regression can call them into use.

What makes attention-getting a good candidate for a higher level construct is that, regardless of the kind of behavior which constitutes help-giving, Beta is always oriented toward and in communicative interaction with Alpha during the nurturing (helping) process. Indeed, any subsidiary or associated behaviors that accompany genuine help-seeking behaviors may be nondiscriminably reinforced and thus create a repertoire of actions which do not have immediate help-seeking intent (i.e., for which there is no expectancy of nurturance or help) but which will occur whenever internal instigation for seeking help is aroused. Such internal instigation may be no more precise than a "feeling of helplessness." Obviously, too, external cues commonly associated with help-giving can serve the same function (e.g., the appearance of a parent, teacher, or older sibling). Any fortuitously-associated responses (e.g., thumb-sucking, touching the caretaker) may persist indefinitely, if they are reinforced simultaneously with instrumental help-seeking, unless the caretaker discriminates between instrumental help-seeking behaviors and mere associated actions, responding discriminatively to them by reinforcing one and extinguishing the other.

In this connection it is interesting to note the age changes in object-choices for securing attention. From three through five, there is a clear shift from adult to child objects when naturalistic observations are made in nursery school settings. If it is assumed that adults provide the major source of help during the first 2 years (in most segments of American culture), then it is not surprising that by stimulus generalization adults other than parents would initially be sought not only for actual help-giving but also for the secondary reinforcer of attention-giving. As a child gets older, however, he finds himself more and more involved in interaction with peer group members who, in turn, are increasingly able to provide some forms of real help and especially attention-giving. Since in the nursery school there are normally many more children than adults, the combination of such direct reinforcement with whatever influence may derive from generalization apparently leads to greater and greater dependence on children as objects of attention-seeking through the nursery school years.

Another kind of higher level construct which may be useful is *seeking admiration or approval.* In the course of early development, even well into middle childhood, a child progresses rapidly through new learning tasks, many of them representing conventional manipulative, cognitive, and language skills. In addition, however, there are social skills, often much less well-defined or labeled, but of considerable importance to parents. When a child performs well, meeting his parents' expectations, he is likely to receive not only orienting reactions from them but also smiles, caresses, verbal admiration, and celebration of success. To the extent that different parents have different goals and expectations for their children, to that extent the repertoire of actions any one child learns to perform is unique. But to the extent that the process of accomplishing new developmental tasks is universal, and parental reinforcement is provided by observable approving or admiring actions, to that extent there is the possibility of the development of a generalized set of behaviors in the child which might be called *seeking admiration*. The role of such learning in the development of achievement motivation, also, should not be overlooked.

In suggesting that Beta's orientations toward the child, or expressions of admiration for his behavior, become secondary reinforcers, I do not mean to imply that there is no direct reinforcement for the child's supplicative or attention-seeking or exhibitionistic actions that produce Beta's responses. On the contrary, as the child gains new talents, or discovers that Beta also responds to being attended to, he can select behavior from his repertoire that will insure direct reinforcement. Thus, while the accompaniment of Beta's orientation-toward-the-child with her actual help-giving may be the vehicle for establishing and shaping Alpha's attention-seeking and creating Beta's reinforcement-by-orientation, the continuation and further development of such behavior is very likely the product of direct reinforcement by other secondary reinforcers besides sheer orientation or admiration.

The above discussions of attention- and admiration-seeking illustrate what I meant by a "quasi-theoretical reason" for hypothesizing higher level constructs about behavior. In the context of the general theory of learning, it is possible to conceive of certain generalities in the nature of the child's actions, the expectations and goals of the parents, and the consequent stability of scheduled reinforcers. Whether, in fact, such constructs as the ones here proposed prove useful, in the sense of seeming to describe some actual action system in children, can only be determined empirically.

Attachment

Attachment is quite different from dependency. It appears to be a process by which a single Beta—the main caretaker in early infancy—attains preeminent status as a love object. As yet there are no data to indicate whether she acquires unusually high potentiality for reinforcing the child's actions, or whether the love relationship is qualitatively unique and perhaps irrelevant to the learning process. The former seems the more reasonable hypothesis in the light of the kinds of actions customarily seen in the child's behavior toward his object. As this has been described by Bowlby (1969), Ainsworth (1967), Heinicke (1956), Heinicke and Westheimer (1966), and others, the infant smiles frequently at her, attempts to keep her as nearly as possible in continuous sight and sound, searches for her visually and auditorally when she is absent, and shows signs of distress (separation anxiety) when she leaves him and of joy and delight when he is reunited with her. This last behavior may be tinctured with temporary resentment, an indication of the ambivalence he seemingly feels because she originally frustrated his love by leaving. These various actions, which constitute the repertoire belonging to the higher level construct of attachment behavior, suggest the operation of very strong instigation to maintain contact and avoid separation; and hence it seems likely that—when a study of the matter is made—the attachment object will be found to have unusually high reinforcing potentiality.

There is little information available, however, on which to found any theory as to the conditions of establishment of attachment. Observations by Bowlby (1969), Ainsworth (1967), Rheingold (1956), and Schaffer and Emerson (1964) suggest that a substantial attachment has been formed in the majority of children by the time they are a year old. Observations of separation prior to age 6 months indicate little evidence of the anxiety so characteristic at later ages; also, the special capacity of the mother to elicit smiling, in contrast to the associated negative instigation provided by strangers, is developed usually in the sixth to eighth months.

These findings suggest that ordinarily the primary attachment occurs during the second half-year of life. But the conditions responsible are not clear. The seeming suddenness, intensity, ardor—even passion—and the prolonged irreversibility of the attachment responses are difficult to reconcile with the orderly progression of learning that characterizes such other action systems as attention-seeking and achievement.

The Bowlby-Ainsworth supposition of some specific genetic propensity (innate bias) for attachment does not seem unreasonable. I myself would go further and suggest that the capacity for forming an attachment is a product of maturation. There is considerable variability in the chronological age at which this capacity develops, however—a variability much greater than that in lower animals whose imprinting behavior has been studied by ethologists—and hence the specific term *critical period* seems inappropriate. On the other hand, such indices of human development as skeletal growth are by no means perfectly correlated with chronological age. A possible hypothesis is that the attachment capacity is a part of some maturational sequence more precisely related to developmental status measured by other indices than by the crude one of chronological age. It is an empirical question as to whether the variability in "age" at which attachment occurs is less when other indices of status than chronological age are used.

The notion of imprinting itself does not seem entirely useful in this context, either, because there is evidence that secondary attachments, i.e., attachments to another object such as father, grandmother, or a sibling, can be formed a little later (Schaffer & Emerson, 1964; Bowlby, 1969). There is, in other words, a certain looseness about both chronological age and objects that distinguishes human attachment formation from the more precise imprinting seen in geese. In any case, whether or not the caretaking reinforcements have any influence on the formation of an attachment, I think we must be alert to the possibility that, if so, they *may* be influential only at a genetically determined stage of the child's development.

The relation of attachment to dependency has been confused in part because groups of investigators, starting with somewhat different experiences and interests, have worked separately on them with little mutual influence in the early stages of research. The attachment researchers, primarily British clinicians with a psychoanalytic background, and the American students of dependency, learning theorists with a nonclinical interest in psychoanalytic theory, chose measures of their respective phenomena that were different even when the phenomena had some similarity. For example, Ainsworth's ingenious series of child-mother-stranger encounters are quite different from the behavior unit observations in nursery school (no mother, few adults, many children) used by Gewirtz, by Heathers, and by Sears. Yet, among the categories in the latter measures are *seeking reassurance, being near,* and *touching and holding,* which could well be actions belonging to the attachment system. Again, it is important, as Gewirtz has emphasized, to be precise with respect to the stimulus objects and settings when operational definitions are being chosen.

This latter point becomes of particular relevance because of another seeming difference between attachment and dependency. There is little doubt that attention-seeking operates according to the laws of stimulus generalization. It is less clear that attachment does, at least to the same extent. That is, a 4-year-old will seek attention from father, teachers, siblings, or other children, depending on their availability and the setting. These people are alternative Betas to the mother. In the nursery school, however, spontaneous proximity-seeking responses are relatively infrequent in comparison with attention-seeking ones. They are directed mainly toward teachers when they do occur, which does suggest stimulus generalization; but the lack of separation reactions when the teacher leaves, or when the child leaves the school to go home, suggests also that the generalization must be very weak. However, one difficulty arises in comparing proximity-seeking and attention-seeking; there is an apparent difference in the reinforcement role that alternative Betas play. Both at home and in the nursery school they all provide in some degree direct reinforcement of attention-seeking by themselves being helpful from time to time. They are not only Betas-for-response, but Betas-for-reinforcement. There is nothing exclusive about the mother in either role.

Not so with attachment, apparently. At the early height of a child's attachment to his mother, he is inconsolable at a separation which implies a loss the temporal span of which he cannot foresee. He can relinquish contact for his own sleep or for her housework (when she stays in auditory contact); but if there is threat of prolonged absence, separation anxiety is evoked. Possibly it is this duration-uncertainty that makes the advent of a younger sibling such a serious instigator of anxiety—and hostility toward both sibling and mother. It is not clear how soon he can be got rid of! Furthermore, at separation there is not an immediate turning to other Betas. In contrast with attention-seeking, attachment seems not to include proximity-seeking responses which are the product of stimulus generalization under conditions of alarm (Rosenthal, 1967a, 1967b). Conceivably, this lack of response to others in a separation-from-mother situation could be accounted for by the strength of supervening "search" responses for the mother which compete successfully with generalization-induced reactions to other Betas. There is still a massive amount of research needed to clarify these issues.

Another set of problems with respect to attachment relates to its fate through the rest of the life span. Most theoretical and investigative considerations of the process have dealt with the earliest years of life, mainly the first two. If it is correct that there is a genetically determined stage at which attachment *can* occur, and that the continued presence of a single caretaker at that stage is the condition required for *actual* occurrence (Ainsworth, 1967), then the issue arises as to what happens to the attachment in subsequent years, and how it relates to other significant dyadic relationships formed at later times. My own unsystematic observations suggest that this primary attachment to the mother/caretaker is one of only three true attachments occurring during life, the second being to an adult peer (usually of the opposite sex), and the third being a multiphased attachment to some or all of Alpha's own children. Because of the incredible complexities introduced by the sexualization of the primary attachment in many, if not most, children, the isolating and identifying of these true attachments is extremely difficult, because the sexualization of so many dyadic relationships makes them at least superficially indiscriminable from attachments. Further, the secondary attachments that often seem to develop shortly after the primary one have much the same persistence and quality of the latter, though the profound effects of permanent separation from these objects appear not to be produced ordinarily (Stolz, 1953).

The fate of the primary attachment is decay, if we may judge by children's behavior. After a year or two at maximum intensity, the initial passion of the love decreases *in expression*. There are various reasons for this. The sexualization of feelings, particularly in boys, is met with social rejection and coped with by repression and denial. Growing cognitive maturity enables the child to understand the necessary causes and limited risks of brief separations, and to use a longer time perspective in his ability to anticipate his mother's return. Through learning, reduced cues become sufficient to signal the mother's presence; symbolic cues develop that provide for a condition of quasi presence. Countering these reducing factors, on the other hand, are the increased verbal facility, capacity for motoric search, and understanding of more subtle cues of impending separation. Until criteria of attachment strength that are independent of these crosscurrents in openness of expression are discovered, it will be difficult to chart finely the decay function during the preschool years, or even unequivocally to assure ourselves that there is such a function.[2] So far, no foolproof criterion has suggested itself to me. One possibility that might be worth exploring is the use of a standardized interruption of a standardized

[2] I am especially grateful to Dr. Eleanor Maccoby for helpful discussion of these points concerning the developmental sequence during the preschool years, as well as for providing me with a prepublication copy of the all-important Maccoby and Masters (1970) paper.

attachment-induced action sequence. Conceivably, if there were a base-line interaction in process, the amount of emotional upset resulting from interference would be less susceptible to variation from the above factors, which seem to influence expression, than would be the case under a more naturalistic situation in which the very nature of the situation itself is partly determined by those factors.

By ages seven or eight, however, there is little doubt that the results of the decay are evident. In spite of the temporary tempest of ambivalence at the onset of adolescence—probably in the main caused by the original sexualization of the attachment—normally the main expressions of the primary attachment disappear in mid-adolescence. The second attachment is usually formed some time in young adulthood, providing, in the most fortunate case, the effective basis for marriage.

One of the most interesting problems is the final near-destruction of the first attachment. During the early adolescent years there are many indications that the child is himself making efforts to break it and is trying experimentally for new attachments. One might hazard a guess that much of adolescent distress, disorganization, aimlessness, blind seeking for new experiences, searching for sexual partners, and alternating periods of euphoria and despair is an indication of the rootlessness of an existence without attachment. These are symptoms of searching for the second object. In the present atmosphere of permissiveness for self-revelation and for the discussion of previously forbidden subjects such as sex, the contemporary adolescent prepossession with love may be simply a final verbalization—a kind of oral epiphenomenon—of this search. In Havighurst's terms, finding a second attachment object is a developmental task. The love generation puts its mouth where its heart is.

Another observation that suggests the mutability of the primary attachment is the phenomenon of pseudo-attachment. Instances of apparent attachment can be observed between children as young as three or four. Two children suddenly become lovers. Sometimes they are boy and girl, sometimes of the same sex. They seem to live, eat, sleep, and breathe for one another. They make plans about marrying when they grow up, or bond themselves in eternal friendship, play together contentedly by the hour, show severe separation distress, and in many ways seem to be acting much as two adolescents suffering "puppy love" or having a "crush." A close study of such episodes might be helpful in discovering some of the conditions relevant to the establishment of true attachments, for it seems possible that these pseudo-attachments, like the earlier secondary attachments, are laid down on the *anlage* of the primary attachment. In spite of their intensity, they tend to be relatively brief and to terminate without the severe disorganization and prolonged despair that ensue from interruption of a primary attachment.

The third attachment is the parents' toward the child as object. David Levy (1958) has charted carefully the affective responses of mothers during early breast-feeding of the child, and has found a considerable degree of consistency among various measures of maternal feeling. There was some evidence that feelings rapidly increased in strength in a quite brief time, although the initial level appears to have had some connection with somatic factors, the strength being positively related ($r = .58$) with duration of menstrual flow (Levy, 1942).

Again the state of affairs is very complex, for the attachment may be multiple if there is more than a single child. Yet one child is no substitute for another, as can be so plainly seen on the occasion of one child's death in a multichild family. As with the second attachment, there also are complications arising from the multiple sources of motivation and kinds of reinforcers operative in parent-to-child attachment. The over-protective mother offers several possible examples, including dependency for attention or admiration, substitution for a parent or husband Beta, and unconscious symbolic sexualization of the child (Levy, 1943). These alternatives to the true attachment make difficult the tracing of the fates of the second and third forms, but it would seem potentially rewarding to try to untangle the mess. Possibly the frank adoption of the present hypotheses might lead observers in research paths somewhat different from those customarily followed through social pathology. Investigators of marital relationships and of the affective quality of parent-child dyads (or polyads) have so commonly focussed on the various pathological alternatives to attachment (divorce, rejection, neglect, etc.) that it sometimes seemed—until Harlow and Bowlby came along—as if plain, simple *love* had never been noticed. Yet a surprisingly large part of the normal population experiences it.

In summary, the propositions worth presenting as hypotheses seem to me to be as follows:

1. Attachment is a process by which the child becomes passionately loving of the mother or other main caretaker and devotes uniquely powerful energy to retaining visual and auditory contact with her, shows severe disorganization and emotional distress at separation, and ultimate joy at reunion. Primary attachment decays during middle adolescence and normally is replaced by a second major attachment in late adolescence or young adulthood.

2. The primary attachment is related to a child's dependency behavior only by the fortuitous fact that the mother is the central figure in both action systems. Dependency behaviors are highly generalizable to other adults and even to children, while attachment behaviors do not appear to be so much so.

3. The necessary conditions for establishing the primary attachment are unknown, but it does not seem unreasonable to speculate about a genetically determined propensity for a rapid and efficient development of the process. Equally, it does not seem unreasonable provisionally to reject the possibility that the primary attachment is established by simple principles of discriminative learning.

4. Three major attachments *can* occur, the first possibly in the last half of the first year of life, the second in late adolescence or early adulthood, and the third, soon after, toward a child or children. Partial, or pseudo-, attachments— brief in time but apparently passonate in intensity—may occur intermittently

along the way. Observation suggests that their passing leaves the major attachments intact.

Frustration and Privation

Most of my discussion so far has dealt with the establishment and development of attachment and dependency. It is clear that certain environmental conditions must be met for these purposes. The crucial role of the mother as an active agent in providing manipulanda and reinforcements for both systems has contributed to the earlier confusion in distinguishing between them. Now, however, if we examine her role as a *non*reinforcer the distinction between them will become clearer.

In a dyadic relationship, Beta can be ineffectual for Alpha's purposes under two distinguishable circumstances. One is failure to be appropriately responsive when Alpha presents the previously rehearsed cues for Beta's next response, that is, when Alpha already has developed a set of actions that require dyadic reactions from Beta. This failure provides a *frustration*, an interference with an on-going action sequence (Dollard et al., 1939). The other way of being ineffectual is by failure to provide the conditions (manipulanda or reinforcements) required for the establishment of a given dyadic action system. This kind of failure provides *privation* for Alpha (as defined by Gewirtz, 1961, pp. 260-264). As examples, a child may suffer frustration if his mother is busy in the kitchen and refuses his request for help in unsnarling his kite string. He suffers privation (in the present use of the word), however, if she never gives him instruction in some foreign language of which she knows nothing and which he does not even know exists. These are perhaps minimal frustrations and privations, but they illustrate the difference between dyadic nonresponsiveness before and after an action system is established.

Every viable child develops a set of actions instrumental to securing help from adults. Otherwise he could not be viable. To what extent he will also develop attention- or admiration-seeking actions is a function of the particular scheduling of reinforcements to which he is subjected for particular forms of behavior. Hence, both "instrumental" and "emotional" dependency actions are susceptible to frustration, but privation (i.e., the lack of opportunity to develop such actions) is a meaningless concept in connection with dependency.

Attachment is another matter. If the Bowlby-Ainsworth view of a genetic bias is correct, there is the possibility that privation may occur and the primary attachment may fail to develop. That such an outcome occasionally happens is suggested by the classical paper of David Levy (1937) on *primary affect hunger*. Levy described several cases of children who, during their first two or three years, were moved from one caretaker to another, receiving little love from any. In later years they appeared to have no significant attachments, regardless of the love and affection they then received. Similar cases were described by Goldfarb (1943, 1945a, 1945b), who was able to secure groups of reasonably comparable nonrejected cases for comparison. People with a so-called psychopathic personality, who show little evidence of making affectionate relationships either with parent or with peer figures, quite commonly have histories of a peripatetic home situation during the first 3 years of life.

It is doubtful that there is the same absolute quality to the relation between developmental stage, caretaking, and attachment, that appears to occur in the classical instances of imprinting in certain birds. So far, human genetics has not discovered such rigidly fixed relationships between experience and behavior establishment. More likely, those clinical cases which might be described as lacking a primary attachment would better be described as extreme cases at the low end of such behavior development. There may well be a range, a continuum, up to a normal degree of attachment.

The wide variations, so brilliantly isolated by the Harlows (1966), in the development of social-emotional and sexual behavior in monkeys, the attachment-appropriateness of whose experiences was varied experimentally, suggests that even in nonhuman primates attachment is not an all-or-none phenomenon. In human children, some of the behaviors developmentally associated with and used in the expression of attachment, e.g., smiling, fear of strangers, motor skills (walking, looking), social responsiveness, and language, have been shown to vary quantitatively in their rate or degree of development with variations in the extent to which loving attention by individual caretakers is provided (Rheingold, 1956; Dennis & Najarian, 1957; Skeels, 1966). In certain extraordinary circumstances even the object of attachment has been shown not to be limited to an adult caretaker, but may be another child or a group of children (Freud & Dann, 1951).

Clinical and naturalistic data on human subjects are less than sufficient to test rigorously such an hypothesis as the all-or-none character of attachment, but these kinds of observations are all we are likely to get for this purpose. The effects of variation beyond rather narrow limits are of such seemingly overriding importance to the welfare of individual children that no one will be disposed to intervene for experimental reasons. The continued analysis of clinical and naturalistic data, however, together with the study of the outcomes of experimental variation of rearing conditions in monkeys or other lower animals (cf., Cairns' work on sheep, 1966), can sharpen the definitions of the relevant parameters and thus can improve the usefulness of naturalistic data for hypothesis-testing.

Levy's use of the term *affect hunger* is reflective of an underlying theoretical position not unlike that of Murray (1938), who spoke of needs (e.g., *n* Succorance), and of the learning theorists' early drive concept of dependency. Levy was clearly concerned with what we now call attachment, however, as was Goldfarb; and it is interesting to note that the latter described certain of his cases who displayed what we would call *nonattachment* as being extremely demanding of attention. Within the clinical materials available there is no indication that the lack of a consistently available love object/caretaker prevents the development of attention- or admiration-seeking in the same way that it prevents attachment. Hence I suggest that even though both attachment and dependency may vary in quantitative degree (and possibly in rate) of development, they develop *according to different principles operating in the same environment and with the same dyadic agents.*

In contrast to privation, frustration clearly applies to both attachment and dependency. Once any action system has been established, interference with it is, by definition, frustration, which creates a hypothetical frustration-induced instigation. This is at once added into the total mélange of instigation affecting the organism. There are two consequences, one quantitative and the other qualitative. One is an increase in total strength of instigation to whatever response occurs next, and the other is the reorganization of the hierarchy of responses which are elicitable by that mélange. Frustration-induced instigation is a determinant not only of *which* responses in the child's hierarchy will now be prepotent, but also of *how strongly* they will be performed—it is a facilitator.

Each action system has its own hierarchy of possible frustration responses. Such a hierarchy is established, in part, because some reactions are more effective than others in helping a child to complete that particular kind of action system, and hence reinforcement makes some of them prepotent over others. Beyond reinforcement, however, it is worth considering the possibility that the internal instigation associated with each action system has a set of genetically predetermined responses to frustration. For example, while interference with aggressive actions appears to increase the instigation to aggression (if the interference does not pose threats of punishment), the frustration of attention-seeking appears to evoke more active efforts to secure the dyadic response. In both cases, of course, the frustration instigates further behavior of the sort that was frustrated, but the frustration reactions are very different from one another in both form and intensity, as well as in the affective experiences accompanying them.

For attachment, some of the more common frustration reactions are clearly congruent with an effort to continue performance of the action system itself. Ainsworth (1969) has shown that in year-old children brief separations are followed by a searching response. Gewirtz (1961), Rheingold (1961), and later Walters and Parke (1964) suggested, probably correctly, that the distance receptors are more important for *maintaining* attachment-comfort than are the tactual ones. It is not surprising, then, that the searching Ainsworth describes is largely a visual searching even in the very young child. I have often observed a kind of head-cocking and apparent listening, which suggests that auditory searching is also common. When the child becomes more mobile and can move around the house or yard, his searching may take on a more motoric character, with aimless wandering about, looking in different rooms, staring out the window, and so on. If the mother leaves the house and the child sees her go, he may sit at a window or on the front steps, apparently oriented toward the outer world from which his mother may return. Such behavior is quite pervasive and characterizes the separation reactions of adults as well as children.

Continued separation inevitably leads to a disorganization of the child's whole behavior system. It is evident that much of his behavior is organized around dyadic interaction with his mother. The signs of interaction may be minimal as long as the mother is present, because the visual and auditory perceptions are the heart of the interaction system, and hence the external observer sees little overt behavior that constitutes the attachment behavior repertoire. Once there has been separation, however, and searching has not restored the object, the lack of the commonly available perceptions represents a disruption in the normal pattern of instigation around which the child's behavior is organized. The emotional response to separation is heavily charged with fear, so it is not surprising that ensuing manipulative and cognitive activities are disorganized. There is a breakdown in constructive action—the regression which Barker, Dembo, and Lewin (1941) described—and an intrusion of crying, flight from strangers, hyperreactiveness to unexpected stimuli, and other responses that have previously been learned to fear-inducing situations. With more and more prolonged separation, depression and finally despair are likely to occur (Heinicke, 1956; see also Yarrow, 1964, for a thorough review).

It is difficult to make direct comparisons between the frustration reactions resulting from interference with different action systems, for researchers have tended to use children of different ages for research on the different systems. Perhaps the best comparisons for attachment are with dependency and with achievement, or task mastery. In both cases, the primary reaction for most children appears to be a strengthened effort to achieve completion of the frustrated action sequence; but the whining, crying, and pleading for help that follow interference with instrumental dependency, and the common intrusion of aggression into renewed performance of a failed task (Keister, 1938; P. S. Sears, 1940), are quite unlike the searching induced by separation. At adolescence, there seem to be few if any separation responses that are similar to the decontextualization seen under experimentally induced failure (Sears, 1942), although the simultaneous autism and motoric inhibition do have their counterparts in attachment frustration reactions.

This suggestion that different action systems have different hierarchies of potential frustration reactions associated with them does not imply that there is no overlap among the action repertoires that constitute the hierarchies. On the contrary, anger and aggression intrude into many frustration reactions, regardless of what action system is frustrated. So do inhibition, autism, regression, depression, displacement, and so on. Rather, the reinforcement histories, the available manipulanda, the expectancies of success or failure, and the nature of the stimulus conditions present at frustration, all influence the character of the acts which are elicited and the order in which they occur. But I suggest, also, that one major difference exists between attachment and either dependency or aggression. It is with respect to stimulus generalization, or displacement, following frustration. Social responsiveness, help-seeking, attention-seeking, and playmate-seeking all generalize to other persons when the primary responder, helper, attention-giver, and playmate disappear. But although there is some kind of *anlage* phenomenon that requires a primary attachment as prerequisite to later love relationships, the evidence is not satisfactory that these later shifts are based on stimulus generalization.

A Propositional Inventory

Some of the statements which have been made in the preceding discussion are firmly based on empirical evidence (A). Others represent only reasonable hypotheses for which there is no evidence contravening but for which direct support does not yet provide full confidence (B). Still others are essentially speculations which have been presented in an attempt to crystallize a position, to define possible variables, or to suggest relationships worth investigation (C). A listing of these statements, with designations of (A), (B), or (C) to indicate to which of these three classes they belong, may help to summarize the present state of our knowledge. It will be understood that for those propositions marked (A) without specific citation of supporting evidence, appropriate evidence can be found in the definitive theoretical research reivew by Maccoby and Masters (1970).

DEPENDENCY

1. Attention from the main caretaker, expressed by means of visual regard or through auditory or tactile stimulation, is observed to be a secondary reinforcer during the first few months of the child's life. (A)
2. The specific forms of attention-giving are unique to each dyadic pair.(B)
3. Attention-seeking actions develop by the sixth month. (A)
4. The specific forms of attention-giving and attention-seeking change with age. (A)
     a. Verbal and auditory seeking of positive attention increases from ages two to five. (A)
5. In group situations, with both adults and children present, attention-seeking toward adults decreases during the preschool years, while that directed toward other children tends to increase. (B)
6. Fear arousal increases proximity-seeking in young children but does not affect attention-seeking. (B)
7. Under the relatively nonstandardized stimulus conditions of a nursery school, the frequency of emission of a given child's attention-seeking acts has more than chance stability over a period of one to four years. (A)
8. Social deprivation increases the frequency of emission of attention-seeking acts. (A)
9. Parental permissiveness and nonpunitiveness is associated with low adult-directed attention-seeking in both girls and boys. (B)
10. Social reinforcement by adults has a stronger effect on children who are

initially higher on attention-seeking or who have undergone social isolation. (A).

ATTACHMENT

1. The primary attachment as defined by separation distress normally occurs between 6 and 18 months of age, the second half-year being the commonest time of formation. (A)

    a. Secondary attachments of less strength may be formed in the same period. (According to Schaffer & Emerson, 1964, 50% of their group developed a second attachment within 12 weeks after the first; and by 18 months, 83% had more than one.) (B)

2. Conditions required for attachment formation include:

    a. Maturation of a specific genetic propensity. (C)

    b. Consistent and extensive expression of love by a caretaker. (B)

    c. Development of a discrimination of the caretaker from other persons (cf. Mussen, Conger, & Kagan, 1969, Ch. 6). (A)

3. The strength of attachment varies positively with the amount of love and caretaking offered by the mother, and with immediacy of her response to supplication. (B)

4. Attachment is evidenced initially by the child's attempts to keep the object in tactual contact; later, visual and auditory contact are used, separation being an instigator initially to searching, and then to depression, agitation, or other expressions of frustration. (A)

5. The primary attachment begins an expressive attenuation within 1 to 3 years, reaching a low asymptote in early adolescence. (B)

6. Proximity-seeking, as a form of attachment behavior under conditions of separation from the primary object (mother), does not appear to operate according to the same principle of stimulus generalization that occurs with dependency (attention-seeking). (B)

    a. Proximity-seeking in a nursery school setting decreases from ages two to five. (A).

7. In many children, particularly boys, there is a sexualization of the primary attachment, eventuating in the familiar phenomena of the Oedipus conflict and early adolescent ambivalence and withdrawal from the family. (A)

8. Pseudo-attachments, particularly between children, may develop during the decay of the primary attachment. They are of relatively brief duration and subside without significant frustration effects. (B)

FRUSTRATION AND PRIVATION

1. The action systems of both attachment and dependency are subject to frustration. (A)

2. Each action system has its own unique hierarchy of potential responses to frustration. (C)

a. For both systems, the most common initial reaction to frustration is a strengthened effort to complete the interrupted action sequence. (B)

3. Privation of opportunity for establishing a primary attachment in the first three years of life produces a character defect such that the second and third major attachments fail to develop. (B)

REFERENCES

Ainsworth, M. D. S. *Infancy in Uganda.* Baltimore: Johns Hopkins Press, 1967.

Ainsworth, M. D. S. Object relations, dependency, and attachment: A theoretical review of the infant-mother relationship. *Child Development,* 1969, **40**, 969-1025.

Baldwin, A. L. The effect of home environment on nursery school behavior. *Child Development,* 1949, **20**, 49-62.

Barker, R., Dembo, T., & Lewin, K. Frustration and regression. *University of Iowa Studies in Child Welfare,* 1941, **18** (1), 1-314.

Becker, W. C. Consequences of different kinds of parental discipline. In M. L. Hoffman & L. W. Hoffman (Eds.), *Review of child development research.* Vol. 1. New York: Russell Sage Foundation, 1964. Pp. 169-208.

Bell, R. Q. A reinterpretation of the direction of effects in studies of socialization. *Psychological Review,* 1968, **75**, 81-95.

Bishop, B. M. Mother-child interaction and the social behavior of children. *Psychological Monographs,* 1951, **65**, No. 328.

Bowlby, J. *Attachment and loss.* Vol. 1. *Attachment.* New York: Basic Books, 1969.

Brackbill, Y. Extinction of the smiling response in infants as a function of reinforcement schedule. *Child Development,* 1958, **29**, 114-124.

Cairns, R. B. Development, maintenance, and extinction of social attachment behavior in sheep. *Journal of Comparative and Physiological Psychology,* 1966, **62**, 298-306.

Davis, H. V., Sears, R. R., Miller, H. C., & Brodbeck, A. J. Effects of cup, bottle and breast-feeding on oral activities of newborn infants. *Pediatrics,* 1948, **3**, 549-558.

Dennis, W., & Najarian, P. Infant development under environmental handicap. *Psychological Monographs,* 1957, **71**, No. 436.

Dollard, J., Doob, L. W., Miller, N. E., Mowrer, O. H., & Sears, R. R. *Frustration and aggression.* New Haven: Yale University Press, 1939.

Dollard, J., & Miller, N. E. *Personality and psychotherapy.* New York: McGraw-Hill, 1950.

Freud, A., & Dann, S. An experiment in group upbringing. *Psychoanalytic Study of the Child,* 1951, **6**, 127-168.

Gewirtz, J. L. A factor analysis of some attention-seeking behaviors of young children. *Child Development,* 1956, **27**, 17-37.

Gewirtz, J. L. A learning analysis of the effects of normal stimulation, privation and deprivation on the acquisition of social motivation and attachment. In B. M. Foss (Ed.), *Determinants of infant behaviour.* London: Methuen, 1961. Pp. 213-299.

Gewirtz, J. L. Deprivation and satiation of social stimuli as determinants of their reinforcing efficacy. In J. P. Hill (Ed.), *Minnesota symposia on child psychology.* Vol. 1. Minneapolis: University of Minnesota Press, 1967. Pp. 3-56.

Gewirtz, J. L. Mechanisms of social learning: Some roles of stimulation and behavior in early human development. In D. A. Goslin (Ed.), *Handbook of socialization theory and research.* Chicago: Rand McNally, 1969. Pp. 57-212.

Goldfarb, W. Infant rearing and problem behavior. *American Journal of Orthopsychiatry,* 1943, **13**, 249-265.

Goldfarb, W. Effects of psychological deprivation in infancy and subsequent stimulation. *American Journal of Psychiatry,* 1945, **102**, 18-23.(a)

Goldfarb, W. Psychological privation in infancy and subsequent adjustment. *American Journal of Orthopsychiatry,* 1945, **15**, 247-255.(b)

Harlow, H. F., & Harlow, M. K. Learning to love. *American Scientist,* 1966, **54**, 244-272.

Hatfield, J. S., Ferguson, L. R., & Alpert, R. Mother-child interaction and the socialization process. *Child Development,* 1967, **38**, 365-414.

Heathers, G. Emotional dependence and independence in nursery school play. *Journal of Genetic Psychology,* 1955, **87**, 37-58.

Heinicke, C. Some effects of separating two-year-old children from their parents: A comparative study. *Human Relations,* 1956, 9, 105-176.

Heinicke, C.M., & Westheimer, I. *Brief separations.* New York: International Universities Press, 1966.

Hull, C. L. *Principles of behavior.* New York: Appleton-Century-Crofts, 1943.

Kagan, J., & Moss, H. A. *Birth to maturity.* New York: Wiley, 1962.

Keister, M. E. The behavior of young children in failure. *University of Iowa Studies in Child Welfare,* 1938, **14**, 27-82.

Levy, D. M. Primary affect hunger. *American Journal of Psychiatry,* 1937, **94**, 643-652.

Levy, D. M. Psychosomatic studies of some aspects of maternal behavior. *Psychosomatic Medicine,* 1942, **4**, 223-227.

Levy, D. M. *Maternal overprotection.* New York: Columbia University Press, 1943.

Levy, D. M. *Behavioral analysis.* Springfield, Ill.: Charles C. Thomas, 1958.

Maccoby, E. E., & Masters, J. C. Attachment and dependency. In P. H. Mussen (Ed.), *Carmichael's manual of child psychology.* (3rd ed.) Vol. 2. New York: Wiley, 1970. Pp. 73-158.

Miller, N. E., & Dollard, J. *Social learning and imitation.* New Haven: Yale University Press, 1941.

Mischel, W. *Personality and assessment.* New York: Wiley, 1968.

Murray, H. A., Jr. *Explorations in personality.* New York: Oxford University Press, 1938.

Mussen, P. H., Conger, J. J., & Kagan, J. *Child development and personality.* (3rd ed.) New York: Harper & Row, 1969.

Rheingold, H. L. The modification of social behavior in institutional babies. *Monographs of the Society for Research in Child Development,* 1956, **21**, No. 63.

Rheingold, H. L. The effect of environmental stimulation upon social and exploratory behaviour in the human infant. In B. M. Foss (Ed.), *Determinants of infant behaviour.* London: Methuen (New York: Wiley), 1961. Pp. 143-171.

Rosenthal, M. K. The generalization of dependency behavior from mother to stranger. *Journal of Child Psychology and Psychiatry,* 1967, **8**, 117-133.(a)

Rosenthal, M. K. The effect of a novel situation and anxiety on two groups of dependency behavior. *British Journal of Psychology,* 1967, **58**, 357-364.(b)

Schaffer, H. R., & Emerson, P. E. The development of social attachments in infancy. *Monographs of the Society for Research in Child Development,* 1964, **29** (3, Serial No. 94).

Sears, P. S. Levels of aspiration in academically successful and unsuccessful children. *Journal of Abnormal and Social Psychology,* 1940, **35**, 498-536.

Sears, R. R. Success and failure: A study of motility. In Q. McNemar & M. Merrill (Eds.), *Studies in personality.* New York: McGraw-Hill, 1942. Pp. 235-258.

Sears, R. R. Personality development in contemporary culture. *Proceedings of the American Philosophical Society,* 1948, **92**, 363-370.

Sears, R. R., Maccoby, E. E., & Levin, H. *Patterns of child rearing.* New York: Harper & Row, 1957.

Sears, R. R., Rau, L., & Alpert, R. *Identification and child rearing.* Stanford, Calif.: Stanford University Press, 1965.

Sears, R. R., Whiting, J. W. M., Nowlis, V., & Sears, P. S. Some child rearing antecedents of aggression and dependency in young children. *Genetic Psychology Monographs,* 1953, **47**, 135-234.

Sears, R. R., & Wise, G. W. Relation of cup feeding in infancy to thumb-sucking and the oral drive. *American Journal of Orthopsychiatry,* 1950, **20,** 123-138.

Skeels, H. M. Adult status of children with contrasting early life experiences. *Monographs of the Society for Research in Child Development,* 1966, **31** (3, Serial No. 105).

Stolz, L. M. *Father relations of war-born children.* Stanford, Calif.: Stanford University Press, 1953.

Walters, R. H., & Parke, R. D. Social motivation, dependency, and susceptibility to social influence. In L. Berkowitz (Ed.), *Advances in experimental social psychology.* Vol. 1. New York: Academic Press, 1964. Pp. 232-276.

Whiting, J. W. M. The frustration complex in Kwoma society. *Man,* 1944, **115,** 140-144.

Yarrow, L. J. Separation from parents during early childhood. In M. L. Hoffman & L. W. Hoffman (Eds.), *Review of child development research.* Vol. 1. New York: Russell Sage Foundation, 1964. Pp. 89-136.

ATTACHMENT AND DEPENDENCY: A PSYCHOBIOLOGICAL AND SOCIAL-LEARNING SYNTHESIS[1]

Robert B. Cairns
Indiana University

Introduction

The concepts of "attachment" and "dependency" refer to phenomena that are fundamental in the social behavior of the individual and the species.

[1] I must express my thanks to my fellow contributors for their helpful comments on this chapter, and particularly to J. L. Gewirtz for his detailed remarks. Much of the paper was written during a leave that I spent at the University of California, Irvine, and I greatly appreciate the kindnesses extended and the facilities that were made available to me. The work was supported in part by National Institute of Child Health and Human Development grant HD 5693-01 and by Office of Education grant 5-71-0069-508.

Questions about their utility, relevance, or relationship to one another cannot help but bring us immediately to the nuclear issues of social behavior description and analysis. Indeed, one of the difficulties of initiating a serious discussion of the concepts is that most of us find it pretty hard to imagine how we can get along without them. That state of affairs in itself seems sufficient cause to be wary of them. If such abstractions are to serve any broader theoretical purpose than that of description, they should be "not only determined, but overdetermined by empirical relationships [Estes, 1958, p. 34]." Failure to anchor the constructs in a network of functional relationships may serve to retard the detailed analysis of the very behaviors that they attempt to explain.

Whatever doubts one might have about the ultimate fate of these theoretical entities, there can be no question about the significance of the elementary phenomena to which they refer. The social orientation behaviors of the immature organism, human or otherwise, and those of his mother, are as basic in the response repertoire of mammalian species as are the various "primary drive" activities.

Now we are in the position of reevaluating concepts that have been instrumental in organizing diverse social behavior phenomena and in stimulating much of the research available on the development of social processes. This kind of theoretical stock-taking, although necessary for the progress and vitality of the science, has certain inherent pitfalls. One of the more significant hazards is *theoretical overkill.* A classic example of overkill is found in the aftermath of the great instinct debate of the 1920s. After the polemics had been heard and the excesses of the instinct models had been exposed, it became theoretically permissible to overlook the contributions of organismic events to behavior. The roles that genetic, neurological, and physiological events play in the development and control of ongoing behavior were difficult to overlook. But most of our behavioral models, up through the recent past, seem to have accomplished the trick. In our present case, there is the danger of a theoretical oscillation in the opposite direction. This would be unfortunate, because significant gains have in fact been made in the application of learning principles to the problems of social behavior.

Another pitfall is that of *nominal resolution.* This occurs when a new term is introduced that is operationally and functionally equivalent to one that has preceded it. Whatever gains are made by thus forcing a reevaluation of an old idea can be cancelled out by the resultant theoretical obfuscation. Pure cases of nominal resolution are hard to find in psychology. But we have a reasonable number of only slightly impure cases in motivational theory; namely, instances where the consequences of two terms are virtually the same. Certain of McDougall's instincts and sentiments, for example, are on formal grounds similar to the fixed action patterns and the motivational systems (e.g., secondary drives, behavior propensities, control systems) that have succeeded them. While this pitfall appears to be rather benign, there seems to be little justification for the generation of additional terms in a discipline that is already generously endowed with redundant concepts.

Finally, in the critical analysis of constructs, it is sometimes possible to forget the functions that they serve and the reasons for their maintenance. Despite generally accepted shortcomings, some concepts endure in psychology because of the services that they perform in describing behavior. The concepts of "intelligence" and "reinforcement" are examples of terms that are retained because no serious competitors have yet evolved to take their place.

Our principal task is to critically examine the concepts of attachment and dependency in the light of ontogenetic analyses of social behavior. The discussion will be taken up in three sections:

Towards an alternative level of analysis
Psychobiological contributions to the development of early social interactions
Dependency and social development in children

Attachment and Dependency: Towards an Alternative Level of Analysis

A great many terms have been introduced to describe and explain social behavior patterns. A sampling would include affectional systems, affiliation drive, bond, cathexis, epimeletic and etepimeletic behavior, gregarious drive, gregarious instinct, herd drive, love (mother, peer, offspring, filial), object relationships, need for approval, succorance, social drive, and so on. In addition, we have the two terms that are currently vying for dominance in the socialization literature; attachment and dependency. While a detailed analysis of the above terms and the theoretical differences that they reflect would be informative and perhaps useful, the exercise is beyond the scope of the paper and of my immediate concern. Nevertheless, it is necessary to be clear about what ground rules can be followed in distinguishing between concepts when the need arises. In particular, as Gewirtz (1961) has pointed out, it would likely help to clarify theoretical discussions in which both attachment and dependency have been involved if the similarities and differences between the two concepts were stated explicitly.

Although the concepts of dependency and attachment both deal with the phenomena of social responsiveness, they have evolved in quite different contexts, both theoretical and methodological. They refer to operationally distinct classes of behavior. Dependency, on the one hand, has ordinarily referred to the behavior of children, adolescents, and adults. The concept has rarely been invoked in empirical studies of nonhuman behavior or in studies of human infants. The concept was originally defined as a learned motivational system, the manifestations of which were help-seeking, approval-seeking, and proximity-seeking behaviors (Sears, Whiting, Nowlis, & Sears, 1953). Later usage extended the concept to nonmotivational habit structures or behavior systems, but these systems encompassed the same behaviors as the motive (see Hartup, 1963). Relationships have been assumed to obtain between this behavioral or motivational system and various distinctively human social behavior patterns.

Dependency thus has been introduced to account for such diverse behaviors as social conformity, verbal reinforcement effectiveness, identification, antisocial aggression, and the development of internal standards. Assessment procedures of dependency normally rely heavily upon verbal statements, judgments, or reports. Some of the measures, such as self-report and projective techniques, are exclusively verbal. In summary, the body of literature concerned with the analysis of dependency deals primarily with the behavior of verbally capable human beings. The concept has rarely been applied to the behavior of infants or nonhuman animals.

In quite a different way, the concept of attachment has also been limited. But where dependency refers to social behavior patterns in organisms that possess distinctively human capabilities (language, symbolic and conceptual mediation, capacity for long-term memory storage and precise retrieval), the term attachment has been used primarily in studies of the social processes of nonhuman animals of all ages and of human infants. The construct is usually involved in connection with the analysis of interactions that occur between infants and their mother or mother-substitutes. While dependency has referred to the nonspecific social orientation of the child, attachment denotes a one-to-one relationship of the infant with a particular other, typically the mother or mother-substitute. Since attachment was not specifically identified with a well-articulated theoretical system, as was dependency, various assumptions have been proposed concerning the motivational and theoretical status of the term. For the same reason, there is less agreement on what behavioral manifestations should be labeled "attachment."

Although the two constructs, attachment and dependency, were both introduced in the context of the analysis of social responsiveness, there are ample grounds for attempting to distinguish between them. One of the bases offered for differentiation has been that "attachment" refers to an emotionally intense relationship that has special motivational properties, whereas "dependency" refers to instrumental interpersonal behaviors. Different principles are presumed to be necessary to account for the establishment and operation of the two behavior dispositions (e.g., Ainsworth, this volume; Sears, this volume). Other writers have taken the position that a single set of principles is adequate to account for the phenomena encompassed by the two terms. Nonetheless, it has been argued, the two concepts should be kept distinct because of essential differences in the types of social interaction patterns to which they refer (Gewirtz, this volume).

On logical grounds, either type of distinction seems permissible, provided that the operational criteria are specified so that individual cases can be reliably classified. In view of the difference in the operations followed in assessment, and in the age-species status of the individuals observed, there appear to be ample grounds for differentiation. However, it appears to me that the question should not be whether these terms can be distinguished, but whether the behaviors to which they refer are in fact related. The critical issues are empirical, not definitional. In particular we need to know whether the several behaviors called "attachment" are precursors to the development of "dependent" response patterns (see pp. 61-62).

Nonetheless, there would be little gain and considerable danger in dismissing the issues of categorization and classification as pseudoproblems. Investigators working in the same area and upon common problems can ill afford to talk past one another. So it seems appropriate to comment on what appears to be the principal problem in the classification debate, namely, the issue of the optimal level of theoretical analysis.

ON CATEGORICAL CONSTRUCTS AND THE OPTIMAL LEVEL OF ANALYSIS

In an excellent discussion of the optimal level of theoretical analysis, Sears et al. (1953) concluded that a "good" developmental construct both should be *economical* and should refer to a *unitary attribute of behavior*. These two criteria—which appear to be of prime importance in their list of six[2]—are often, if not always, in conflict. The criterial tug-of-war is between generality and precision. The construct that is most economical (in summarizing disparate behaviors) is typically not unitary (in referring to a single phenomenon or process). The authors saw the problem as a serious one, and warned that "constructs that do not provide consistent antecedent-consequent relationships often fail to do so because they do not refer to any unitary attribute of behavior [p. 141]." In retrospect, the warning stands out as prophetic.

One other assumption, on why construct selection is so important, was implicit in the Sears et al. (1953) discussion. A "good" construct was presumed to refer to a distinctive process or single theoretical mechanism which underlies and accounts for the coherence, stability, and intensity of the behaviors subsumed by it. Hence dependency gave rise to the notion of a secondary dependency motive, and later, attachment gave rise to the idea of a unitary biogenic disposition. This "one-construct = one-process" equation implies that a direct relationship obtains between the construct label and an underlying motivational or dispositional mechanism. Once a classification or categorical system is established, its terms have been presumed to represent the principal explanatory mechanisms.

In practice, a major dilemma has arisen in the application of the construct selection criteria of Sears et al. (1953). The construct that is unitary tends not to be economical, and vice versa. Hence the discrete variable that permits the establishment of antecedent-consequent relationships, and which supports the

---

[2] The six criteria for a good construct listed by Sears et al. (1953) are: economical, important, universally applicable, nonevaluative, reducible to an operational definition, and demonstrably useful in the discovery of antecedent-consequent relations (i.e., it should refer to a unitary attribute).

"one construct = one process" equation, tends to be too narrow or limited for the description of general personality or adaptational dispositions. By way of example, consider the behaviors that have been subsumed by the economical constructs "sexual drive" and "reproduction." One of the obstacles to productive research in the area of sexual behavior was the search for a unitary "sexual motive" that accounted for sexual differences between individuals and species. When research turned to the semiautonomous biological and learning phenomena that were involved in the several components of sexual activity (e.g., partner selection, peripheral sensitization, motor coordination, and reflex facilitation), the accounts became at once more precise and more powerful (Aronson, 1959; Beach, 1970).

Perhaps a similar resolution can be reached in the analysis of the behaviors to which such constructs as "attachment" and "dependency" refer. Given that a real conflict exists among the criteria for construct selection, a first step may be the recognition that the criteria themselves refer to two separable objectives. These are (a) the need to distill an exceedingly large number of observations into a small number of dispositional variables, and (b) the need to establish cross-individual and cross-specific explanatory mechanisms. Both objectives are worthy, and one need not be subordinated to the other. It is not obvious, however, that one set of terms must serve both objectives. Nor is it self-evident that the criterion of unity and explanatory precision must necessarily give way to economy.

On a priori grounds, there seems to be a reasonable basis to expect that the major adaptations of the individual and the species, including reproduction, species-identification, and aggression, will turn out to be the outcome of multiple processes. In evolution, the most important or critical problems of adaptation are usually solved in a variety of ways. Moreover, given the sometimes contradictory demands of different settings, the individual must evolve over ontogeny ways of responding that are specific to the context in which he is placed (Mischel, 1969). Accordingly, it should not be surprising to find that the distinctive social adaptations of the individual reflect a personal mosaic of experimental, situational, and maturational processes. While the substance of the adaptations may differ, the mechanisms by which they are achieved can be general.

One implication of the preceding comments is that we can well afford two levels of analysis in social behavior development. Because of their utility in the description of molar behavior patterns, the "higher order" constructs of dependency and attachment can possibly serve a useful orientation function. Such global constructs permit the identification of developmental and individual difference consistencies that are not easily seen in precise phenomenon-linked analyses. "Reducing values" are not inherently bad (see Mischel, 1969). For certain descriptive purposes, they can be quite useful. But, as Sears et al. (1953) observed, the most attractive constructs in terms of economy and meaningfulness are also the poorest candidates for the demonstration of precise antecedent-consequent relationships. A principal hazard in higher order constructs is the tacit acceptance of the proposition that each refers to a unitary motivational disposition that is generalized directly across space and time. The latter assumption appears not only unnecessary, but also, in the case of the concepts of attachment and dependency, likely wrong.

The second level of analysis would be closer to the several events to which global constructs refer. A basic problem will be to determine how narrow or discrete alternative categorizations should be. As a starting point, the categorical units might be the phenomena that have been considered as the "indices" of attachment/dependency. This would involve considering separately such diverse behaviors as response-to-social-reinforcement, approaching-and-remaining-with-others, and crying-when-mother-departs. Once the phenomena have been identified, the empirical problem will be to specify the events that bear a functional relationship to the so-called "index" behaviors. The search for antecedent-consequent relations in the dyadic sequences in which the behavior is embedded can be conducted without tautological recourse to the higher order construct to which the behavior was assigned. That is, it becomes insufficient to "explain" the behavior because it denotes a particular state of attachment or dependency. More substantive information on the immediate antecedents and consequents of the behavior would be required, including data on the origins and maintenance of the "index" behaviors themselves.

In summary, the dyadic phenomena of social development can be accepted as problems of interest in their own right, and not merely because they serve to "index" a higher order theoretical construct and are "explained" by it. Questions on the interrelations among the several types of dyadic events subsumed by a given term (or different terms) become issues for direct analysis of the relevant processes. This analytic strategy leads to a shift in attention away from global constructs and their validity to a direct analysis of the behaviors that the terms were invented to explain.

The issues will likely be brought into focus by the critical examination of one such global construct, attachment.

ATTACHMENT: ITS MEANINGS AND FUNCTIONS

As the term attachment has been used by recent writers, it has had two separable meanings. On the one hand, attachment behavior has been used to denote particular classes of responses that occur in dyadic relationships, especially those involving the mother and her offspring. These responses include (a) the maintenance of proximity and (b) behavioral disruption when the two members of the dyad are separated nonvoluntarily. In this sense, the term attachment serves to identify specific response tendencies that require explication. Although it is possible to use the concept at this descriptive or taxonomic level, few theorists have settled for such a modest use. More frequently, the term has been assumed to refer to a unitary process that serves to energize, regulate, and direct the several phenomena subsumed by it (Ainsworth, 1969; Bowlby, 1969).

In the past ten years, considerable attention has been given to attachment in the latter sense. Rather separate lines of influence seem to have been responsible, and it would be inappropriate to credit one set of investigators or one theoretical orientation. Animal researchers and theorists, because of their diverse origins and methods, speak with one voice no more than do researchers in child behavior. In particular, although some writers in the ethological tradition have endorsed attachment as a primary explanatory construct, other ethologists have been sharply critical of proposing hypothetical unitary structures to explain the motivation, direction, and control of complex social behaviors (see Hinde, 1956, 1960, 1963; Klopfer & Hailman, 1967). Similar differences in theoretical orientation have been expressed among writers in psychology.

Discussions of the origins of attachment have, for the most part, emphasized its genetic and evolutionary roots. The propensity is thus assumed to be endogenous and immanent (i.e., inborn). Some learning is necessary in view of the fact that species-atypical attachments can be produced and, under some conditions, the object of the attachment can be switched. The central structure itself, however, is assumed to be an inevitable outcome of maturational-developmental processes, in a fashion that is analogous to the development of physical structures. Environmental influences presumably play only a permissive role in the development of the structure. However, the assumption of genetic determination is not a necessary one. Within social-learning accounts, analogous and functionally equivalent motivational structures have been assumed to be the product of individual, not phyletic, experience.

Regardless of the presumed genesis of attachment-as-a-unitary-process (whether genetic, evolutionary, learned, or unspecified), there has been a general consensus among writers with respect to the kinds of services that it performs. Some of the more basic functions include:

1. *Behavior continuity over time and space.* The central structure is presumed to remain relatively stable, regardless of the contingencies of environmental events. Although outward manifestations of the tendency might shift over time as the organism changes in physical structure and in modes of expression, there remains a unitary motivational state through ontogeny (see Emmerich, 1969). In the specific instance of continued separation, the attachment structure will remain intact because it is not directly subject to contemporaneous stimulus conditions. Similarly, the stability of an attachment across situations is assured by virtue of the stable endogenous state.

2. *Differential responsiveness to social events.* Variations in the intensity of attachment behaviors are also attributed to the central state. While it appears paradoxical that the same structure is called upon to account for both stability and variability, the latter property of the construct is entirely in keeping with the functions that are usually assigned to primary drive states. The differential readiness to consume food as a function of hours of deprivation, for instance, is

accounted for by differences in the strength of the hunger drive. The question remains, however, as to whether the structure itself changes, or whether the structure remains invariant and the processes under its control shift. Within the framework of classical ethological theory, it would appear to be the latter. According to Tinbergen (1951), the energy associated with biogenic propensities is "action specific," i.e., available to be used in the performance of a particular activity (see also Dollard, Doob, Miller, Mowrer, & Sears, 1939). Accordingly, attachment "strength" may not only not diminish during periods of separation, it could increase. By the same reasoning, different levels of response to one event by the same individual but at two different times can be attributed to momentary fluctuations in attachment "strength," i.e., energy distribution.

3. *Maintenance of proximity.* The tendency for a young animal to remain with its mother, and vice versa, is a primary justification for, and at the same time is explained by, the internal propensity. On a more general level, the structure itself has been justified in terms of the survival properties of the behavior both for the individual and for the species.

4. *Behavior disruption upon separation.* Like proximity-maintenance, heightened vocalization and increased activity observed when a young animal has been separated from its mother are evidence for, and are explained in terms of, their evolutionary significance and survival functions.

5. *Coherence of attachment behaviors.* A final function that might be assigned to attachment-as-a-process is that it can account for why disparate behaviors are integrated and organized to perform a given response (e.g., maintenance of an optimal distance with respect to the mother).

Difficulties inherent in the postulation of unitary biogenic or motivational structures in order to account for complex social behavior patterns have been discussed in detail elsewhere (e.g., Brown, 1953; Lehrman, 1970; Mischel, 1969; Schneirla, 1959). The issues have concerned the unrestrained generation of central constructs, the negative evidence for the generality and stability of social behaviors, and the hazards of employing a single underlying mechanism to explain diverse characteristics of behavior. Within ethology, the most telling criticisms have been offered by Hinde (1956, 1960), who observed that nothing that we know about the central nervous system corresponds to Tinbergen's model of neural centers and energy displacement. Detailed experimental analysis of the phenomena attributed to "energy displacement," on the other hand, can be directly and parsimoniously interpreted in terms of more immediate stimulus and contextual factors (Andrew, 1956; Zeigler, 1964). But since several secondary sources (e.g., Bolles, 1958; Cofer & Appley, 1964) discuss the issues at length, it does not seem necessary to review them here.

What does need to be said is that the basic issue of the utility of a unitary structure of attachment is *not* whether biophysical events influence behavior. Nor is it whether evolutionary factors or survival properties are involved in the propensity to form social relationships. The issue at stake is whether the hypothesis of a global state is adequate as *an answer sufficient in itself.* If it is not, then we will have to be concerned about the exact mechanisms that account for the stability of social interaction patterns. We will have to ask what is the role of the stimulus context in producing continuity and change. To what extent do drastic shifts in rearing circumstances produce concomitant changes in social behavior? Similarly, we will have to be concerned about morphological and hormonal stability and change, and what effects alterations in internal states have upon dyadic interactions. We will have to be concerned about the extent to which habit structure consistency helps to maintain continuity in behavior in the absence of external contextual supports. We will have to reassess the effects of separation, and to determine precisely what behavior changes occur and the conditions under which they can be inhibited. In sum, we will be required to identify the several organismic, developmental, contextual, and experiential mechanisms that lead to the establishment and maintenance of the behaviors that have been attributed to the unitary process.

Relevant here is the observation of Bolles (1967) that general motivation variables usually provide answers at a point where questions are called for. When specific queries on the contribution of developmental and associative mechanisms are answered, the postulation of attachment as a unitary process may prove to be unnecessary.

Psychobiological Contributions to the Development of Early Social Interactions

Discussions of developmental phenomena nowadays seem incomplete without some reference to the genetic and biological substrates of behavior. This emphasis is a timely one in view of the spectacular advances in molecular biology. But those who aspire to use findings from genetic research for direct guidelines in the analysis of social behavior face an awesome translation task (Dobzhansky, 1967). Happily for developmental psychology, the impact of biological research has been more general. On the one hand, it appears to have inspired a reevaluation of the role of phyletic and evolutionary processes in the control of behavior. On the other hand, renewed interest has been aroused in the tracing of the interactions between morphological, neurophysiological, contextual, and associational determinants of social behavior (Kuo, 1967). The outcomes of this work have begun to yield a preliminary, yet coherent, picture of the particular ways in which endogenous and exogenous influences operate together to determine the course of social interactions.

This information is directly relevant to the problem of how it is that the young animal or infant develops its first social relationships and interaction patterns. These include, of course, the principal phenomena assigned to the attachment construct (e.g., mutual approach, separation-disruption).

Of basic importance for the present chapter is the fact that considerable similarity exists among mammalian infants in the form and type of these initial relationships. The primary features of human infant "attachment behavior" are observed in part or in toto in several other species, from rodents to primates. That adaptations which are apparently homologous to those of human young take place among nonhuman infants suggests that caution should be exercised in the type of construct invoked to explain primitive human social interactions. Especially suspect are such attractive but distinctively human concepts as "separation anxiety," "love," and "cognitive representation."

More important, the occurrence of apparently homologous phenomena in different species of the same class permits the introduction of experimental procedures to examine the mechanisms of control. Whether or not common processes are involved in human and nonhuman forms becomes a question to be answered by accounts of specific phenomena in each group. It seems not unreasonable to expect that some basic and class-universal behaviors are related to events fundamental to the biological adaptation of the mammalian neonate (Schneirla & Rosenblatt, 1961).

ESTABLISHMENT OF DYADIC RESPONDING

The logical place to initiate a psychobiological analysis of social behavior development is at birth (or before). What events are significant in the establishment of interaction patterns at parturition and in the *postpartum* period?

Biogenic factors. Some of our best information on the development of early maternal-infant interactions in mammals has been obtained in studies of the laboratory rat. Detailed accounts of the birth process and the activities of the mother prior to and following parturition indicate that her biological status and that of her offspring are primary determinants of the nature and type of interactions that occur. Even the *prepartum* period may contribute significantly to later maternal-infant adaptations. According to Roth and Rosenblatt (1967), striking changes occur in a pregnant rat's self-licking activities. Whereas nongravid rats concentrate the greatest portion of their "washing" time to the forepaws, back, and sides, pregnant females tend to lick the pelvic area, nipple lines and ano-genital region. Later, during parturition, the licking contributes importantly to the birth process and to the immediate *postpartum* care of the young. At parturition, the maternal animal persists in bursts of licking at the vaginal opening. Upon appearance of the fetus, she draws it to her with her mouth, while licking and rotating it. Turning then to the placenta, she engorges it while holding the pup away with her forepaws. The birth fluids and membranes are licked from the fetus. In the process of licking the pup, the maternal animal gradually begins to concentrate upon the neonate's anal-genital area. This stimulation serves to evoke urination and defecation. The products of elimination are consumed by the mother, and the area thereafter becomes one of "special attractiveness" (Rosenblatt & Lehrman, 1963).

Maternal stimulation thus serves to arouse and maintain activity in the young. There is some evidence to suggest that the adult animal's stimulation serves a directive function as well, in that the offspring are brought into close proximity to the mammary areas as a byproduct of maternal grooming (Blauvelt, 1955). In one experimental analysis of this proposal with sheep, maternal ewes were restricted so that they could neither groom their offspring nor otherwise orient them toward the nipple area. The young lambs, however, were free to move about the enclosure and to suckle. Other ewe-lamb pairs were not restricted. During the first 12 hours following birth, the experimental lambs (whose mothers' heads had been restricted) gained significantly less weight and showed less "teat-seeking activity" than did the offspring of ewes that had not been restricted (Alexander & Williams, 1964). For the purposes of an interaction analysis, it should be observed that the suckling behavior of the young probably serves a dual function. Suckling reduces hydraulic pressure in the mammary glands of the mother while simultaneously providing a preferred substance for the offspring. It seems likely that the anal-genital stimulation of the offspring by the mother has precisely the same dyadic significance. In both instances, essential physiological functions are involved for both.

The picture that emerges in the analysis of immediate *postpartum* interactions is one in which there is rapid evolution of a behavioral interdependence between the mother and her offspring. The interaction chains that occur do not represent a smooth flow of events, but rather ones in which the behaviors of the offspring (and the mother) serve to elicit a reciprocal response in the other. As the interactions recur, the sequences themselves become more predictable, and the behavioral episodes more regular.

How general is this process for mammals? While the above account was drawn primarily from studies of rodents and ungulates, comparable observations have been reported for other domestic species, including dogs (Fuller & Fox, 1969; Rheingold, 1963), cats (Schneirla, Rosenblatt, & Tobach, 1963), and goats (Collias, 1956). While parallel information is obviously more difficult to obtain with nondomesticated species, those reports that are available from observations of primates (Tinklepaugh & Hartman, 1932) and wild ungulates (Altmann, 1963) suggest that the basic elements of the early *postpartum* interactions are relatively general. However, it should be observed that not *all* mammals exhibit all aspects of the behavior described (Lehrman, 1961). The camel, for instance, is not a placentaphage (i.e., does not consume placenta and afterbirth). Furthermore, not all animals within the same litter are treated alike. The last arrival in a litter typically is given less maternal attention than the first-born animal. Clearly there must be some diversity in the physiological and behavioral mechanisms that are operative. The processes that evoke and maintain mutual responding must be sufficiently redundant so that one process can fail without producing disastrous consequences. It is not uncommon, of course, for biological systems to have "fail-safe" features, particularly in those systems that are essential for survival.

One such process involves the thermal regulatory behavior of the neonate itself. Heat loss is a primary cause of mortality in young mammals. Most mammalian species are poikilothermal at birth, and some do not achieve a homeothermal capability for some time afterwards. Rats, for instance, do not develop the capacity to maintain constant body temperatures until at least 18 days of age (Barnett, 1963). It has been proposed that the near universal tendency toward social aggregations observed in the day-old animal—offspring of multiparous species heap themselves against and upon each other—serves a critical thermal-regulatory function. Social stimuli thus could help to modulate and cushion extremes in environmental temperature.

At least some evidence is consistent with the proposal that the neonate varies its closeness to others as a direct function of ambient heat. What is particularly striking is the age and degree of immaturity at which the behavior occurs. Young mice, as far as the receptor-effector apparatus is concerned, are primitive creatures. In the initial 24 hours *postpartum,* the visual, auditory, and olfactory systems are virtually nonfunctional, and the capability for locomotion is poor indeed. Nonetheless, increments in temperature only 7 to 8°C. above the normal state (of 24.5°C.) are sufficient to elicit agitation and dispersion from others in day-old mice. Conversely, a drop in temperature below the normal state serves to increase activity within the "clump" but does not produce increased interanimal distance (R. B. Cairns, S. D. Scholz, & A. Einsiedel, unpublished). Welker (1959) earlier reported that neonatal puppies show tendencies toward aggregation as a direct function of environmental temperature variations.

"Clumping" behavior cannot be exclusively attributed to the actions of young, however. The maternal animal's retrieval of the offspring contributes significantly to the maintenance of cohesiveness of the group. Even more interesting, the heaping that is observed in the neonatal animals continues through to adulthood. The mechanisms that maintain the behavior in the mature animals are probably not the same as those that were responsible for its development, in that the animals are then homeothermal and hardly the objects of retrieval.

Associational factors. What role do experience and learning play in the development, integration, and persistence of the interactions? With the recurrence of a given interaction sequence, the response of each individual in the dyad should acquire the capacity to elicit an anticipatory response in the other (Sears, 1951). A dyadic sequence develops when the behaviors of the two become interdependent, such that a response sequence of the one is enchained to a particular response sequence of the other. In the feeding sequence, for instance, the responses of the mother may become significant cues for the elicitation, maintenance, and inhibition of the suckling responses of the infant. Similarly, the mother begins to discriminate and respond to nuances in the behavior of the young. Since there are a great many repetitions of the feeding interaction every week (e.g., approximately 7 times for rabbits, 480 times for lambs, and 28 times for humans), there should be ample opportunity for discrimination and learning on the part of both members of the dyad. Presumably the mother's responses, at least initially, would be more rapidly conditioned than those of her offspring. Whether or not individual preferences evolve should depend in part upon the extent to which the behaviors and characteristics of the young are distinguishable, and upon whether the maternal animal is capable of the appropriate discriminations.

Studies of the conditioning process in both human and nonhuman infants support the above speculations. Events preparatory to, and during, the feeding sequence acquire elicitory and behavior control properties (e.g., Lipsitt, 1967; Papousek, 1966; Satinoff & Stanley, 1963; Thoman, Wetzel, & Levine, 1968). These cue properties, once established, serve to elicit and organize the behavior, as well as to provide signals for its termination. From analyses of non-feeding dyadic sequences, it appears that such mutual response patterns as play, grooming, and mother-infant transport are formed in the same way as are dyadic sequences involving feeding (Harlow & Harlow, 1965; Kummer, 1968; van Lawick-Goodall, 1968; Nowlis, 1941).

But response synchrony does not tell the whole story of how social events can control the behavior of others. A significant amount of evidence has accumulated which demonstrates that social stimuli can acquire significant cue properties for some species even in the absence of physical interaction (Cairns, 1966a; Walters & Parke, 1965). Apparently social and nonsocial events can support behavior patterns in which they are not directly involved as manipulanda. For example, the response of drinking is conditioned not only to the internal state (hunger cues) and to the manipulanda (nipple or cup), but also to the setting in which the feeding typically occurs. Sharp changes in temperature, in light intensity, or in sound level, or *any* abrupt change in contextual conditions should disrupt the behavior. The idea that the context plays a critical role in behavior support is not a new one, although it has rarely been invoked in discussions of social behavior. The phenomenon that Pavlov (1927) labeled external inhibition reflects the significance of background events in the support of conditioned responses. Later writers, including Tolman (1932) and Logan (1961), have emphasized that a response becomes conditioned not only to the focal stimulus but also to the context in which the behavior occurs. The point to be emphasized is that other individuals can serve as "behavioral supports" for activities in which they are not immediately involved.

This property of pattern conditioning takes on considerable importance when one reviews the actual conditions in which the offspring of most mammals are maintained. During the *postpartum* period, and sometimes considerably beyond, the infants are functionally isolated by the mother from interactions with others. This functional isolation is produced in species that bear precocial young by physical separation from the other members of the group prior to parturition. The mother and her infant remain apart from the conspecific group for periods ranging up to several days or weeks before rejoining. In the case of altricial young (i.e., relatively helpless at birth), continued interaction is required because of the incompetence of the offspring. In both instances the mother-as-a-stimulus is a ubiquitous event, and can potentially become involved in diverse behavioral activities of the young. That is to say, she is likely to become a significant component in most of those stimulus configurations that support the offspring's normal maintenance behaviors. These would include even those response patterns, such as play and grooming, in which she was not directly involved (see Cairns, 1966a, for a more detailed discussion).

MAINTENANCE AND DYNAMICS OF DYADIC RESPONDING

Organismic and associational factors continue to interact to control the direction and course of the young animal's dyadic behavior through ontogeny. The notion of a "critical period" in social development has had, simultaneously, a stimulating and an inhibiting effect upon developmental analyses. It has stimulated ontogenetic work by emphasizing that biogenic factors serve to determine the impact of experiential events, and that the nature of the interaction between endogenous and exogenous events is paced by the maturational status of the young. Unfortunately, the concept focused attention upon only a restricted period of such interaction, early in the life of the individual. The focus upon early effects has tended to shift attention away from the fact that there is a continuous interaction between biogenic and associational events through ontogeny. In discussions of "critical periods," there is a tendency to overlook the fact that the organism is continuously adjusting to changing patterns of internal and external stimulation.

An examination of the young animal's behavior as he progresses from infancy through adolescence to early adulthood indicates that some of the more important changes in dyadic interactions are linked to alterations in his biophysical state. The analysis is complicated by the fact that shifts in organic status can be either a *determinant* or an *outcome* of changes in dyadic interaction patterns. The type of social-physiological feedback patterns that occur is nicely illustrated in the outcome obtained when rat mothers are prematurely separated from their young. Compared with a group of control mothers (i.e., those who kept their litters), mothers whose young have been kidnapped show a sharp decrement in their readiness to nurse, retrieve, or build nests. Correlated changes occur in their physiological status. Normally, estrous cycles are inhibited in maternal rats until about the fourth week after they give birth. In the case of females whose litters have been removed, however, estrous cycling begins shortly after parturition (Rothchild, 1960). Even more remarkable, the physiological state of the mother—in terms of lactation, retrieval, and nest-building—can be prolonged indefinitely by constantly replacing her growing litter with pups less than 10 days of age (Wiesner & Sheard, 1933). Filial interactions provide the feedback for the maintenance of the "maternal condition," which in turn leads to a persistence in the filial interaction, and so on. The resultant behavioral → endocrinological → tissue change → behavioral feedback loop provides a sensitive mechanism for coordinating physiological status with current adaptational requirements.

Under normal conditions, the maturational status of the offspring is a primary pacemaker in the system. Changes in the morphology and nutritional needs of the young, for instance, set into action the chain of maternal responses that leads to weaning. Whether a young dog's gnawing and chasing will elicit reciprocal play and grooming or avoidance depends upon its size and strength. The chewing of a toothless 28-day-old puppy has effects markedly different from those of topographically similar behavior when the same animal is 4 months old (Cairns & Werboff, 1967). Finally, as the recent literature has amply documented, young animals and infants show an increasing tendency to orient toward perceptually salient events in their environment. As their motor and sensory capacities develop, this orientation is reflected in increased locomotion toward such events. Such unlearned, maturation-determined structural changes play a critical role in the extinction and revision of earlier dyadic chains, and set the conditions for the learning of alternative responses.

Even in these instances, however, it would be gratuitous to assert that maturational events "determined" the particular form of dyadic patterns that evolve. Responses of the adult to altered dyadic responding by the young apparently serve to consolidate and to modify further the behavior of the offspring. Although learned response tendencies serve to provide stability in any given relationship, the interaction sequences between two organisms are dynamic and are continuously vulnerable to modification from within and from without.

DISRUPTION AND EXTINCTION OF DYADIC INTERACTIONS

Filial interactions are not only established and maintained; they also diminish in frequency and change in form. The processes that govern the eventual movement of the animal away from the mother and litter mates must be considered of primary importance in any overview of the ontogeny of social responsiveness. There are sharp differences among species, and within species, in the timing and course of such separations. Some feral-reared animals, such as female sheep (Grubb & Jewell, 1966) and certain chimpanzees (van Lawick-Goodall, 1968) tend to remain with the mother through adulthood. Other closely related animals, including male sheep and various primates, become dissociated from the mother almost as soon as they can maintain themselves independently.

The most direct and certainly the most economical account of this process is in terms of a "waning" of strength of an underlying "attachment" propensity (Bowlby, 1969). The waning has been presumed by some writers to be paced by an internal neurophysiological disposition that is immediately linked to the maturational status of the individual. This explanation tells us little about the details of the process, however, and fails to indicate how internal or experiential events can contribute to the "waning."

Empirical information on the processes involved has been provided by studies of the young animal's reactions during and following separation from the mother. Because a psychobiological analysis has implications that are immediately pertinent to such operations, a recapitulation of some of the more important expectations seems in order. Within the framework of the analysis, the young animal's behavior patterns would be expected to be disrupted by maternal removal to the extent that she had become a significant stimulus in the support of his responses. The support could be in either of two forms. On the one hand, the mother's behavior could serve as an essential component in the formation and performance of particular dyadic response sequences. Following the repetition of these sequences, the behavior of the one would become enchained to the behavior of the other in the completion of that dyadic sequence. The elimination of one or the other would make it impossible to perform any of these sequences in which the two had served as reciprocal partners. In addition, stimuli distinctive to the mother may also serve a more general role in the support of response patterns of the young in which she was not directly involved. To the extent that she has become a significant feature of the context in which nondyadic or maintenance activities are performed, then those activities should be at least temporarily disrupted by her absence. To put the distinction succinctly, maternal events can serve as *focal* or as *contextual* stimuli in the support of behavior.

Certain expectations for what should happen during, and following, extended maternal-offspring separation follow directly from this analysis. In the case of dyadic sequences where the mother had been involved as a reciprocating partner, it would be expected that "those habits that S had acquired specifically with respect to [her] presumably would remain relatively intact [Cairns, 1966a, p. 414]." This means that insofar as the conditioning assumptions are concerned, she would maintain whatever specific dyadic cue properties that had been originally established, if organismic and contextual factors could be held relatively constant. The adequacy of this prediction would be determined by the behavior of the two animals *following* a period of separation.

On the other hand, the analysis requires that her function as a contextual stimulus would be directly affected by the forced separation. During the period that the young animal is required to remain away from the mother, presumably a new conditioning process is initiated. And the longer that the young animal remains in the "motherless" context, the fewer will be the response patterns that remain exclusively conditioned to her presence. That is, maternal-produced events will be represented in progressively fewer of the stimulus configurations that support the animal's ongoing behaviors. Whether or not contextual conditioning occurs would be determined by the animal's behavior *during* the period of separation.

Fortunately for the purposes of evaluating the adequacy of the above analysis, the effects of maternal-separation have been studied in both ways. One set of studies has involved tracing the animal's adaptation to a motherless environment during separation, and another set of investigations has been concerned with the behavior at and following reunion (i.e., termination of the separation). The results of the two procedures can be best summarized separately.

Behavior during separation. A reasonable amount of research has accumulated on the behavior of young that have been shifted to a motherless context. In general, the results indicate that an adaptation or behavioral reorganization process is initiated following separation (e.g., Mason, 1967; Hinde & Spencer-Booth, 1967; Rosenblum & Kaufman, 1968). In some instances, as in the case of young sheep and dogs, the conditioning to new contextual support stimuli occurs very rapidly (i.e., within 96 hours in the case of dogs, Cairns & Werboff, 1967; within 72 hours in the case of 8-week-old sheep, R. B. Cairns & S. D. Scholz, unpublished). It would be inaccurate to assert, however, that the course of adaptation is equally rapid in all species, regardless of age or species-typical social organization. Significant individual—and subspecies—differences have been reported (Elliot & Scott, 1961).

Such variability points up the need to specify the precise conditions under which the individual is maintained during the time that he is separated from the mother. Attention to contemporary maintenance circumstances is especially important if the infant is left with other animals. The interaction characteristics and social organization of the group with which he is left should be significant determinants of the course of the adaptation process. The time course of the process, the similarity of his behavior to that observed in the preseparation period, and the extent to which he demonstrates aberrant responses (e.g., withdrawal, motor depression) would all be influenced by the activities of others with respect to him.

Recent studies of the differential response of two species of macaque monkeys to short-term maternal separation underscore the importance of the maintenance circumstances (e.g., Rosenblum & Kaufman, 1968). The pigtail macaque infant usually responds to maternal-separation first with extreme agitation, then with marked depression, and finally with a gradual recovery of preseparation levels of activity. The depression stage is marked by virtual cessation of activity, by withdrawal, and by nonresponsiveness to stimulation. Bonnet monkeys, on the other hand, typically fail to show "anything remotely resembling the severe depressive reaction" of the pigtails (Rosenblum & Kaufman, 1968, p. 425). Following a period of agitation, bonnet infants settle down to an activity level that compares favorably to that observed in the preseparation periods. Rosenblum and Kaufman (1968) observed that these separation-induced behavioral differences in the infants were directly correlated with differences in the way that the nonmaternal animals responded to them the motherless context. The adult pigtail macaques more or less ignored the orphaned infants, while the adult bonnet macaques freely interacted with the young. The joint effects of differences in the maternal and nonmaternal care combined to produce dramatic differences in the offspring, including their response to maternal separation. The lesson that the investigators saw in their work was that "the line between phylogenetic and ontogenetic forces, as is so often the case, becomes at least increasingly blurred with intensive study. It seems evident here that behaviors which, because of their species specificity ... might appear to have a specific genetic base, may well be highly influenced by ontogenetic factors, in ways that might be overlooked without detailed comparative studies [Rosenblum & Kaufman, 1968, p. 426]."

Reactions to reunion. Studies of "reunion" following brief periods of separation (relative to the normal life span of the species) provide support for the assumption that separation leaves the habits acquired directly with respect to the "mother" for the most part intact. Unfortunately, experimental reports of reunion typically fail to indicate who initiates the interaction: mother or offspring (Hinde, 1969; Mason, 1965). Re-presentation of the other would be expected to momentarily heighten its salience, and thus to elicit those dyadic activities that had been specifically conditioned to the other. Once these responses have been elicited, it does not necessarily follow that the behavior of the two would revert to preseparation levels. Instead, it would be expected that the behavior of each would be ordered around the contemporaneous activity of the other. The nature of the dyads that form, and the relative probability of their recurrence, would reflect the current biophysical status of both members of the pair.

In the analysis of maternal-separation studies, it is important not to ignore the continuing contribution of endogenous states. If the period of removal is long enough, there will be biophysical changes in both the mother and her progeny. Either set of changes may serve to alter succeeding dyadic interactions. Relevant here are some unpublished findings that we obtained on the effects of maternal-offspring separation in dogs. The experiment was a simple one: the pups were removed from their mothers at 4 weeks of age, and permitted to interact with her at the end of 5 weeks of separation. We found that the pups (like Mason's chimpanzees and Hinde's rhesus monkeys) did not forget. When the pups were given the choice of approaching their mothers or an empty goal area in a Y-maze, they demonstrated a strong tendency to select the mothers. What was surprising to me was the observation that mother love didn't persist. The bitches attempted to avoid their offspring, and if this failed, they nipped at, pushed away, and otherwise discouraged the pups. The treatment worked, at least for the mothers, and the pups ceased to approach. Why the rejection? Observation of the pups' reactions to their mothers suggests an answer. Immediately upon sighting her in the goal areas, the pups attempted to suckle. The mothers, however, had long since stopped lactating because they were no longer being stimulated by the litter. The feeding interaction sequence was, in effect, impossible to maintain and possibly even painful to the mother.

Furthermore, the offspring had changed. Significant differences had occurred in response topography and physical appearance during the period of separation. Such "unlearned" factors made the resumption of the previously established reciprocal sequences impossible. Although stimulus-response associations can remain relatively intact during periods of separation, the responses will not be evoked if the stimuli themselves have been irrevocably altered.

Note should be made of the seemingly paradoxical outcomes that have been obtained in studies of brief separations. If one considers behavioral disruption to be an index of "attachment," it would appear that attachment strength is diminished as a function of length of separation. On the other hand, if the tendency to approach and remain with another is the index, then brief separations leave the attachment strength unchanged or even intensified. The paradox arises if both behaviors are assumed to be controlled by a single underlying mechanism. Detailed consideration of the behaviors indicates, again, that overlapping but separable conditioning processes control the two responses.

Detachment. The behaviors of the mother and the offspring ordinarily become increasingly independent of each other; there is a behavioral detachment[3] of the two. While this outcome can be produced experimentally by withdrawing the young from the mother, the question can be raised as to what produces separations in natural circumstances. Some writers have proposed that maternal punishment of the offspring plays the critical role in detachment (e.g., Hansen, 1966). Others have focused upon the behavior of the infant (e.g., Ainsworth 1969; Bell, 1968; Rosenblum & Kaufman, 1968; Rheingold & Eckerman, 1970).

In a discussion of this matter, Hinde and Spencer-Booth (1967) write that "we feel that it cannot be too strongly emphasized that the relationship between mother and infant is a developing, interacting pattern [p. 195]." Clearly both are involved and contribute to the "detachment." As the behavior of the one changes, in response to endogenous biophysical events as well as to external contingencies, reciprocal adjustments occur in the behavior and the structures of the other. The reciprocal feedback then serves to augment and to stabilize the change. Although the fact that the child or young animal helps to shape his own future has been too long ignored, it would be just as specious to overlook the continuing contributions of those with whom he interacts.

Some Theoretical Comments on Early Social Development

ON REINFORCEMENT AND THE RESPONSE-SUPPORT PROPERTIES OF ENVIRONMENTAL EVENTS

Since Harlow's (1958) demonstration that primary reinforcement in the form of hunger-tension reduction was not an essential component in the establishment

---

[3] It should be noted that Ainsworth's use of "detachment" differs from its meaning in this chapter. Here the term refers to the species-typical developmental pattern whereby the young spend less time in close proximity to their parents as a function of age.

of surrogate preferences, hedonic and reinforcement models have been on the defensive. But the concept of reinforcement is too useful and powerful to be eliminated by just one type of disconfirming evidence. It is, therefore, important to observe that additional evidence gained over the past decade has been equally embarrassing for hedonic-reinforcement accounts. The findings include:

1. Social preferences develop even when the mother is severely punitive with respect to the young (Kummer, 1968; Rosenblum & Harlow, 1963; Sackett, 1967; Seay, Alexander, & Harlow, 1964).

2. Behavioral disruption in human infants appears to vary with the variety and number of interactions that occur between the child and its caretaker. Evidence for an effect of the quality of such interactions (e.g., "warmth") remains equivocal (Ainsworth, 1967; Fleener & Cairns, 1970; Schaffer & Emerson, 1964).

3. Young animals acquire a preference for, and are disturbed by, the removal of events which have been continuously present in the area in which they have lived. The properties are established even if the subject is not permitted to interact physically with the object (Cairns, 1966b; Cairns & Werboff, 1967; Cairns & Johnson, 1965; Walters & Parke, 1965, review related evidence).

4. Events that are perceptually salient or novel have the capacity to elicit perceptual and motor approach responses in young animal and human infants (e.g., Cantor, Cantor, & Ditrichs, 1963; Fantz, 1967; McCall, 1969; Parry, 1972; Rheingold & Eckerman, 1970).

Again, no single set of results can be considered in itself crucial for the appetitional-reinforcement assumption. But taken together, the findings are sufficient at least to raise doubts about its unchallenged acceptance as an essential feature in the establishment of reciprocal response patterns.

The picture is complicated by the equally well-established findings that some properties of events facilitate the formation of interactions, and that these properties are also positively correlated with the establishment of preferences. For instance, events that can elicit and maintain sucking (e.g., "pacifier," nipple, thumb) tend to become preferred objects. If they are presented during periods of separation-disruption, they also have the capacity to inhibit distress. Similarly, objects which are mildly reactive to stimulation (e.g., mobiles, most living objects) and which elicit and maintain play, have the same dual influence upon behavior. And as Harlow (1958) originally emphasized, soft, furry objects which have the capacity to elicit and maintain a variety of behaviors (e.g., grooming, lying down, clinging) also serve to determine preferences and to inhibit behavioral disruption.

The problem of how to conceptualize these properties of events that influence the phenomena of social interaction has not been a trivial one. The usual solution has been to assign these events, or the activities that they evoke, primary reinforcement status. This "explanation" suggests more problems than it solves. While it preserves the hedonic-reinforcement account of social interactions, it opens the door for the expedient of "explaining" the social control properties of any event by its a posteriori classification as a primary reinforcer. Given such freedom in the introduction of reinforcement properties, the idea that interactions are cemented together through the action of some primary reinforcement event becomes virtually impossible to disprove.

As observed earlier, certain concepts tend to give us answers when further questions would be more valuable. The use of the term "reinforcement" in this context may be a case in point. Examination of events that have the dual properties of eliciting approach and inhibiting distress suggests that a factor common to them is the capacity to elicit and maintain organized responding in the young subject. Many of these organized activities (e.g., play, grooming) do not have any obvious relationship to endogenous homeostatic tension states. It might be that the behavior organization capability of the event is itself the feature that facilitates dyadic conditioning. That is, the event would not necessarily be seen as "reinforcing" interaction, but as providing the occasion and the setting for the support of the interaction. Other events associated with it would acquire the capacity to elicit and maintain components of the interaction sequence. Similarly, the reason why presentation of particular events during a period of behavioral disorganization serves to inhibit crying and other forms of distress is that they elicit organized responses with respect to themselves (see Wolff, 1969, who has offered a similar argument). A "pacifier" is one such event for infants. Alternatively, the event may provide the contextual support for some pattern of organized responding.

This proposal is not intended to diminish the importance of "reinforcement" processes so much as it is intended to offer research guidelines for investigating their effective mechanism in social interactions. The analysis focuses attention upon the response-support properties of environmental events, and upon their capacity to elicit and maintain response sequences.

Certain psychobiological implications of the response-support analysis require comment. Organisms that differ in terms of structure and encoding processes doubtless also differ in terms of the kinds of events that can support and maintain their response patterns. For example, among those species with finely differentiated structures for grasping, environmental events that permit clinging and grooming should have particular behavior support properties. Other species that do not have the required morphological structures, such as ungulates, would be relatively uninfluenced by this feature of stimulus event. The stimulus properties that are most relevant for a lamb are not necessarily of equivalent importance for a young monkey.

On the other hand, it should be possible to identify certain environmental events that have response-support properties that are general to all species in the *class*. Since all mammals have at least one behavior in common, it would be expected that events which support sucking would have response-organization properties for all mammalian young. But even though an event has the capacity to support one response pattern, it does not follow that the organism will spend all or even most of its time around the event. While not eating or suckling, it likely will be in the presence of those events that support other activities in its repertoire, including grooming, sleeping, and climbing. While suckling-feeding interactions are important because of their universality and individual survival properties, they constitute but one set of a population of interactions in which the young and objects in its environment might become involved.

A parallel case can be made for expecting that changes will occur through ontogeny in the response-support properties of events. With development-paced modifications in the response and sensory apparatus, there should be concomitant differences in the extent that particular environmental events are effective in evoking and maintaining behavior. In the early stages of infancy, for instance, the rhesus monkey infant spends a great deal of time either sleeping or suckling. These physiologically determined behaviors have a high probability of occurrence, and environmental events that support their performance likely will be those with which the most time is spent (Harlow, 1961). But as the response and sensory capabilities of the organism mature, a greater variety of responses is possible. To the extent that these "new" behaviors become linked to alternative events in the environment, either because the performance of the response requires it or because of contextual conditioning, new preferences and interaction sequences will evolve. Responses, not organisms, become "attached" to stimuli. As response patterns change, so must the events that support them.

ON THE PARADOXICAL EFFECTS OF PUNISHMENT

It is of interest to extend the response-support analysis to the curious effects of maternal punishment upon infant social preferences. Several reports of mammalian social development have demonstrated that social approach and proximity-maintenance are not necessarily inhibited or extinguished by punishment. On the contrary, studies of monkey infants indicate strongest preferences are demonstrated with respect to punitive mothers (Arling & Harlow, 1967; Sackett, 1967; Seay, Alexander, & Harlow, 1964). "Motherless-monkey mothers" (i.e., females that have been raised in isolation and at maturity bear young) behave in an entirely unmotherly fashion toward their offspring. They either abuse their infants or are indifferent and ignore them. Seay et al. (1964) report that few of the infants would have survived if intervention measures had not been taken by the laboratory staff. In one instance, "the mother passively accepted the baby to the breast by Day 3 [after birth] , and attempts to remove and hand feed the baby were abandoned on Day 4 since such efforts provoked violent attacks directed against her infant." The attacks included "crushing the infant's head and body against the floor . . . and jumping up and down with her full weight on the infant [p. 347] ." Despite the abusive treatment, the infants persisted in clinging to the mother's body, and were disrupted when separated from her.

The detailed observations of Seay et al. (1964) suggest that the clinging behavior might have been, at least initially, an adaptive species-typical escape response. The report indicates that the more violent attacks occurred when attempts were made to remove the infant or when it attempted to separate itself from her. One of the more effective defensive responses that the infant had available to minimize such treatment may have involved clinging to the mother's body. Maintenance of proximity could have originally served, among other things, an attack-inhibiting function. Similarly, in another observation of the offspring of motherless monkeys, Sackett (1967) reports that extreme aggression occurred only during the first 2 to 3 months of life. "After this time overt hostility by the mothers rarely occurred *because the infants learned to avoid attacks by the mother* [Sackett, 1967, p. 365, my italics]."

Observations of what happens in the young of other species that are placed with a punitive adult suggest that they also develop adaptive dyadic responses. For instance, if a 6-week-old infant lamb is placed in a small compartment with an unfamiliar adult ewe, she will vigorously and violently rebuff approaches by battering the lamb against the walls. Since the ewe uses her head to butt, the lamb can avoid those onslaughts by remaining behind her. In fact, the young rapidly learn to follow, rather than remain in front of, the rejecting females. Again, the behavior of the adult provides the occasion for the development of reciprocal adaptive responses in the young. Once these interaction sequences are acquired, they are—like avoidance responses in general—highly resistant to change. They also provide the occasion for the subsequent development of other interdependent behaviors in the mother-infant dyad.

The above observations were made, it should be noted, under special conditions of environmental restriction. Neither the young nor the "mothers" were permitted to escape, and alternative objects were not available which would support the performance of the young animals' response patterns. Quite a different outcome is obtained under less restrictive circumstances. In the naturalistic or seminaturalistic setting, continued punishment by the mother for approach of the young is typically associated with physical separation and diminution of the filial bond (Altmann, 1963). And observations of ungulates indicate that rebuffs by other potential mothers for approach to them serve to maintain the coherence of the relationship between a lamb and its *real* mother (who does not reject). The young, in this case, do not prefer the punishing female. Finally, pain *contingency* (i.e., whether punishment is elicited by approach or withdrawal) is a primary determinant of its dyadic effects. In the Hymadryas baboon, for instance, harem cohesion is maintained in part by attacks by the male "leader" upon females that stray (Kummer, 1968). In brief, the "punitive" behaviors themselves support dyadic responses in the young. Whether the net outcome is an increment, or decrement, in mutual preference depends upon such factors as the contingency of the punishment, its intensity, its context, and the developmental status of the young.

LOVE AND AROUSAL

One of the less compelling features of social-learning analyses of social development analysis is that they ignore the visceral features of the phenomenon. Four-week-old beagle pups are so uncoordinated that they are unable to walk and must move about by "swimming" movements. Yet if these young animals are removed from their mother and litter-mates, they show almost adult levels of excitement and duress. Similarly, in the pigtail macaque, maternal-infant separation leads to frantic, nondirected activity in both members of the pair, mother and infant alike. For most of us, the depth of emotional response observed in the animals can be readily apprehended. Any parent who has experienced the terror of not being able to find his 4-year-old at dusk on an unfamiliar seashore *knows* the degree of arousal that separation can evoke.

How might such common arousal experiences fit with a psychobiological analysis of the processes of early social interactions? A review of the theoretical models that have been offered indicates that emotional states—love, affection, anxiety—have been frequently assigned the basic responsibility for the phenomenon. One of the early proposals on the emotional control of "gregarious" behavior was offered by Tolman (1942). He argued that "the individual, when separated from the flock or herd, or group, seeks to get back into it in order to prevent an internal sufferance which in gregarious species seems to result directly from lack of surrounding animals [Tolman, 1942, p. 21]." Similar proposals have been offered by Dollard and Miller (1950) as well as Brown (1953), except that for these writers "internal sufferance" becomes anxiety, and the biological drive becomes a learnable one. In any event, all of these proposals point to the negative emotional arousal engendered by separation, and make it the cornerstone of a theoretical account of dyadic and group cohesion.

Theoretical accounts of human social behavior have, on the other hand, emphasized the operation of positive emotional states. Even the radical behavioral account offered by Watson (1928) invoked "love" as the primary factor in the maintenance of the filial relationship. More recently, Ainsworth (1969) has expanded upon this theme. This view of social relationships resonates pretty well with common experience. We might ask, then, why have not all theoretical accounts given primary attention to the control features of positive emotional states? The answer seems to be two-fold. The first reason is related to the hegemony of drive reduction models of motivation in psychology which held, in effect, that social behavior was instigated and maintained to the extent that it served to reduce tension states. Such models do not easily assimilate the possibility that some behaviors are maintained because of their affect *producing* properties. Then there is the empirical ambiguity of the concepts of "love" and "affection." Analyses of nonhuman behavior can readily detect the operation of heightened emotional arousal of a disrupting and mobilizing nature. The concepts of "fear" and "anxiety" are anchored by parallels across species in terms of the patterns of autonomic reactivity observed and the types of stimulus conditions that evoke them. No such cross-specific patterns have been identified in the "positive" emotional states.

Simply that emotional consequences are difficult to identify and integrate into existing theoretical structures does not mean that we can afford to ignore them. Recent theoretical analyses, in conjunction with a highly perceptive early one, offer some promising guidelines for their integration into social processes. In the recent literature, the proposal of Mandler (1964) on the effects of behavioral interruption seems immediately relevant to understanding the relationship between separation and emotional arousal. According to Mandler, the interruption of an "organized" behavior sequence is sufficient to produce a state of arousal and "emotional behavior" (Mandler, 1964). Following Schacter and Singer (1962), Mandler assumes that visceral arousal has no emotional specificity in itself. The labeling of the arousal state, and the behaviors that it elicits, are determined by situational-contextual events.

Even though the model was not stated in terms of the maintenance or disruption of social relationships, it can be extended to encompass them. Consider, for instance, the phenomenon of separation. Abrupt removal of the mother may, at once, elicit responses directed toward her but at the same time ensure that the elicited response sequence cannot be completed. The primary manipulanda (the mother) is no longer present. Emotional behavior (e.g., crying, thrashing about in the infant) follows from behavioral interruption. The arousal state is maintained until another organized response pattern is elicited in her absence, or until she returns.

Although Mandler (1964) views the essential process to be behavioral interruption → arousal → behavioral disorganization, there is a reasonable basis for arguing that the proper sequence of the last two phases is the other way around. That is, behavioral disorganization may follow directly from the removal of environmental events that can support organized response sequences, and the emotional arousal is just one aspect of more general response "disintegration." If some alternative response sequences could be performed in the context, such as clinging or sucking, they should lead to response organization and a general "pacifying." In effect, the occurrence of an integrated response sequence would provide the occasion for the synchronization of internal as well as effector-receptor processes.

Doubtless experience plays an important role in the integration of internal as well as external processes. To the extent that environmental events become reliable precursors of change, they themselves should acquire the capacity to elicit appropriate levels of internal response. After the repeated occurrence of, say, separation, it would be difficult to disentangle the initial or original succession of events. Emotional responses thereby become part of the total configuration of events that control the individual's behavior.

Emotion as dynamic background. Some of the basic problems of the involvement of emotions in behavior were outlined in an early (1928) essay by Knight Dunlap. In an obscure and almost forgotten paper entitled "Emotion as a

Dynamic Background," Dunlap objects to the common practice (then and now) of considering "emotions" to be absolute qualities that are divorced from the context and organism in which they occur. According to Dunlap, "emotional states" can most appropriately be viewed as stimulus patterns or configurations that have the capacity to "bring about or check" the activities of the organism. He thus argues that emotions can participate in the determination of all responses of the individual.

Of particular interest for the analysis offered in the present chapter is Dunlap's interpretation of emotions as background. He argues that the sense of our internal states—or the total of visceral occurrences—is the typical "background" against which our activities are performed. He writes, "Visceral content is normally background. External content is normally foreground. Somatic content is normally integrated with the background, but may from time to time emerge into the foreground, or even into the focus." The same point is made succinctly when he states that "auditory and visual stimuli may come and go, but our guts are always with us . . . ." Then he adds that ". . . at various times large parts of the external world are as much a part of the background as are the visceral factors. There is thus no organic division, no anatomical one, of perception from feeling. The distinction is one of integration [Dunlap, 1928, pp. 155-156]."

Although Dunlap did not take up the problem of the development of emotional states, it seems consistent with his general outline to propose that the basic stuff out of which emotions are made is with the individual through ontogeny. What does change over time are: (a) modifications in the hormonal-visceral apparatus itself and its controls, (b) the types of external events that can recruit and/or diminish internal states, and (c) the capacity to differentiate and label internal states. Accordingly, the several human emotions of love, anger, anxiety, and so on, do not develop as entities which are disembodied from the behavior of the individual. Rather, they are internal states that participate in and become synchronized with particular social and nonsocial activities. Symbolization in the human permits increasingly finer differentiation of bodily states, and provides for the extension of the range of events and settings that can elicit them.

The importance of emotional states in the analysis of behavior interactions cannot be denied. There are nonetheless hazards in singling out a particular emotion, whether love or fear or anxiety, and assigning to it the burden of "explaining" the acquisition and maintenance of diverse patterns of social behavior. The main problems are that the development of the arousal state itself is left unresolved, and the essential integration of cognitive, biochemical, and effector events is obscured. Doubtless visceral changes do promote and accompany dyadic interactions in the neonate and young infant. But to attribute the conspecific and maternal preferences of young rats or monkeys simply to "love" or "fear" can hardly clarify either the behavior or the emotional state.

Summary: Early Interaction Development

By way of summary, it should be useful to distinguish between the *establishment* of maternal-infant interaction patterns and the *maintenance* of these patterns. The events that make for the initial establishment of the relationship may not be the same as those that provide for its maintenance. Interaction chains apparently can be elicited by many different events, according to the species and the age of the individuals involved. And once interchange has been elicited, by whatever mechanism, the response patterns of the members of the dyad are altered via learning mechanisms.

What makes the summary task challenging is the fact that the eliciting events are not limited to simply one stage of ontogeny. During each developmental phase, significant changes in structure, hormonal status, and perceptual and cognitive capabilities can trigger changes in interaction patterns. Similarly, the repeated occurrence of a given interaction sequence provides the occasion for modifications in the individual's structural and perceptual-cognitive status. Nonetheless, there is some advantage in focusing upon the initial establishment of the relationship. Although reciprocal interchanges between structure and behavior are not limited to infancy, they are in some instances more readily disentangled in the early periods of life than at maturity.

ESTABLISHMENT OF EARLY INTERACTIONS

Among the events that have been shown to contribute to the initial establishment of nonhuman parent-infant social relationships, the following appear to be of rather general importance.

1. *Phasic processes at birth.* Behaviors evoked in the mother by events surrounding parturition (e.g., self-grooming, placentaphagous activity, licking of young) heighten the probability of mutual contact and acceptance.

2. *Temperature regulation.* The thermal control activity of the mother and neonate supports such behaviors as nest-building, clumping, neonatal aggregation and dispersion, and maternal retrieval.

3. *Neural reflexes.* Reflexive responding of the mother and neonate provide for the initial synchronization of neonatal activities (e.g., orientation, rooting, and sucking) and maternal stimulation and nursing.

4. *Cyclic processes.* Rhythmic engorgement of maternal mammary glands and the digestive tract of the offspring promotes reciprocal and coordinated maternal-neonatal consummatory behavior.

5. *Hormonal and humoral processes.* Biochemical states of the mother are correlated with several components of maternal behavior (Moltz, 1970; Rosenblatt, 1970).

In brief, the stimuli of the "other" provide the occasion for the performance of prepotent response patterns and, thereby, the development of mutual dependencies in behavior. The principal attachment phenomena of nonhumans (e.g., initiation of contact, maintenance of proximity) observed in the *postpartum* period reflect dyadic events promoted by basic thermal, reflexive, nutritive, and hormonal processes.

A major question arises on the role of prior experience, either specific or nonspecific, in determining whether these biological events will elicit maternal-infant interactions. For some mammalian species, including rats, apparently no particular experience with young animals is required for the evocation of adequate maternal care patterns. Maternal rats reared in total conspecific isolation turn out to be reasonably adequate in the basic parameters of maternal care (Thoman & Arnold, 1968). In primates, however, rearing with others of their kind seems important for the initial development of appropriate care patterns (Seay et al., 1964). Precisely why species-typical maternal patterns are not evoked in rhesus monkeys who have not been reared with others of their kind remains to be discovered. What is known is that experience with a young offspring serves to alter the response patterns of maternal animals when they are presented with another opportunity at caretaking. Even motherless monkeys who were brutal with respect to the firstborn adequately care for their second-born offspring. Similarly, rat mothers change with experience, treating offspring from the second and later litters differently from the way they do the first litter. It is plausible, but not necessary, to assume that these changes reflect learning processes. Increased readiness for maternal behavior could be also due to experience-produced changes in the biological states of the female (e.g., ease of delivery, readiness to lactate, lowered sensitivity).

MAINTENANCE OF DYADIC INTERACTIONS AND PREFERENCES

What are the events that serve to *maintain* specific parental-infant interactions? Presumably whatever events lead to the maintenance of a particular interaction sequence are also responsible for the development of specific preferences, i.e., attachment behaviors.

As indicated in the preceding discussion, repeated participation in a given interchange promotes in both individuals changes in the stimulus properties of the other, as well as changes in the form and motor coordination of the response itself. It is the change in the stimulus properties of others that appears to be basic to the phenomena of attachment. Such changes come about through the following processes:

1. *Synchronization of dyadic behaviors.* Once distinctive mutual response sequences have been established, they tend to be self-perpetuating. The more distinctive the form of interaction and the behavior of the participants, the more likely it is that the specific relationship will evolve. In the highly distinctive case, only certain "social" manipulanda and background stimuli will permit the performance of organized response sequences. In terms of social attachment

behavior this means that a particular "other" will become preferred, and that behavior disruption will occur upon the removal of the "other." The associational mechanisms underlying this phenomenon have been elaborated elsewhere (Cairns, 1966a).

2. *Ecological and genetic processes.* Maternal animals in several species isolate themselves and their offspring from others following parturition. Such isolation promotes, among other things, the establishment of individual recognition and mutually supportive response patterns. In addition, exclusive infant-maternal preferences tend to evolve among species that bear single offspring (e.g., sheep, monkeys) as opposed to multiple offspring (e.g., rodents, dogs). Such an outcome seems consistent with the proposal that mutual discriminations develop most readily in the course of insulated and exclusive interactions.

3. *Reciprocal biophysical maintenance.* The behaviors of the neonate serve to maintain the maternal animal in that biological state that is required for the continued performance of its own (the infant's) responses. Such a feedback loop occurs, for instance, in the maintenance of maternal hormonal states for lactation. By virtue of its own activities, the young shapes and maintains salient features of its environment. Those features are thereby peculiarly suited to support the behaviors of the young at precisely the level required by its current morphological-biophysical development.

The phenomena of "attachment" are embedded in specific response sequences and occur in particular contexts. What manipulanda and discriminanda are "preferred" (i.e., approached) for the performance of responses of one class need not be the same as those preferred for alternative response patterns. In some contexts, the mother does not prefer to approach the infant, and vice versa. The appropriate study of such phenomena in any species requires a functional analysis of the behavior, its antecedents, and its dyadic consequences.

DEVELOPMENTAL MODIFICATION OF MATERNAL–OFFSPRING INTERACTIONS AND PREFERENCES

Social interactions (and related preferences) are not only established and maintained; they are also modified and extinguished. An overview of the developmental-comparative literature implicates certain major pacemakers of the modification process, including the following changes.

Changes in the effector apparatus. As the basic response capabilities of the individual are modified, so must be the events in the environment capable of supporting those responses. For example, when suckling ceases to be the primary consummatory response, nondyadic food sources become salient. In addition, changes in the effector apparatus evoke changes in reciprocal responding, thus modifying response form in both individuals. Another effector change involves locomotion. "Learning to walk" has manifold consequences for the modification of previously existing interaction patterns, as well as for the development of new ones.

Changes in sensory-perceptual capabilities. Maturational changes in perception and sensory discrimination are of fundamental importance in pacing the specificity of early social interactions. That monumental perceptual changes occur over development cannot be disputed. What have been lacking up to this point are precise attempts to disentangle the effects due to sensory-perceptual changes from those due to correlated effector apparatus changes. The species-typical onset of some attachment phenomena (e.g., orientation toward familiar individuals, disruption upon visual separation from them) implies the development of new levels of sensory differentiation.

Changes in biochemical status. For the growing infant, social behaviors are directly influenced by developmentally linked changes in internal regulatory mechanisms. These include changes in temperature control (from poikilothermal to homeothermal), in adrenal function and secretion, and in the central control of hormones. Although the postnatal modifications that occur vary as a function of the particular system and species involved, the general patterns of hormonal action and development are reasonably similar across mammals (Gorbman & Bern, 1962). The behavior effects of such internal changes can be mediated through various pathways. The effects can be direct, as in the use of social stimuli to modulate temperature, or indirect, as in the conditioning of different visceral states.

Changes in conditioning and retention capacities. Some controversy remains with respect to the timing and nature of the changes in conditioning and retention that take place over development (see Campbell, 1967, and Sameroff, 1971). But it cannot be gainsaid that significant modifications do occur in both processes, and that these are reflected in the nature of the dyadic relationships that evolve. The synchronization of idiosyncratic interaction sequences, for instance, requires the development of the basic capabilities for the modification of stimulus properties through association. However, the development of associational processes—either instrumental or classical, or elements of both—seems not to be an all-or-none affair. With the development of relevant perceptual and motor differentiation and with central nervous system maturation, learning becomes increasingly more efficient. Hence the development of specific dyadic cue properties (for the support of both effector and hormonal patterns) is paced in part by the maturation of associational capabilities. In addition, the continuity and transituational stability of interaction sequences require the development of basic discrimination and generalization processes. An increased efficiency in learning and retention permits more rapid adaptation to new settings and to unique interaction demands.

Cognitive changes and language in children. In addition to the above events, the social interactions of children are influenced and paced by uniquely human cognitive processes. With the development of the capacity for language and higher order symbolization of social events, the child's capabilities for retention, generalization, and differentiation are enormously increased. So are the potentialities for learning from the experiences of others through observational learning and imitation. Such processes greatly extend the range and complexity of social interchanges that are possible. As the children approach mastery of language, direct parallels to the social behavior of nonhumans become increasingly hazardous.

CONCLUDING COMMENT ON EARLY DYADIC INTERACTIONS

A summary account of the several biological events that contribute to the establishment and change of early interactions may partially correct for their omission in an earlier paper (Cairns, 1966a). Psychobiological mechanisms were then implicated, but were not elaborated. That account was unfortunately representative of the attention ordinarily given by social-learning statements to developmental events. Social-learning discussions (of aggression, sex-typing, etc.) have traditionally contained some vague admission that maturational-organismic factors must play a role in social development. However, after the disclaimers, the significant problems of socialization are treated as if they fell into the exclusive domain of learning processes (e.g., modeling, reinforcement, discrimination). To admit that developmental events are important, but to fail to link them to key explanatory constructs, is tantamount to ignoring them in the first place. More positively, the delineation of the precise roles that developmental processes play in dyadic control should clear the way for a fresh look at social-learning contributions and constructs.

On Dependency and Social Development in Children

Up to this point, the discussion has been concerned with the early foundations of social behavior. Analyses of infant human and nonhuman mammals indicate that the responses of the very young and those with whom they interact become mutually dependent. The relationship, once formed, is not a static one. Its course is paced by biophysical and maturational changes in the infant and in those with whom they interact. The particular kinds of interaction that develop, and the extent to which they are maintained, are determined in part by the context in which the behavior occurs. Our analysis thus has been concerned with the integration of social-learning processes with developmental changes in the control and organization of dyadic sequences.

Now we can return to the issue raised earlier in this chapter—the relationship of dyadic phenomena observed in infancy to those behaviors that have been subsumed by the concept of dependency. Earlier, on page 33, the problem was left open. It was observed that the concepts of attachment and dependency had been developed in mutually insulated research orientations, by investigators concerned with different methods, issues, species, and behavior. Although both concepts were concerned with "other-directed" or "social" phenomena, there was meager ground on which to argue that one should give way, or be subsumed by, the other.

The logical point of contact between these two research orientations is the social behavior development *of children*. If only the peaceful coexistence of two concepts of social behavior were at stake, the problem could be solved by definition. This would involve generalizing each term from the methodological and theoretical domain in which it was originally established and indicating its implications for the domain of the other. For definitional clarity, overlap between the two concepts could be minimized or eliminated at each stage of development. Such a general partitioning of social behavior into two separate categories, while possible, serves to raise some nontrivial problems for the theorist, including:

1. *Why only two?* Considering the substantial evidence that indicates that both "dependency" and "attachment" are multidimensional, a taxonomy of person-oriented behavior in preschool children would appear to require several nonoverlapping categories. The number of factors increases as a function of the number of settings or response patterns sampled, and as the age-developmental status of the child increases.

2. *Criteria for assignment.* Certain behaviors appear basic to both concepts. Consider the response "approach and remaining near others," an activity that has been a measure of choice for indexing both dependency and attachment constructs. How might one distinguish between "approach" behavior motivated by attachment or by dependency? More generally, simply because an individual approaches and remains with another does not mean that the behavior is supported by a positive regard for the other. Children also approach each other to fight, to threaten, or to take something away. Mere approach, or interaction, is not an infallible index of either attachment or dependency, although it has been commonly assumed to be unique to both. The uncritical use of proximity measures has not been limited to the analysis of child behavior. For instance, Salazar (1968) found that isolated rats tend to approach other animals more rapidly than do nonisolated rats. He argued from these results that isolation produced a heightened attachment motive through social deprivation. This interpretation is challenged by the observation of the nature of the interaction that occurs once the "deprived" rodents reach the other. If they are permitted to physically interact with the other animal, previously isolated mice vigorously explore the other. In a high proportion of the instances, the exploration escalates into fighting (Cairns & Nakelski, 1971; R. B. Cairns & J. L. Milakovich, unpublished). In general, whether a given instance of approach is labeled attachment, dependency, investigation, exploration, general activity, or aggression appears to be determined principally by the investigator's expectations and the consequences of the act. Walters and Parke (1964) have explored the role of social judgment in the definition of functional behavior categories.

3. *Orthogonal dispositions or developmental-emergent response patterns?* Basic to the partitioning of dependency and attachment into categories is the assumption that the various phenomena subsumed by these two terms are independent. The position seems to be inspired by, and constitutes a reaction to, the alternative social-learning assumption that dependent behaviors are generalized attachment responses. As we have already observed, there are ample grounds to reject the latter assumption in its original form because the very phenomena of "attachment" are themselves controlled by semiautonomous mechanisms. There remains, however, the question of how the early specific social adaptations of the infant relate to subsequent adaptations (specific and general) of the child. To argue that there is no relationship whatsoever and that the other-oriented behaviors which occur at different stages of the individual's life are independent would be curious for a developmental analysis. Moreover, it seems unnecessary. One can reject the specific proposal that the phenomena of dependency are simply generalized mother-infant interaction patterns without undercutting the more fundamental assumption of developmental continuity.

Both attachment and dependency are *economical* constructs in that they refer to multidimensional other-oriented phenomena in which the infant and child become involved. Hence neither construct is particularly suited for the assumption that it represents a single or unitary underlying process. Given that there are multiple determinants of both "attachment" and "dependency" behaviors, it seems not unreasonable to expect some overlap in the several mechanisms involved. Psychobiological processes, for instance, are doubtless active in pacing the behaviors delineated by both descriptive constructs. It seems likely, moreover, that such processes act more directly in the case of "attachment" phenomena than of "dependency."

The problems posed by the analysis of behaviors called dependency and attachment are broader ones than matters of definition. Two basic issues can be identified. One involves the developmental continuity of mother-infant adaptations. The problem is to determine the extent to which early social adaptations of the child serve as precursors of, and are primary to, his subsequent dyadic interactions. The second issue concerns the establishment of more precise accounts of the behaviors that have been subsumed by the construct "dependency." When there is generalized dissatisfaction with a construct, as appears to be the case with dependency nowadays, there is also strong pressure toward nominal resolution. In the present case, this has led to the introduction of such "new" terms as attachment and detachment. The alternative strategy would be to reevaluate the functions assigned to the construct, and to develop miniature systems that provide more powerful (i.e., precise) accounts of the behaviors "explained" by it.

This final section of the chapter will be subdivided into two parts. The first will be concerned with the issue of social behavior continuity (and discontinuity) in children, including the contributions of maturational factors and rearing experiences. The second subsection will review the mechanisms that have been proposed to account for the different aspects of dependency behavior in children.

Continuity in Social Development: From Attachment to Dependency

One of the more regrettable deficiencies in developmental research with children has been the failure to trace the ontogeny of primary patterns of social responding. This deficit is remarkable in the light of the hegemony of social-learning models in socialization research. Without exception, behavioral accounts have assumed that early interaction patterns (including mother-infant relationships) provide the basis for the emergence of dependency behavior (Bandura & Walters, 1959, 1963; Bijou & Baer, 1965; Gewirtz, 1961, 1969; Sears, Maccoby, & Levin, 1957; Sears, Rau, & Alpert, 1965). Until the recent past, the orientation has failed to attempt a convincing test of its claim. The work of Sears (1961), Kagan and Moss (1962), and the symposium reports of Coates, Anderson, and Hartup (1971), Maccoby (1971), and Lewis and Ban (1971) constitute important steps toward providing such evidence.

ATTACHMENT: LABORATORY STUDIES OF STABILITY AND CHANGE

Up until the very recent past, reliable information on the stability of behaviors taken as indices of social attachment has been hard to come by. A significant improvement in our state of knowledge on the processes in human infants occurred in 1971 when three closely related but independent laboratory studies of stability of change were reported (Coates et al., 1971; Lewis & Ban, 1971; Maccoby, 1971). Taken in conjunction with the earlier work of Fleener (1967), these reports yield a clear but disappointing picture of the extent to which individual differences in maternal-child interactions are subject to variation over time.

Despite the fact that the relevant investigations were carried out in different laboratories, there was considerable similarity in procedures followed, measures used, and results obtained. Basically, each of the studies involved direct observation of mother-child interactions under seminatural conditions in a test-retest short-term longitudinal design. In two of the studies (Coates et al., 1971; Maccoby, 1971), the maternal-infant interaction was also manipulated by having the mother absent herself from the room and/or by having a stranger enter. The observation periods themselves were rather brief, lasting from 10 to 20 minutes in each test period. The intervals between observations ranged from 1 day to 1 year.

Since the studies were not precise replications of each other, the consistency in the results obtained is impressive. Overall, the work indicates:

1. There is only modest stability of differences among individual children in the interaction measures of maternal-offspring relationship over a 3- to 6-month period. Moreover, the degree of relationship typically diminishes to nonsignificance as the length of time between observations is extended to 1 year. The measures that involve the assessment of behaviors that occur directly between the mother and child (touching, smiling, vocalization) seemed especially unstable over the long run. Nonetheless, there is a suggestion in the data that the experimental manipulation of introducing a stranger or of having the mother remove herself from the room serves, in Maccoby's terms, "as a catalyst that produces consistency." For example, even though remaining-close-to-mother is not a very stable characteristic over time, remaining-close-to-mother when a stranger is present is moderately predictable from 2 years of age to 2½ or 3 years of age.

2. Individual differences in attachment behavior at one stage are not transformed into differences in more mature behaviors at a later stage. It has been proposed (Ainsworth, 1969; Bowlby, 1969) that even though the actual form of the overt or phenotypic behavior might change over time, the underlying "attachment structure" would remain relatively stable. Thus stability would be reflected in parallel individual differences in behavior that would be appropriate for the child at the time in which he was observed. The specific hypothesis evaluated by two of the investigators (Lewis & Ban, 1971; Maccoby, 1971) was that the basic motivational difference would remain relatively stable, but that children would shift from proximal expressions of attachment (e.g., touching, proximity-seeking) to distal forms (e.g., looking, smiling) over time. Virtually no support was found in either study for this proposal, with the relevant correlations typically not differing from zero. In one instance, the proposal was embarrassed by the correlations which were significant in a direction opposite to that expected on the "transformational" hypothesis. Maccoby (1971) thus found that the most mature forms of attachment were, at an initial stage, predictable of subsequent immature forms of attachment at a later age. For example, children who vocalized to their mothers at age two ("distal" attachment behaviors) were the ones who were most likely to remain close to her at age two and one-half ("proximal" attachment behaviors). There is some confirmation of this reversal-of-prediction in the Lewis and Ban (1971) study, but the relevant correlation was reliable only in the case of boys, not girls.

3. The behaviors of the children with respect to their mothers, and vice versa, show consistent shifts during the first year of life, and from the first to the second year. As several investigators have documented, the onset of discriminative crying by infants upon maternal departure typically occurs in the second half of the first year (Ainsworth, 1967; Fleener & Cairns, 1970; Schaffer & Emerson, 1964; Tennis & Lampl, 1964). Similarly, looking-at-the-mother in a normal interchange is more frequent at 25 months than at 13 months (Lewis & Ban, 1971). Over the shorter term—3 to 6 months—the changes in expression are more difficult to discern (Coates et al., 1971). In overview, there are significant

age-related changes in terms of maternal-infant interaction over time, but the differences among infant-mother pairs at one stage are not very predictive of differences that are observed at a later stage.

Two comments seem called for on the stability-change findings. First, the measures themselves were only of the child's behavior. No attempt was made, in any of the studies, to track changes in the maternal activities that might be responsible for alterations in the behaviors of the children. In view of the fact that the child's responses were in fact dyadic ones, it would appear that the interchange in which they occurred would be a significant determinant of their recurrence or absence. In brief, the issue is not merely one of stability of behavior in the child, but of stability of behavior in the mother, and the stability of the relationship between these two interacting events. The dynamic interaction matrix in which both the child's and the mother's behaviors are embedded would appear to be key to the problem of stability and change. More generally, such findings emphasize that the notion of attachment is a relational concept, involving the contributions of two individuals, as opposed to a monadic, internally controlled "structure."

Secondly, given the above considerations, the essential problem of stability and change is to identify precisely how it is that the interaction sequences at one point in time are modified over time. The matter involves specifying processes by which dyadic interactions are themselves maintained and changed. As in the case of nonhumans, there appear to be both developmental pacemakers and interaction-specific determinants of change. We will now turn to a consideration of these two major sources of interaction continuity and change in children.

ROLE OF MATURATIONAL-ORGANISMIC FACTORS

Developmental variables, and, specifically, changes in the organism as a function of maturation, have never played a very critical role in social-learning models of socialization. While the impact of constitutional variables has rarely been denied, the primary burden for continuity and change in social behavior has been assigned to learned motivation and response structures.

The view that constitutional-maturational factors are not very important in human social development has been vigorously challenged. In a review of the possible effects of children upon parental behavior, Bell (1968) argues that many of the primary individual differences in social behavior that are observed in children reflect constitutional factors. Accordingly, Bell proposes that person-orientation differences are linked to genetic-constitutional factors, and that these are translated into later differential levels of dependency behaviors. Further, interspecific comparisons in rodents have suggested to some investigators that "sociability" is a heritable characteristic (Lindzey, Winston, & Roberts, 1965). Unfortunately, behavioral research with humans is less clear. Although there are individual differences among infants in irritability and social reactivity, attempts to determine the stability of these dispositions have yielded equivocal results (Freedman, 1965; Kagan & Moss, 1962; Lipton & Steinschneider, 1964; Thomas, Chess, & Birch, 1968; but see Scarr, 1969, for a provocative discussion of the evidence). Just how much individual difference variance in preschool dependency behaviors can be attributed to genetic or constitutional variables remains unknown. It likely varies as a function of the particular interaction phenomena considered.

Such findings do not necessarily detract from the general proposition that the constitution-linked characteristics of the child help to determine his dyadic behaviors and responses to them. To be influential in the developmental process, early social dispositions do not have to be viewed as performed and unmodifiable orientations. To the extent that there is a continuing interplay between biophysical states and social experiences throughout ontogeny—with progressive reorganizations in both behavior and structure—early observed individual differences would *not* be automatically preserved.

Turning from the problem of individual differences, it can hardly be disputed that maturation-related changes profoundly influence the basic course of social development. Chronological age is strongly associated with the amount, form, direction, and type of person-oriented behavior observed in children as well as in infants. These modifications are significantly determined by the child's increasing capacities for processing and transmitting verbal information. At a more mundane but equally important level, they also reflect changes in the effector apparatus and sensorimotor coordination of the preschool and early school-age child. With the development of new skills in self-care, locomotion, and object manipulation, the child becomes less tied to the immediate caretaking activities of adults. The older child is, realistically, less dependent. Both the child's behaviors and responses to them are further shaped by normative expectations. Social-normative attitudes are themselves maintained because they are roughly congruent with the child's developmental capabilities and response limitations.

EFFECTS OF CHILD REARING

Recent critical evaluations of the socialization literature indicate that there have been few winners in attempts to analyze child-rearing determinants of dependency. Discussing the association between maternal behavior and measures of preschool dependency, Yarrow, Campbell, and Burton (1968) conclude that "Slim and doubtful are the relations detected in our data and those of parallel studies in the field [p. 53]." In their incisive analysis of the problems of child-rearing research, Yarrow et al. suggest that the difficulties were inevitable given the limitations of the measurement procedures employed. Dependency indices typically fail even minimal tests of internal and cross-situational consistency. They conclude that "at the very least, the unitary nature of the concept, or the interchangeability of its measures, has been placed in doubt [p. 53]."

More generally, child-rearing studies have shown that the processes by which parents influence their children's behaviors are considerably more complex than was first assumed to be the case. Summary variables, like "maternal warmth," and "dependency" were selected because it seemed likely that concepts at this level of abstraction would yield stable antecedent-consequent relations. That expectation has not, for the most part, been confirmed.

In the face of such negative results, there has been a tendency among recent writers to detract from the importance of learning mechanisms in social development in order to emphasize maturational-constitutional factors. From what studies of nonhuman mammals teach us, however, such a dichotomy hardly seems justified. Both social learning and endogenous physiological events are implicated at succeeding developmental levels.

How might child rearing analyses begin to disentangle the specific contributions of interactional and maturational variables in behavior continuity? From the foregoing it appears that methods should be particularly concerned with:

1. *Detailed accounts of the reciprocal interaction sequences.* Parent-child or child-parent relationships apparently can be reduced to the fundamental units of component dyadic sequences (Sears, 1951). The problem of identifying child-rearing determinants of social behavior then becomes one of specifying the immediate effects of particular parent-produced events upon the child's responsiveness. Recent advances in the sequential analysis of behavior offer promising methodological and statistical tools for the task (e.g., Bobbitt, Gourevitch, Miller, & Jensen, 1969; Kaufman & Rosenblum, 1966; Nelson, 1964; the discussion of Hutt & Hutt, 1970, is of particular value).

2. *Tracing temporal (developmental) shifts in interaction patterns.* At any developmental period, parental behaviors are contingent upon the child's responses, and vice versa. As the behaviors shift, so do the responses contingent upon them. Research techniques that fail to identify long-term changes in parent-child interactions will, according to Yarrow et al. (1968), miss the essence of the developmental process. Children in the 1 to 3-year-old age range have infrequently been studied in settings that are comparable either to younger children (infants) or to older children (4 to 6 years old).

3. *Formation of "new" dyadic sequences.* Students of primate behavior have proposed that the early interaction patterns serve to prepare the young animal for adult social adaptations (e.g., Hinde, 1970; Kummer, 1968). Comparable processes by which components of prior interaction sequences are merged into "new" relations in children have yet to be identified. Analyses could be concerned either with the generalization of specific behaviors across persons, holding the child's age constant; or with the generalization of particular responses over time, holding the relationship constant.

4. *Experimental intervention.* While the traditional methods of animal experimentation (e.g., dyadic isolation for varying periods, neurological or physiological blockage of development) are not available, an important range of

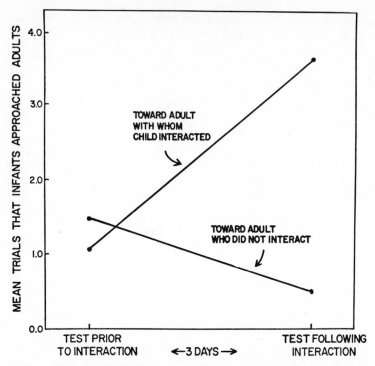

Fig. a. Twenty infants, 10-14 months old, were permitted to approach one of two women in a two-choice apparatus. Four trials were given each test day (T_1 and T_2). On T_1, both women were unfamiliar. Between the first and second tests each child spent 2½ hours on each of three consecutive days interacting with (playing, looking at, being held by, etc.) one of the two women. The second test was given at the end of the third day. Following the interaction series the infants crawled or toddled to the "interactor" with a speed and intensity like that shown to their real mothers. (From Fleener, 1967).

less drastic intervention procedures can be employed by the child psychologist. For instance, the experimental establishment of interindividual social preferences in infants has been nicely demonstrated by Rheingold (1956) and Fleener (1967). The latter investigator showed that even a short period of intensive interaction (approximately 7½ hours) between an unfamiliar adult and a 10- to 14-month-old infant is sufficient to produce dramatic changes in the child's orientation and preferences. Following interaction, the infants became distressed when the woman left, and consistently approached her when she was present (see accompanying figures). In a counterbalanced design using two adult females, the infants developed a preference for only the woman with whom they had interacted. Apparently infants adapt to new social contingencies much more rapidly than they have been given credit for. Such findings, if extended, could have significant implications for the analysis of mother-infant separations.

5. *Contextual divergence.* Social-learning models predict that the child's initial response in a new setting would be generalized from prior experiences in

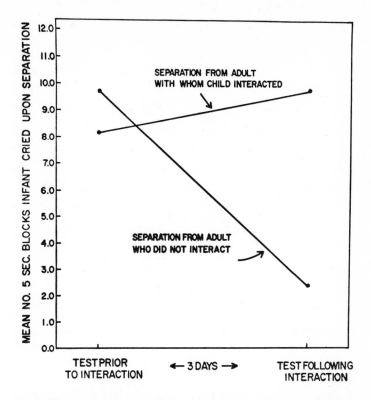

Fig. b. The same infants were also tested in their response to brief separation. In the first series (T_1), immediately after being separated from their real mothers, the infants cried indiscriminately, regardless of which adult left the room. But after the experimental manipulations crying was typically observed only when separated from the woman who had interacted 7½ hours with them. Again, the phenomenon was similar in terms of intensity of the disruption to that observed when the infants were separated from their actual mothers. (From Fleener, 1967).

similar settings. Such generalization would make for the stability of social responding. Moreover, it seems reasonable to expect that his subsequent reactions *in that context* would be shaped by the particular reactions that they elicit and/or provoke. Social actions thus become adapted to the settings in which they occur. Furthermore, as the child's capacities for making precise discriminations between persons and situations develop, his social behaviors can become person- or situation-specific. The verbal human's capacity for discrimination, abstraction, and recall set him apart from other animals. Such characteristics permit—but do not require—considerable variability and intraindividual independence in dyadic responding. They also permit generalization on the basis of subtle features of seemingly disparate interpersonal encounters and contexts.

How then might differences in rearing practices influence the social reactivity of the child in interaction away from home? At this point, the answer must be tentative. It appears, however, that the strongest effects are obtained where the criterion interaction shares common elements with the interaction observed (or reported upon) in the home. What appear to generalize across situations for the young child are specific dyadic response tendencies and cognitive sets. And once the behavior has occurred in the new situation—the school or the laboratory—whether the child will persist in it is significantly determined by the counterresponses that it evokes in others.

Social interactions are vulnerable to change, in both the child and nonhumans. Prior experience and learned reaction tendencies bias responses so that some dyadic behaviors are more probable than others in a new setting. The extent to which this bias is maintained, however, will be a function of the events that are operative in *that* context. The same dyadic learning processes that were operative in the child-rearing interactions with the parents will continue to be operative in the child's relationship with friends and adults. And some behaviors are self-perpetuating by virtue of the responses they reliably elicit from others.

Dependency Reevaluated

A reading of the recent literature shows that the concept of dependency as a unitary mechanism or response system has been virtually abandoned (Gewirtz, 1969; Hartup, 1963; Sears, 1963). The term itself might have also been jettisoned had it not been for the apparent centrality of the construct in socialization theory. In any event, the burden now rests upon the researcher to develop adequate alternative explanations for those behavioral phenomena that have been heretofore accounted for by appealing to a dependency motive or system or generalized trait.

The task has been taken up with vigor. Consider, for instance, the analysis of events labeled "social reinforcement." One of the more important services performed by the dependency construct was to explain why "social reinforcers" (i.e., assent-approval words) were reinforcing. Much of the earlier research was concerned with establishing a functional relationship between dependency motivation or "social drive," on the one hand, and the efficacy of social reinforcement events, on the other. The initial empirical findings were sufficiently positive to encourage many of us to use dependency as an explanatory construct. The basic results included:

1. A moderately positive and significant correlation between behavioral and personality measures of dependency and the child's rate of learning under conditions of social approval (Cairns, 1961; Endsley & Hartup, 1960).

2. A higher level of acquisition (in a choice task where the correct response elicited approval) following social "deprivation" (i.e., the child was left alone 20 minutes prior to testing) than following a nondeprivation manipulation (Gewirtz & Baer, 1958; see Eisenberger, 1970).

3. A lower level of acquisition in the choice task where correct responses elicited approval following social "satiation" (i.e., frequent, indiscriminate approval) as compared to "nonsatiation" (Gewirtz, 1967; Landau & Gewirtz, 1967).

Despite the early positive returns, the research nonetheless encountered serious pitfalls as it progressed. The problems were methodological, empirical, and theoretical. Some of the more important methodological deficiencies of the work have been outlined by Parton and Ross (1965, 1967; see also Stevenson & Hill, 1966). These included such oversights as the recurrent failure to include random reinforcement or no-reinforcement control groups, and the confounding of experimental manipulations. Equally disturbing was the failure to replicate some of the primary effects, as well as the unclarity of the theoretical status of such constructs as "satiation" and "deprivation" when applied to nonhomeostatic motivational systems (see Cairns, 1966a; 1970; Gewirtz, 1967; Maccoby & Masters, 1970).

From the standpoint of the theoretical analysis of the effective processes, doubtless the most important shortcoming was the failure of the work to pinpoint the behavioral mediators of the correlational and experimental effects. This is essentially the problem of establishing the behavioral linkage between the predispositional measure (or manipulation) and the child's actual performance. For instance, does the "deprived" child perform better because he is paying closer attention, because he is actively testing hypotheses, because he "values" approval at a higher level, or because he is in a state of high arousal? The empirical problem thus becomes one of establishing the link (*a*) between the predispositional measure (or manipulation) and a potential behavioral mediator; and (*b*) between the behavioral mediator (e.g., attention, hypothesis testing, incentive value) and performance on the task. Once these relationships are identified, the modest correlations between measures of "dependency" and social reinforcement may themselves be accounted for.

To deal with these questions, much of the recent research has shifted from attempts to replicate gross dependency or deprivation-satiation relationships to ask what in fact are the immediate controls of social reinforcer effectiveness. The work has yielded some promising returns. One of the more interesting outcomes suggests that a primary determinant of effectiveness is simply whether or not the child considers the approval comments to be relevant to his specific choices in the test context. Operations that serve merely to draw the child's attention to the relevance of the "approval" words (i.e., "good," "fine," "right") for his behavior markedly enhance their effectiveness (Cairns, 1967; Hamilton, 1969; Spence, 1966). Conversely, operations in which approval words occur initially in a random or nondiscriminant fashion tend to diminish their effectiveness. In this regard, the effects that have been assigned to "social satiation" may not be due to the fact that the words occurred repeatedly so much as to the fact that they occurred randomly and nondiscriminatively (Cairns, 1970; Warren & Cairns, 1972).

Further analyses of social reinforcers in everyday life indicate that approval comments occur much more frequently than do negative or disapproval remarks. Boucher and Osgood (1969) labeled this effect the "Pollyana phenomenon." The ratio of approval comments to disapproval ones was 7:1 in one study of normal classrooms (Cairns & Paris, 1971) and 8:1 in a study of special classrooms (Paris & Cairns, 1972). In both settings, the approval words served multiple functions, including a surprisingly high incidence (39%) where their occurrence did not refer to any particular praiseworthy performance of the child. Negative comments, though they occurred less frequently, virtually always referred to a particular response of an individual child. When a teacher said wrong, she *really* meant it. The same did not hold for such expressions as "good," "OK," and "all right." It seems relevant that studies of relative effectiveness of reinforcement combinations have repeatedly demonstrated that negative comments are vastly superior to positive ones in promoting learning and concept identification (e.g., Curry, 1960; Hamilton, 1969). Such results are consistent with the general interpretation that the prior signal or informational properties of verbal events are the principal determininants of their reinforcement effectiveness.

How might such mediators be linked to dependency states or deprivation-satiation manipulations? Walters and Parke (1964), among others, have proposed that a major characteristic of children labeled "dependent" is their tendency to attend to or orient toward the interpersonal behaviors of others. It would follow that the modest correlations that have been obtained between measures of dependency and social reinforcement reflect principally a bias toward attending to the interpersonal behaviors of others, including the "social reinforcement" behaviors of the experimenter. Whether or not all of the social reinforcement phenomena attributed to dependency states can be accounted for in terms of the attentional-informational properties of the event and the orientational patterns of the child remains to be determined. Nevertheless, it is clear that both historical and situational factors play important roles in determining the momentary effectiveness of these events.

Comparable attempts have been made, with varying success, to provide more explicit accounts of other phenomena that were originally assigned to the general dependency construct. In each instance, the common strategy has involved a detailed analysis of the intervening behavioral processes. Notable recent contributions include specification of the processes of imitation and modeling (Bandura, 1969; Gewirtz & Stingle, 1968), reanalyses of self-criticism (Aronfreed, 1968), and revised treatments of antisocial aggression (e.g., Feshbach, 1970). Each of these behavioral phenomena had, at one point, been explained by social-learning theories in terms of a dependency or dependency-inhibition process.

In overview, the functions assigned to the global motivational construct of dependency are currently being taken over by miniature systems that are more directly linked to relevant dyadic behaviors. The dependency construct performed a valuable service in focusing attention upon significant social behavior patterns in children. Intensive investigations of the phenomena, in turn, have given rise to more detailed accounts of the essential processes that underlie them. The more that has been learned about the events that control dependency behaviors, the less compelling has seemed the need to retain the term as an explanatory device.

Concluding Comments

To continue to be useful in developmental analyses, social-learning theory requires major revisions in both methodology and orientation. A burden of this chapter was to focus attention upon the revisions that are now under way or seem called for in understanding the foundations of social development. Of primary importance is the dual problem of how ontogenetic-linked biophysical events help to determine what is learned, and how experiential events serve to initiate and maintain developmental changes. Traditional analyses of social learning typically have held ontogenetic factors constant empirically, then ignored them theoretically. The fiction that maturation-paced changes in social interactions are uninteresting, irrelevant, or beyond our comprehension is no longer acceptable. While it seems unlikely that concepts of learning have outlived their usefulness, as Kuo (1967) has maintained, his point that they must be integrated with the processes of behavioral epigenesis is well taken.

A second area of revision, in this case methodological, concerns the analysis of dyadic sequences. Notwithstanding its importance, work has only begun on the formal analysis of interaction response chains. Despite Sears' (1951) clear statement of the need for such analyses in social development, progress has been disappointingly slow. But the validity of the original statement has yet to be challenged. Fundamental to such analyses is the need for a revised conception of the effective stimulus. Dyadic responses are controlled not only by the behavior of the other, but by the context in which the interaction occurs, the developmental status of the individuals, and their momentary endogenous states. A key to understanding developmental and contextual continuity in social behavior is the specification of how dyadic patterns are generalized and modified.

Finally, the basic concepts of social-learning models are being evaluated from a broader and more rigorous perspective. This reevaluation has been augmented by the evolution of a toleration, and mutual respect, between developmental researchers who work with animals and those who work with children. The importance of the convergence of interest, ideas, and their joint application to the basic problems of social development can hardly be too strongly emphasized. Continued interchanges can help to keep both areas focused on the main problems of social development and to protect each from becoming mired in conceptual side issues. Such cross-fertilization is an obvious and necessary step toward a coherent and unified science of development.

REFERENCES

Ainsworth, M. D. S. *Infancy in Uganda: Infant care and the growth of love.* Baltimore: Johns Hopkins Press, 1967.

Ainsworth, M. D. S. Object relations, dependency, and attachment: A theoretical review of the infant-mother relationship. *Child Development,* 1969, **40**, 969-1025.

Alexander, G., & Williams, D. Maternal facilitation of sucking drive in newborn lambs. *Science,* 1964, **146**, 665-666.

Altmann, M. Naturalistic studies of maternal care in moose and elk. In H. L. Rheingold (Ed.), *Maternal behavior in mammals.* New York: Wiley, 1963. Pp. 233-253.

Andrew, R. J. Normal and irrelevant toilet behavior in *Emberiza* spp. *British Journal of Animal Behaviour,* 1956, **4**, 85-91.

Arling, G. L., & Harlow, H. F. Effects of social deprivation on maternal behavior of rhesus monkeys. *Journal of Comparative and Physiological Psychology,* 1967, **64**, 371-377.

Aronfreed, J. *Conduct and conscience.* New York: Academic Press, 1968.

Aronson, L. A. Hormones and reproductive behavior: Some phylogenetic considerations. In A. Gorbman (Ed.), *Comparative endocrinology.* New York: Wiley, 1959. Pp. 98-120.

Bandura, A. *Principles of behavior modification.* New York: Holt, Rinehart, & Winston, 1969.

Bandura, A., & Walters, R. H. *Adolescent aggression.* New York: Ronald Press, 1959.

Bandura, A., & Walters, R. H. *Social learning and personality development.* New York: Holt, Rinehart, & Winston, 1963.

Barnett, S. A. *The rat: A study in behaviour.* Chicago: Aldine, 1963.

Beach, F. A. Coital behavior in dogs: VI. Long-term effects of castration upon mating in the male. *Journal of Comparative and Physiological Psychology,* 1970, **70** (3, Pt. 2).

Bell, R. Q. A reinterpretation of the direction of effects in studies of socialization. *Psychological Review,* 1968, **75**, 81-95.

Bijou, S. W., & Baer, D. M. *Child development.* Vol. 2. *Universal stage of infancy.* New York: Appleton-Century-Crofts, 1965.

Blauvelt, H. Dynamics of the mother-newborn relationship in goats. In B. Schaffner (Ed.), *Group processes: Transactions of the First Conference.* New York: Josiah Macy, Jr. Foundation, 1955. Pp. 251-258.

Bobbitt, A., Gourevitch, V. P., Miller, L. E., & Jensen, G. D. Dynamics of social interactive behavior: A computerized procedure for analyzing trends, patterns, and sequences. *Psychological Bulletin,* 1969, **71**, 110-119.

Bolles, R. C. The usefulness of the drive concept. *Nebraska Symposium on Motivation,* 1958, **6**, 1-33.

Bolles, R. C. *Theory of motivation.* New York: Harper & Row, 1967.

Boucher, J., & Osgood, C. E. The Pollyanna hypothesis. *Journal of Verbal Learning and Verbal Behavior,* 1969, **8**, 1-8.

Bowlby, J. *Attachment and loss.* Vol. 1. *Attachment.* London: Hogarth, 1969.

Brown, J. S. Problems presented by the concept of acquired drive. *Nebraska Symposium on Motivation,* 1953, **1**, 1-23.

Cairns, R. B. The influence of dependency inhibition on the effectiveness of social reinforcement. *Journal of Personality,* 1961, **29**, 466-488.

Cairns, R. B. Attachment behavior of mammals. *Psychological Review,* 1966, **73**, 409-426.(a)

Cairns, R. B. Development, maintenance, and extinction of social attachment behavior in sheep. *Journal of Comparative and Physiological Psychology,* 1966, **62**, 298-306.(b)

Cairns, R. B. The information properties of verbal and nonverbal events. *Journal of Personality and Social Psychology,* 1967, **5**, 353-357.

Cairns, R. B. Attention and meaning as determinants of social reinforcer efficacy. *Child Development,* 1970, **41**, 1067-1082.

Cairns, R. B., & Johnson, D. E. The development of interspecies social attachments. *Psychonomic Science*, 1965, **2**, 337-338.

Cairns, R. B., & Nakelski, J. S. On fighting in mice: Ontogenetic and experiential determinants. *Journal of Comparative and Physiological Psychology*, 1971, 74, 354-364.

Cairns, R. B., & Paris, S. G. The multiple functions of social reinforcement events. Unpublished manuscript, Indiana University, 1971.

Cairns, R. B., & Werboff, J. A. Behavior development in the dog: An interspecific analysis. *Science*, 1967, **158**, 1070-1072.

Campbell, B. A. Developmental studies of learning and motivation in infraprimate mammals. In H. W. Stevenson, E. H. Hess, & H. L. Rheingold (Eds.), *Early behavior: Comparative and developmental approaches*. New York: Wiley, 1967. Pp. 43-71.

Cantor, G. N., Cantor, J. H., & Ditrichs, R. Observing behavior in preschool children as a function of stimulus complexity. *Child Development*, 1963, 34, 683-689.

Coates, R., Anderson, E. P., & Hartup, W. W. Interrelations and stability in the attachment behavior of human infants. Symposium paper read at the Biennial Meeting of the Society for Research in Child Development, Minneapolis, Minn., April 1971.

Cofer, C. N., & Appley, M. H. *Motivation: Theory and research*. New York: Wiley, 1964.

Collias, N. E. The analysis of socialization in sheep and goats. *Ecology*, 1956, 37, 228-239.

Curry, C. The effects of verbal reinforcement combinations on learning in children. *Journal of Experimental Psychology*, 1960, 59, 434.

Dobzhansky, T. Of flies and men. *American Psychologist*, 1967, **22**, 41-48.

Dollard, J., Doob, L. W., Miller, N. E., Mowrer, O. H., & Sears, R. R. *Frustration and aggression*. New Haven, Conn.: Yale University Press, 1939.

Dollard, J., & Miller, N. E. *Personality and psychotherapy*. New York: McGraw-Hill, 1950.

Dunlap, K. Emotion as a dynamic background. In M. L. Reymert (Ed.), *Feelings and emotions: The Wittenberg symposium*: Worcester, Mass: Clark University Press, 1928. Pp. 150-157.

Eisenberger, R. Is there a deprivation-satiation function for social approval? *Psychological Bulletin*, 1970, 74, 225-275.

Elliot, O., & Scott, J. P. The development of emotional distress reactions to separation in puppies. *Journal of Genetic Psychology*, 1961, 99, 3-22.

Emmerich, W. Models of continuity and change in development. Symposium paper read at the Biennial Meeting of the Society for Research in Child Development, Santa Monica, Calif., March 1969.

Endsley, R. C., & Hartup, W. W. Dependency and performance by preschool children on a socially reinforced task. *American Psychologist*, 1960, **15**, 399. (Abstract)

Estes, W. K. Comments on Doctor Bolles's paper. *Nebraska Symposium on Motivation*, 1958, 6, 33-34.

Fantz, R. L. Visual perception and experience in early infancy: A look at the hidden side of behavior development. In H. W. Stevenson, E. H. Hess, & H. L. Rheingold (Eds.), *Early behavior: Comparative and developmental approaches*. New York: Wiley, 1967. Pp. 181-224.

Feshbach, S. Aggression. In P. H. Mussen (Ed.), *Carmichael's manual of child psychology*. (3rd ed.) Vol. 2. New York: Wiley, 1970. Pp. 159-260.

Fleener, D. E. Attachment formation in human infants. (Doctoral dissertation, Indiana University) Ann Arbor, Mich.: University Microfilms, 1967, No. 6872-12.

Fleener, D. E., & Cairns, R. B. Attachment behavior in human infants: Discriminative vocalization upon maternal separation. *Developmental Psychology*, 1970, **2**, 215-223.

Freedman, D. An ethological approach to the genetical study of human behavior. In S. G. Vandenberg (Ed.), *Methods and goals in human behavior genetics*. New York: Academic Press, 1965. Pp. 141-161.

Fuller, J. L., & Fox, M. W. The behaviour of dogs. In E. S. E. Hafez (Ed.), *The behaviour of domestic animals*. (Rev. ed.) Baltimore: Williams & Wilkins, 1969. Pp. 438-481.

Gewirtz, J. L. A learning analysis of the effects of normal stimulation, privation and deprivation on the acquisition of social motivation and attachment. In B. M. Foss (Ed.), *Determinants of infant behaviour.* London: Methuen (New York: Wiley), 1961. Pp. 213-299.

Gewirtz, J. L. Deprivation and satiation of social stimuli as determinants of their reinforcing efficacy. In J. P. Hill (Ed.), *Minnesota symposia on child psychology.* Vol. 1. Minneapolis: University of Minnesota Press, 1967. Pp. 3-56.

Gewirtz, J. L. Mechanisms of social learning: Some roles of stimulation and behavior in early human development. In D. A. Goslin (Ed.), *Handbook of socialization theory and research.* Chicago: Rand McNally, 1969. Pp. 57-212.

Gewirtz, J. L., & Baer, D. M. Deprivation and satiation of social reinforcers as drive conditions. *Journal of Abnormal and Social Psychology,* 1958, 57, 165-172.

Gewirtz, J. L., & Stingle, K. G. Learning of generalized imitation as the basis of identification. *Psychological Review,* 1968, 75, 374-397.

Gorbman, A., & Bern, H. A. *A textbook of comparative endocrinology.* New York: Wiley, 1962.

Grubb, P., & Jewell, P. A. Social grouping and home range in feral Soay sheep. *Symposium of the Zoological Society of London,* 1966, No. 18.

Hamilton, M. L. Reward and Punishment in child discrimination learning. *Developmental Psychology,* 1969, 1, 735-738.

Hansen, E. W. The development of maternal and infant behavior in the rhesus monkey. *Behaviour,* 1966, 27, 107-149.

Harlow, H. F. The nature of love. *American Psychologist,* 1958, 13, 673-685.

Harlow, H. F. The development of affectional patterns in infant monkeys. In B. M. Foss (Ed.), *Determinants of infant behaviour.* London: Methuen (New York: Wiley), 1961. Pp. 75-88.

Harlow, H. F., & Harlow, M. K. The affectional systems. In A. M. Schrier, H. F. Harlow, & F. Stollnitz (Eds.), *Behavior of nonhuman primates: Modern research trends.* Vol. 2. New York: Academic Press, 1965. Pp. 287-334.

Hartup, W. W. Dependence and independence. In H. W. Stevenson (Ed.), *Child psychology: The sixty-second yearbook of the National Society for the Study of Education.* Part I. Chicago: University of Chicago Press, 1963. Pp. 333-363.

Hinde, R. A. Ethological models and the concept of "drive". *British Journal of the Philosophy of Science,* 1956, 6, 321-331.

Hinde, R. A. Energy models of motivation. *Symposium of the Society of Experimental Biology,* 1960, 14, 199-213.

Hinde, R. A. Discussion following Dr. Ainsworth's paper. In B. M. Foss (Ed.), *Determinants of infant behaviour II.* London: Methuen (New York: Wiley), 1963, P. 110.

Hinde, R. A. Influence of social companions and of temporary separation on mother-infant relations in rhesus monkeys. In B. M. Foss (Ed.), *Determinants of infant behaviour IV.* London: Methuen (New York: Wiley), 1969. Pp. 37-40.

Hinde, R. A. *Animal Behaviour.* (2nd ed.) New York: McGraw-Hill, 1970.

Hinde, R. A., & Spencer-Booth, Y. The behaviour of social living rhesus monkeys in their first two and a half years. *Animal Behaviour,* 1967, 15, 169-196.

Hutt, S. J., & Hutt, C. *Direct observation and measurement of behavior.* Springfield, Ill.: Charles C. Thomas, 1970.

Kagan, J., & Moss, H. A. *Birth to maturity.* New York: Wiley, 1962.

Kaufman, I.C., & Rosenblum, L.A. A behavioral taxonomy for *Macaca nemestrina* and *Macaca radiata*: Based on longitudinal observation of family groups in the laboratory. *Primates,* 1966, 7, 205-258.

Klopfer, P. H., & Hailman, J. P. *An introduction to animal behavior: Ethology's first century.* Englewood Cliffs, N. J.: Prentice-Hall, 1967.

Kummer, H. *The social organization of the hamadryas baboon.* Chicago: University of Chicago Press, 1968.

Kuo, Z. Y. *The dynamics of behavior development: An epigenetic view.* New York: Random House, 1967.

Landau, R., & Gewirtz, J. L. Differential satiation for a social reinforcing stimulus as a determinant of its efficacy in conditioning. *Journal of Experimental Child Psychology,* 1967, 5, 391-405.

Lehrman, D. S. Hormonal regulation of parental behavior in birds and infra-human mammals. In W. C. Young (Ed.), *Sex and internal secretions.* (3rd ed.) Baltimore: Williams & Wilkins, 1961. Pp. 1268-1382.

Lehrman, D. S. Semantic and conceptual issues in the nature-nurture problem in L. R. Aronson, E. Tobach, D. S. Lehrman, & J. S. Rosenblatt (Eds.), *Development and evolution of behavior.* San Francisco: W. H. Freeman, 1970. Pp. 17-52.

Lewis, M., & Ban, P. Stability of attachment behavior: A transformational analysis. Symposium paper read at the Biennial Meeting of the Society for Research in Child Development, Minneapolis, Minn., April 1971.

Lindzey, G., Winston, H. D., & Roberts, L. E. Sociability, fearfulness, and genetic variation in the mouse. *Journal of Personality and Social Psychology,* 1965, 1, 642-645.

Lipsitt, L. P. Learning in the human infant. In H. W. Stevenson, E. H. Hess, & H. L. Rheingold (Eds.), *Early behavior: Comparative and developmental approaches.* New York: Wiley, 1967. Pp. 147-180.

Lipton, E. L., & Steinschneider, A. Studies on the psychophysiology of infancy. *Merrill-Palmer Quarterly,* 1964, 10, 102-117.

Logan, F. A. Specificity of discrimination learning to the original context. *Science,* 1961, 133, 1355-1356.

Maccoby, E. E. Stability and change in attachment-to-mother during the third year of life. Symposium paper read at the Biennial Meeting of the Society for Research in Child Development. Minneapolis, Minn., April 1971.

Maccoby, E. E., & Masters, J. C. Attachment and dependency. In P. H. Mussen (Ed.), *Carmichael's manual of child psychology.* (3rd ed.) Vol. 2. New York: Wiley, 1970. Pp. 73-157.

Mandler, G. The interruption of behavior. *Nebraska Symposium on Motivation,* 1964, 12, 163-219.

Mason, W. A. Determinants of social behavior in young chimpanzees. In A. M. Schrier, H. F. Harlow, & F. Stollnitz (Eds.), *Behavior of nonhuman primates.* Vol. 2. New York: Academic Press, 1965. Pp. 335-364.

Mason, W. A. Motivational aspects of social responsiveness in young chimpanzees. In H. W. Stevenson, E. H. Hess, & H. L. Rheingold (Eds.), *Early behavior: Comparative and developmental approaches.* New York: Wiley, 1967. Pp. 103-126.

McCall, R. B. Models of attention in infants. Symposium paper read at the Biennial Meeting of the Society for Research in Child Development, Santa Monica, Calif., March, 1969.

Mischel, W. Continuity and change in personality. *American Psychologist,* 1969, 24, 1012-1017.

Moltz, H. Some effects of previous breeding experience on the maternal behavior in the rat. In L. R. Aronson, E. Tobach, D. S. Lehrman, & J. S. Rosenblatt (Eds.), *Development and evolution of behavior.* San Francisco: W. H. Freeman, 1970. Pp. 489-515.

Nelson, K. The temporal patterning of courtship behavior in the glandulocaudine fishes. *Behaviour,* 1964, 24, 90-145.

Nowlis, V. Companionship preferences and dominance in the social interaction of young chimpanzees. *Comparative Psychological Monographs,* 1941, 17, (1, Whole No. 85).

Papousek, H. Conditioning during early postnatal development. In Y. Brackbill & G. G. Thompson (Eds.), *Behavior in infancy and early childhood.* New York: Free Press, 1966. Pp. 259-274.

Paris, S. G., & Cairns, R. B. An experimental and ethological analysis of social reinforcement with retarded children. *Child Development,* 1972, 43, in press.

Parry, M. H. Infants' responses to novelty in familiar and unfamiliar settings. *Child Development,* 1972, **43**, 233-236.

Parton, D. A., & Ross, A. O. Social reinforcement of children's motor behavior: A review. *Psychological Bulletin,* 1965, **64**, 65-73.

Parton, D. A., & Ross, A. O. A reply to "The use of rate as a measure of response in studies of social reinforcement." *Psychological Bulletin,* 1967, **67**, 323-325.

Pavlov, I. P. *Conditioned reflexes.* Trans. by G. V. Anrep. London: Oxford University Press, 1927.

Rheingold, H. L. The modification of social responsiveness in institutional babies. *Monographs of the Society for Research in Child Development,* 1956, **21** (2, Whole No. 63).

Rheingold, H. L. Maternal behavior in the dog. In H. L. Rheingold (Ed.), *Maternal behavior in mammals.* New York: Wiley, 1963. Pp. 169-202.

Rheingold, H. L., & Eckerman, C. O. The infant separates himself from his mother. *Science,* 1970, **168**, 78-83.

Rosenblatt, J. S. Views on the onset and maintenance of maternal behavior in the rat. In L. R. Aronson, E. Tobach, D. S. Lehrman, & J. S. Rosenblatt (Eds.), *Development and evolution of behavior.* San Francisco: W. H. Freeman, 1970. Pp. 489-515.

Rosenblatt, J. S., & Lehrman, D. S. Maternal behavior of the laboratory rat. In H. L. Rheingold (Ed.), *Maternal behavior in mammals.* New York: Wiley, 1963. Pp. 8-57.

Rosenblum, L. A., & Harlow, H. F. Approach-avoidance conflict in the mother-surrogate situation. *Psychological Reports,* 1963, **12**, 83-85.

Rosenblum, L. A., & Kaufman, I. C. Variations in infant development and response to maternal loss in monkeys. *American Journal of Orthopsychiatry,* 1968, **38**, 418-426.

Roth, L. L., & Rosenblatt, J. S. Changes in self-licking during pregnancy in the rat. *Journal of Comparative and Physiological Psychology,* 1967, **63**, 397-400.

Rothchild, L. The corpus luteum-pituitary relationship: The association between the cause of luteotrophin secretion and the cause of follicular quiescence during lactation: The basis for a tentative theory of the corpus luteum-pituitary relationship in the rat. *Endocrinology,* 1960, **67**, 9-41.

Sackett, G. P. Some persistent effects of different rearing conditions on preadult social behavior of monkeys. *Journal of Comparative and Physiological Psychology,* 1967, **64**, 363-365.

Salazar, J. M. Gregariousness in young rats. *Psychonomic Science,* 1968, **10**, 391-392.

Sameroff, A. J. Can conditioned responses be established in the newborn infant: 1971? *Developmental Psychology,* 1971, **5**, 1-12.

Satinoff, E., & Stanley, W. C. Effect of stomach loading on sucking behavior in neonatal puppies. *Journal of Comparative and Physiological Psychology,* 1963, **56**, 66-68.

Scarr, S. Social introversion-extroversion as a heritable response. *Child Development,* 1969, **40**, 823-832.

Schachter, S., & Singer, J. Cognitive, social and physiological determinants of emotional states. *Psychological Review,* 1962, **69**, 379-399.

Schaffer, H. R., & Emerson, P. E. The development of social attachments in infancy. *Monographs of the Society for Research in Child Development,* 1964, 29 (3, Whole No. 94).

Schneirla, T. C. An evolutionary developmental theory of biphasic processes underlying approach and withdrawal. *Nebraska Symposium on Motivation,* 1959, **7**, 1-42.

Schneirla, T. C., & Rosenblatt, J. S. Behavioral organization and genesis of the social bond in insects and mammals. *American Journal of Orthopsychiatry,* 1961, **31**, 233-253.

Schneirla, T. C., Rosenblatt, J. S., & Tobach, E. Maternal behavior in the cat. In H. L. Rheingold (Ed.), *Maternal behavior in mammals.* New York: Wiley, 1963. Pp. 122-168.

Sears, R. R. A theoretical framework for personality and social behavior. *American Psychologist,* 1951, **6**, 476-483.

Sears, R. R. Relation of early socialization experiences to aggression in early childhood. *Journal of Abnormal and Social Psychology,* 1961, 63, 466-492.

Sears, R. R. Dependency motivation. *Nebraska Symposium on Motivation,* 1963, 11, 25-65.

Sears, R. R., Maccoby, E. E., & Levin, H. *Patterns of child rearing.* Evanston, Ill.: Row, Peterson, 1957.

Sears, R. R., Rau, L., & Alpert, R. *Identification and child rearing.* Stanford, Calif.: Stanford University Press, 1965.

Sears, R. R., Whiting, J. W. M., Nowlis, V., & Sears, P. S. Some child rearing antecedents of aggression and dependency in young children. *Genetic Psychology Monographs,* 1953, 47, 135-234.

Seay, B., Alexander, B. K., & Harlow, H. F. Maternal behavior of socially deprived rhesus monkeys. *Journal of Abnormal and Social Psychology,* 1964, 69, 345-354.

Spence, J. T. Verbal discrimination performance as a function of instructions and verbal-reinforcement combination of normal and retarded children. *Child Development,* 1966, 37, 269-281.

Stevenson, H. W., & Hill, K. T. Use of rate as a measure of response in studies of social reinforcement. *Psychological Bulletin,* 1966, 66, 321-326.

Tennes, K. H., & Lampl, E. E. Stranger and separation anxiety in infancy. *Journal of Nervous and Mental Diseases,* 1964, 139, 247-254.

Thoman, E. B., & Arnold, W. J. Effects of incubator rearing with social deprivation on maternal behavior in rats. *Journal of Comparative and Physiological Psychology,* 1968, 65, 441-446.

Thoman, E., Wetzel, A., & Levine, S. Learning in the neonate rat. *Animal Behaviour,* 1968, 16, 54-57.

Thomas, A., Chess, S., & Birch, H. G. *Temperament and behavior disorders in children.* New York: New York University Press, 1968.

Tinbergen, N. *The study of instinct.* London: Oxford University Press, 1951.

Tinklepaugh, O. L., & Hartman, C. G. Behavior and maternal care of the newborn monkey (*Macaca mulatta*—"*M. rhesus*"). *Journal of Genetic Psychology,* 1932, 40, 257-286.

Tolman, E. C. *Purposive behavior in animals and men.* New York: Century, 1932.

Tolman, E. C. *Drives toward war.* New York: Appleton-Century, 1942.

van Lawick-Goodall, J. The behaviour of free-living chimpanzees in the Gombe Stream Reserve. *Animal Behaviour Monographs,* 1968, 1 (part 3), 161-311.

Walters, R. H., & Parke, R. D. Social motivation, dependency and susceptibility to social influence. In L. Berkowitz (Ed.), *Advances in experimental social psychology.* Vol. 1. New York: Academic Press, 1964. Pp. 231-276.

Walters, R. H., & Parke, R. D. The role of the distance receptors in the development of social responsiveness. In L. P. Lipsitt & C. C. Spiker (Eds.), *Advances in child development and behavior.* Vol. 2. New York: Academic Press, 1965. Pp. 59-96.

Warren, V. L., & Cairns, R. B. Social reinforcement satiation: An outcome of frequency or ambiguity? *Journal of Experimental Child Psychology,* 1972, 10, in press.

Watson, J. B. *Psychological care of infant and child.* New York: Norton, 1928.

Welker, W. I. Factors affecting aggregation of neonatal puppies. *Journal of Comparative and Physiological Psychology,* 1959, 52, 376-380.

Wiesner, B. P., & Sheard, N. M. *Maternal behavior in the rat.* London: Oliver and Boyd, 1933.

Wolff, P. H. The natural history of crying and vocalization in early infancy. In B. M. Foss (Ed.), *Determinants of infant behaviour IV.* London: Methuen (New York: Wiley), 1969. Pp. 81-110.

Yarrow, M. R., Campbell, J. D., & Burton, R. V. *Child rearing: An inquiry into research and methods.* San Francisco: Jossey-Bass, 1968.

Zeigler, H. P. Displacement activity and motivational theory: A case study in the history of ethology. *Psychological Bulletin,* 1964, **61,** 362-376.

ATTACHMENT AND DEPENDENCY: A DEVELOPMENTAL PERSPECTIVE

Leon J. Yarrow

Social and Behavioral Sciences Branch
National Institute of Child Health and
Human Development

Introduction

Although the development of interpersonal relationships is one of the most significant aspects of human development, our knowledge of the process and the underlying mechanisms is still very limited. There has been much speculation in the clinical and psychopathological literature about the process (Spitz, 1950; Benjamin, 1963; Murphy, 1964; Mahler & La Perriere, 1965), and many theories and a varied assortment of terms have been used to designate the basic concept (Ainsworth, 1969; Bowlby, 1969; Maccoby & Masters, 1970). Of the many terms in the psychological literature on relationships, there are three which have been most common: "attachment," "dependency," and "object relationships." The original meanings of these terms can probably be best understood in the theoretical frameworks from which they have emerged. *Object relationships* has its roots in psychoanalytic theory (Freud, 1905); *dependency* is identified with social-learning theory (Sears, Whiting, Nowlis, & Sears, 1953); while the term *attachment* is associated with Bowlby's (1958) attempts to integrate concepts from psychoanalysis and ethology. It seems clear that the distinctions between these terms have evolved from the specific kinds of research and the clinical or field observations that have been carried out from these varied theoretical perspectives. There is considerable overlap in meaning; the differences seem to be chiefly in the specific dimensions of interpersonal relationships on which the

81

research and observations have focused, and, to some extent, in the mechanisms postulated to account for their development and maintenance.

In psychoanalysis, the concept of *object relations* is part of Freud's theory of instincts, the object being the thing in regard to which or through which an instinct achieves its aim (Freud, 1915). Freud describes the course of development of object relationships beginning with a gradual awareness by the helpless infant of his dependence for relief of tension on an object outside of himself; in time, positive feelings become focused on this object. The mother or caretaker becomes the first love object, the prototype of all later object relationships. Freud implicitly subscribed to a secondary drive theory. In the psychoanalytic formulation, instrumental dependency and positive affect are intertwined, at least in early infancy. The Freudian theory of object relationships has been considerably elaborated and revised by Balint (1949), Fairbairn (1954), and Klein (1952).

The earliest work on *dependency* attempted to deal with the development of object relationships within a learning theory framework (Sears, 1951; Sears et al., 1953; Beller, 1955; Gewirtz, 1956, 1961). The learning theorists were more explicit in specifying the behaviors included in this concept and the conditions under which these behaviors were elicited. Fundamentally, dependency on the mother developed as a secondary drive because of its association with caretaking, particularly feeding. Some investigators, working from a learning theory orientation, distinguished two types of dependency: emotional and instrumental (e.g., Heathers, 1955). In instrumental dependency the focus is on another person's instrumental acts required for gratification; presumably anyone could perform these acts. In emotional dependency the emphasis is on obtaining reassurance, attention, or approval from another person; presumably the number of people who could provide these psychological rewards is more limited. During the past ten years there have been significant revisions and elaborations of learning theory formulations by Jack Gewirtz (1969 and this volume), Robert Sears (1963 and this volume), and Robert Cairns (1966 and this volume).

The concept of *attachment* (Bowlby, 1958) also evolved from the psychoanalytic theory of object relationships. Bowlby (1969) attempts to blend concepts from psychoanalysis, ethology, and control-systems theory to account for the development of the child's distinctive emotional tie to the mother. He limits attachment to a relatively few intense and enduring relationships, such as the mother, father, caretaker, siblings, and spouse. In distinction from the secondary drive formulation, Bowlby's emphasis is on the instinctive bases or built-in characteristics of the organism which initiate the process of attachment. These instinctive behaviors, e.g., clinging, following, and smiling, serve to keep the child in close physical contact with his mother and evoke nurturant behavior from her. In time these behaviors somehow become incorporated into complex feedback systems which regulate the child's subsequent responses. (Bowlby has not yet specified the principles by which these complex systems come into being.)

There may be some heuristic value in attempting to make critical distinctions among the terms attachment, dependency, and object relationship, to the extent that such attempts force us to be more precise and more analytical about the dimensions of interpersonal relationships. If we are to study systematically the determinants of various aspects of interpersonal relationships and to analyze the process by which early relationships are established, it is necessary to be clear about the core concept and to specify the range and limits of behaviors included in the concept. I believe that this kind of conceptualization and specification can be done most meaningfully within a developmental framework.

My primary concern in this paper will be to describe the behaviors which define the early stages of the development of significant interpersonal relationships. Concurrent and closely related to the behavior changes associated with the development of focused relationships are changes in perceptual and cognitive functions. I shall describe the cognitive correlates of the development of focused interpersonal relationships and point out the interdependence of social and cognitive functions. I shall not attempt to distinguish among the terms attachment, emotional dependency, and object relationships; but I shall, where it is appropriate, note some distinctions between these terms and instrumental dependency. Inasmuch as I view the development of interpersonal relationships as an aspect of early social development, I prefer the term "focused relationship" (Yarrow, 1956, 1967) to the terms attachment or emotional dependency. However, since attachment has come into such wide usage, I shall use the terms attachment and focused relationship interchangeably.

SOME BASIC ASSUMPTIONS FROM A
DEVELOPMENTAL PERSPECTIVE

Inherent in a developmental orientation is the premise that attachment is not a unique set of behaviors with special or unique determinants; rather it is part of a chain of social and cognitive developmental changes. Attachment has often been treated as an end point, as a developmental milestone, like the achievement of upright posture or the ability to cruise on all fours. It does not seem useful to conceptualize attachment in this way. It is more meaningful to view attachment as an organizing concept that indexes a broad range of behaviors extending across a wide developmental time span. It encompasses dynamically similar but phenotypically different behaviors at different developmental periods through-out the life history. This means that the behaviors defining attachment will change at different developmental levels. It is an interactional concept in which reciprocity is central. It includes the mother's or some other responsive person's behavior and feelings towards the infant, and the infant's behavior and feelings towards these objects of attachment. In middle childhood and adolescence it includes a wider circle of social beings—siblings and peers of both sexes, and other significant adults. At any one developmental point, the relevant behaviors will vary in intensity and on a number of qualitative dimensions. These varied behaviors have a common conceptual core. They refer to a relationship between two human beings in which there is a strong interdependence and a strong affective component. Although the development of intense interpersonal relationships occurs at many ages, in this paper I shall limit my discussion to the infancy period and to the earliest focused relationship, the initial attachment between mother and infant.

Clearly, attachment or focused relationship is a dyadic concept; it refers to an interaction between two people. The mother does not simply elicit response from the child; the child through his behavior and characteristics elicits response from the mother. It is necessary, however, to distinguish behavioral criteria that are useful for defining a concept from criteria that are most meaningful for analysis of the processes underlying the acquisition of these behaviors. In analyzing the mechanisms by which these behaviors are acquired and maintained, the unidirectional model is clearly inadequate; an interactional model is necessary (as Gewirtz, Sears, and Cairns indicate in this volume). For defining the concept, it is easier to work from a unidirectional framework in which the behavior of one member of the dyad is used as the criterion. I have chosen to define the criteria of attachment in terms of the infant's behavior.

Early Social and Perceptual-Cognitive Developments

The many normative studies of early social and visual-perceptual development have delineated a sequence of behaviors which parallel developmentally (and at some points are identical to) the behaviors designated as attachment behaviors. Some selected norms on social development are summarized in the table. These attachment-related behaviors range from very simple responses to very complex behaviors indexing the infant's differential response to mother and stranger. On the whole, there is substantial agreement among investigators on the age of appearance of the simple, more discrete behaviors, such as sustained visual regard, which can be defined with some precision. There is less agreement on the more complex behaviors, on differential response to mother and stranger, and on stranger anxiety. There are probably many bases for these discrepancies. There are variations in stimulus-conditions eliciting these behaviors and in the broader contexts in which the behaviors occur, i.e., familiar, strange. The criteria defining the responses differ from one investigator to another. In some studies the norms are based on the first manifestation of a response; other studies require a definite well-established response that occurs with a high degree of consistency. The methods and subjects also differ; some of these data are based on cross-sectional studies of different children at different ages; some are based on longitudinal data from the same subjects; still others are partly cross-sectional and partly longitudinal. Nevertheless this table shows an essential agreement on the sequences of development of these aspects of social behavior.

DEVELOPMENTAL PRECURSORS OF ATTACHMENT

From a developmental perspective we have tried to conceptualize a number of steps in the development of attachment or focused relationships, and have

Selected Normative Data on Early Social Development

Investigator	Sustained Visual Regard of Person Mean (weeks)	Differential Response to Person and Object		Social Smile		Differential Response to Mother and Stranger		Stranger Anxiety (Marked Distress)		Separation Anxiety (Marked Distress)	
		Mean (weeks)	Range*	Mean (weeks)	Range	Mean (weeks)	Range	Mean (weeks)	Range	Mean (weeks)	Range
Bayley (1969)	4	—	—	6	—	21	—	—	—	—	—
Bridges (1933)	—	—	—	17	—	21	—	28	—	—	—
Bronson (1971)	—	—	—	—	—	—	13-21	28	—	—	—
Carpenter, Tecce, Stechler, & Friedman (1970)	—	2	—	—	—	—	—	—	—	—	—
Gesell & Amatruda (1947)	4	—	—	8	—	24	—	28	—	—	—
Griffiths (1954)	4	—	—	8	—	14	13-17	—	—	—	—
Schaffer & Emerson (1964)	—	—	—	—	—	—	—	34	25-78	—	22-78
Shirley (1933)	—	—	—	8	4-26	—	—	—	21-26	—	—
Spitz (1965)	4	—	—	8	—	26	—	32	—	34	—
Spitz & Wolf (1946)	—	13	—	8	—	26	—	—	—	—	—
Tennes & Lampl (1964, 1966)	—	—	—	—	—	21	13-39	39	13-60	35	17-60
Yarrow (1967)	—	—	4-13	—	—	—	13-22	—	13-34	—	21+

*Range in age of appearance

85

attempted to tie these concepts to observable behaviors of the infant. There are a number of basic cognitive achievements which must be attained first or which are concurrent with these social-emotional developments. At times it is difficult to make clear distinctions between cognitive achievements and social-emotional developments. These earliest perceptual-cognitive achievements might be considered precursors of the social responses which index attachment.

Externalization of the Environment: Differentiation of Self from the External Environment. A first step in the development of the infant's responsiveness to people involves the externalization of the environment—the differentiation of himself from other people and from the inanimate environment. There are several aspects of this externalization process. As with many developmental changes which appear to be partly maturational and partly learned, these achievements are not manifested suddenly in final form but are preceded by fluid and partial responses which are gradually consolidated and strengthened during the first half year of life. Since we have no definitive normative data, we can only extrapolate from our knowledge of related developmental achievements. Probably one of the earliest steps involves differentiation between internal and external sources of stimulation. Although there is probably a large maturational component in the emergence of this capacity, it undoubtedly is also influenced by experiential factors. Both frustration and gratification are probably necessary antecedents. The child's awareness of his own body is heightened by feelings of hunger, cold, and mild discomfort which are then followed by satiety, warmth, and comfort. Caretaking activities involving tactile, kinesthetic, auditory, and visual stimulation, as well as the infant's experiences in manipulation and simultaneous visual regard of objects, also contribute to the externalization of the environment.

Another aspect of the differentiation of the self from the external environment is the development of associations between one's actions and changes in the environment. That is, the infant becomes aware that his actions can have some perceptible impact on the environment. There are nonsocial as well as social aspects of this development. Crying or vocalization can bring about changes in the environment through the mediation of other human beings. The manipulation of objects produces effects; for example, shaking a rattle makes sounds. This stage of cognitive development in which the infant repeats activities with objects which produce interesting effects (Piaget's secondary circular reactions) is apparently well established by 5 or 6 months of age.

Before this time, during the very earliest weeks of life, the essentially helpless infant has extremely limited capacity to manipulate his environment directly, but he can bring about change indirectly by giving the appropriate cues, usually vocal, which may lead to his caretaker's interventions. At this time the infant begins to associate his actions with changes in his internal states. He may have some vague perception that the change in state which he experiences comes about as a result of some force external to himself. This marks the beginning of the infant's sense of separateness from the external environment. The boundaries between his body and the outside world become more sharply defined.

Paralleling this definition of the boundaries of the self is a developing sense of awareness by the infant of his reliance on the external world. At this developmental point, one might theoretically distinguish instrumental dependency and attachment. The infant is aware that changes in his internal states are associated with certain instrumental acts by an external source, without clear differentiation of this external agent or special affect directed towards this person. The infant is dependent on an undifferentiated external object (person) for some change in internal state. One might consider this awareness instrumental dependency. The crucial point is that these changes are not associated with a specific person. However, one can think of these early developments as precursors of attachment rather than as a separate and distinct behavior system. In doing so, we emphasize the continuity between stages in the development of focused relationships. It is likely that these behaviors are not completely consolidated before the earliest forms of focused relationships occur.

Steps in the Development of Focused Relationships

Much of the research on the development of attachment in human infants has used indirect criteria, such as fear of strangers or disturbed reactions to separation from the mother (Bowlby, 1960; Schaffer & Emerson, 1964). It seems more meaningful to try to identify more direct criteria of attachment (Gewirtz, 1961; Yarrow, 1967). Conceptualizing attachment within the broader framework of the development of social responsiveness, we can see an orderly progression of increasingly differentiated and discriminating responses which come to be focused on a special person. Thus, we find that the infant gives indications of his capacity to discriminate strange from familiar persons, particularly his mother, long before overt stranger anxiety in the form of withdrawal or protest is evident. As with the externalization of the environment, the development of focused relationships can be analyzed in a number of steps, and the behaviors indexing these steps can be specified.

SELECTIVE RESPONSIVENESS TO FAMILIAR AND UNFAMILIAR PEOPLE

One of the earliest evidences of the development of a focused relationship is selective responsiveness to the mother or familiar caretaker and to unfamiliar people. Two levels of selective responsiveness can be distinguished: passive and active. Passive responsiveness is manifested by differential visual attention to the mother or caretaker; for example, in the presence of mother and stranger, the infant orients towards his mother and looks at her more than momentarily, whereas he gives only fleeting visual regard to the stranger. At the level of active responsiveness the infant exhibits more overt preferential behavior towards the mother in the presence of a stranger, such as making approach movements toward his mother, smiling or vocalizing to her. Early developmental norms indicate that differential response to the mother is in evidence sometime between 13 and 24 weeks (Bridges, 1933; Gesell & Amatruda, 1947; Griffiths, 1954). Somewhat earlier, infants show discriminating responses to unfamiliar or discrepant visual stimuli. In studying the development of focused relationships through direct observations in natural situations, I have used such indices of active differentiation as vocalization, approach movements, and postural adjustments in anticipation of being picked up (Yarrow, 1967).

Clearly these kinds of discriminating social responses in infants presuppose certain perceptual, motor, and cognitive abilities. For the infant to show selective responsiveness to his mother, he must be capable of making complex perceptual-sensory discriminations, and he must have developed at least a primitive schema of the mother. He must also have a repertoire of responses—smiling, cooing, reaching out to her—in terms of which he can show preference for her. Recent data indicate that the infant's capacities for complex perceptual discriminations develop much earlier than we had thought (Fantz & Nevis, 1967). Although for a long time we assumed that these capacities were primarily maturationally determined, in recent years we have begun to recognize the contribution of experiential factors (White, Castle, & Held, 1964). We have, however, only begun to identify some of the specific environmental conditions which facilitate and maintain these capacities for perceptual discrimination. Both laboratory studies and differentiated observations of mother-infant interactions in natural situations should help elucidate this process. These responses of the infant to the mother and the stranger are also tied in with other cognitive changes, such as his differential attention to novel and familiar stimuli. There is evidence that very early in life the infant shows visual preference for a novel stimulus. This preferential attention varies with the degree of discrepancy of the novel stimulus from stimuli to which he has previously been exposed.

DEVELOPMENT OF SPECIFIC EXPECTATIONS
OF THE MOTHER

The next level of social responsiveness is characterized by behavior indicating specific expectations towards the mother or familiar caretaker. The infant shows consistent and sustained expectations of being gratified by his mother. For example, when in distress, he expects to be soothed; when she appears he may stop crying, or he may cry more intensely, at least momentarily, until she engages in the expected behaviors. When approached by his mother he may make postural adjustments indicating that he expects to be picked up. He has learned that certain behaviors on his part elicit specific responses from his caretaker. For instance, a smile, a coo, reaching out, or a more complex repertoire of "tricks" will elicit from his mother smiles, talking, touching, bouncing, or play. At the next developmental level, if the expected responses from his caretaker are not immediately forthcoming, the infant is able to wait, confident that his needs will be met. This level of relationship, with its implication of basic trust, which is similar to Benedek's (1938) "confidence relationship," probably represents the attainment of a true focused relationship.

Just as the infant must have acquired the capacity for perceptual discrimination to be able to respond differentially to mother and stranger, the acquisition of specific expectations towards the mother is dependent on several cognitive attainments: the development of a rudimentary memory, the acquisition of the concept of the existence of objects outside of his immediate perceptual field, some elementary concept of means-ends relationships, and a differentiated schema of the mother. As with other cognitive developments, there are probably differing degrees of stability of object permanence before it is fully established and consolidated. These different levels of cognitive functioning with regard to object permanence are probably paralleled by differing expectations towards the mother. Detailed studies of infant behavior and mother-infant interaction are needed to attain greater clarity about the cognitive underpinnings of the "confidence relationship" and to specifiy the conditions under which this level of focused relationship is developed and maintained.

STRANGER AND SEPARATION ANXIETY

Indices of attachment which involve aversive behaviors and negative affect are counterparts of the direct measures of attachment based on approach behaviors and positive affect. Stranger anxiety and anxiety when separated from the mother have until recently been the major indices of attachment used in research. There is some rationale for the use of these indices. When the child shows stranger anxiety he is indicating that he can distinguish between his familiar caretaker and a stranger. When he manifests disturbance on being separated from his mother, he is demonstrating that his mother has a special meaning to him. There seems to be clear sequences in the appearance of these negative indices of attachment which parallel the stages of the positive indices.

In a longitudinal study of young infants (Yarrow, 1967), we have noted behaviors which distinguish several levels of differentiation of the mother and the stranger. These behaviors range from passive visual fixation on strangers to active fear responses. Probably the earliest precursors of stranger anxiety are those behaviors showing discrimination between familiar and unfamiliar persons. At the level of passive differentiation we find such behaviors as intent visual concentration on the stranger (without overt affect), or apparent deliberate ignoring of the stranger and concentration of attention on the mother. This level of passive differentiation can be distinguished from overt anxiety responses. At this level of active differentiation there is great variety in form and intensity of these overt responses. They range from ambivalent approach towards and withdrawal from the stranger to behavior characterized by intense negative affect, e.g., vigorous and prolonged crying. In addition to variations in intensity and type of response, these behaviors differ on dimensions such as latency of response and time required for their habituation. These variations in response characteristics are not always simple direct reflections of the degree of anxiety. Variation in these response dimensions may also be related to individual differences in modes of expression, and they may be partly related to the immediate state of the infant. They will vary with such characteristics of the immediate situation as the degree of strangeness of the surroundings and the person. There are also significant developmental changes in form and intensity of expression.

Inasmuch as infants during the first months of life are sensitive to perceptual incongruity and are capable of distinguishing familiar from strange or novel stimuli, it seems likely that the affective bases for stranger anxiety are at least as important as the perceptual-cognitive determinants. More complex cognitive factors than the ability to make simple perceptual discriminations may be associated with the manifestation of stranger anxiety. For example, if the infant has developed expectations of specific kinds of behavior from another person and the stranger does not show the expected behavior, this violation of expectancies may induce fear responses.

There are many problems in the use of separation protest and stranger anxiety as indices of strength of attachment. Although we do not have precise data, the evidence seems to indicate that the environmental conditions which influence the strength of positive attachment behaviors differ from the factors determining the strength and character of responses to separation and to stranger anxiety. The available research shows that the infant's smiling, vocalizations, and approach movements can be brought under the control of very specific social-environmental conditions (Rheingold, Gewirtz, & Ross, 1959; Weisberg, 1963; Brossard & Décarie, 1969). Data on a very different level suggest that the appearance or the intensity of stranger anxiety may be influenced by several life history variables, such as the number of different people in the child's environment who take responsibility for his care and the variety of strange situations to which he has been exposed (Schaffer, 1966). It is also significantly influenced by a number of situational factors, such as the familiarity or strangeness of the immediate setting, the presence or absence of the mother (Morgan & Ricciuti, 1969), and the gradualness or suddenness of approach by the stranger. The relative significance of these factors may vary at different developmental points (Bronson, 1971).

Similarly, with regard to separation protest, not only are there differences in intensity and type of response to separation at different developmental periods, but there is also a wide range of environmental conditions that influence separation protest (Yarrow, 1964). Like the positive indices of attachment and like stranger anxiety, separation protest does not appear suddenly full-blown. In our studies of separation (Yarrow & Goodwin, in press) involving a change in mother figures, we have found disturbances in young infants following separation even before there are clear-cut positive signs of a focused relationship with the mother. It is quite possible that these disruptions in infant functioning may be reactions to broad environmental changes. Rather than simply being protests at the loss of a specific person, these infant disturbances may be reactions to changes in the scheduling of routines and in the timing of response to his distress signals, as well as to changes in the kinds of tactile and auditory stimulation provided by the new caretaker. Moreover, there are indications that the intensity of separation protest is inversely related to the amount of experience the infant has had with multiple caretakers. On the other hand, our data show that reactions to separation are directly related to the intensity of the relationship with the previous caretaker. They are more severe in infants who have had close relationships with their caretakers. In this sense, severity of separation protest may be directly related to the intensity of attachment. However, we also found that some infants who show severe initial separation reactions are able to become attached quickly to a new caretaker. Other investigators have also pointed out that the relationship between the level of attachment to the mother and intensity of separation anxiety is not a simple one (Benjamin, 1963; Ainsworth, 1969).

The Role of Environmental Influences

In concentrating on the orderly sequences in the development of focused relationships, there is an implication that this is a wholly maturational process. There are, however, important environmental influences. The data on the environmental factors influencing the distinctive bond between mother and infant are sparse and tend to be somewhat equivocal.

Some inferences can be made about the conditions that impede the formation of attachments from studies of infants in residential child-care institutions. In such institutions there is often no single, consistent caretaker with whom the infant can establish a relationship. The quality of care is so routinized that there is little variety of stimulation, minimal contingent responsiveness, and very little adaptation of the caretaker's behavior to the child's individual characteristics and sensitivities. Infants in these settings do not form deep or enduring relationships with their caretakers. They are also delayed in the cognitive processes underlying attachments, such as the development of object permanence (Paraskevopoulos & Hunt, 1971).

Findings from studies of infants in home environments (Schaffer & Emerson, 1964; Ainsworth, Bell, & Stayton, 1971) might be interpreted as indicating that high contingent responsiveness of the mother, varied stimulation, and a special sensitivity of the mother to the baby's signals are positively related to the development of attachment. These findings, together with the findings on institutional environments, point to some of the characteristics of maternal care that seem to be important for the development of focused relationships.

We should also recognize that environmental influences cannot be seen as a simple antecedent-consequent relationship; rather, there is an interaction between the child's characteristics and the kinds of stimulation he receives.

Some characteristics of the child are more likely to elicit varied social stimulation and higher levels of responsiveness from mothers. For instance, alert, active infants who smile, vocalize, and make approach movements towards their mothers are apt to receive more attention than infants who are quiet and apathetic and who show little responsiveness. Probably the "fit" between mother and infant is also important (Yarrow, 1963). The extent to which the mother and infant are similar or complementary in characteristics may affect the amount and kinds of stimulation the infant receives, and thus may influence the formation of attachment. For example, if both mother and infant enjoy tactile contact, the mutually satisfactory adaptation that results is likely to facilitate the development of a focused relationship; and conversely, a poor "fit" between mother and infant may impede the relationship.

Attachment and Dependency Beyond the First Year

In this discussion, I have concentrated on the development of focused relationships during the first year of life. Considering the concepts of attachment and dependency at developmental periods beyond infancy, after the child has acquired the capacity to handle and manipulate his environment more effectively, one might expect an even more complex relationship between instrumental dependency and attachment. A strong attachment to the mother may facilitate the child's autonomy. The child who has developed confident expectations towards his mother and who sees his environment as essentially predictable, may be capable of greater instrumental *independence* than the child who does not have these secure expectations. Similarly, in regard to emotionally dependent behaviors, during infancy such behaviors may be meaningful indices of the strength of attachment, whereas in later childhood, similar behaviors, such as seeking physical contact, may indicate a basic insecurity in the child's feelings about his relationship with his mother. The meaning of clinging behavior changes as the child grows older. The child who wants to be near his mother constantly, may cling to her (physically or symbolically) because he feels the relationship is a tenuous one. This example merely suggests the difficulties in using simple behavioral indices of attachment, without any consideration of their dynamic meaning.

Concluding Remarks

The concept of attachment had been analyzed within the broader framework of social development during infancy. We have described the varieties of social-relational behaviors characteristic of different developmental periods during the first year of life, and we have emphasized the strong interdependence between social behaviors and cognitive capacities. It seems reasonable to assume that some cognitive developments may underlie, that is, may be necessary conditions for, the development of focused relationships. The differentiation of self from the environment is partly dependent on the development of the child's awareness that he can have an effect on the environment. The growth of social discrimination is intimately tied to the development of basic perceptual discriminations in the visual and auditory modalities, and possibly also in the tactile and kinesthetic modalities. The growth of the confidence relationship is linked to the development of the capacity for mental representation of objects in their absence. It is likely, however, that these are not simple one-way relationships in which the cognitive developments always precede the social and affective changes. They may appear concurrently and simply be different expressions of the same structural changes. In other cases, some cognitive functions, such as object permanence, may be strengthened or consolidated by the formation of social attachments. The data on institution-reared infants indicating retardation in the achievement of object permanence might be interpreted as supporting this conjecture.

In analyzing in detail the behavioral criteria for early focused relationships, I have implied that attempting to distinguish between attachment and emotional dependency may not be too useful. The distinctions that have been made tend to be rather arbitrary, and do not seem to facilitate theoretical understanding of the origins of these behaviors or of the factors influencing their developmental course. At this stage in our theoretical thinking it may be more meaningful to define the various precursors of attachment and to distinguish the various levels of focused relationships. Such analysis has an apparent heuristic value. It simplifies formulation of hypotheses regarding antecedents at different developmental levels, and thus it provides a framework for specification of the environmental parameters which might be systematically studied.

REFERENCES

Ainsworth, M.D.S. Object relations, dependency and attachment: A theoretical review of the infant-mother relationship. *Child Development*, 1969, **40**, 969-1025.

Ainsworth, M. D. S., Bell, S. M., & Stayton, D. J. Individual differences in strange-situation behavior of one-year-olds. In H. R. Schaffer (Ed.), *The origins of human social relations*. London: Academic Press, 1971. Pp. 17-52.

Balint, A. Love for the mother and mother love. *International Journal of Psycho-Analysis*, 1949, **30**, 251-259.

Bayley, N. *Bayley scales of infant development: Birth to two years*. New York: Psychological Corp., 1969.

Beller, E. K. Dependency and independence in young children. *Journal of Genetic Psychology*, 1955, **87**, 25-35.

Benedek, T. Adaptation to reality in early infancy. *Psychoanalytic Quaterly*, 1938, **7**, 200-215.

Benjamin, J. D. Further comments on some developmental aspects of anxiety. In H. S. Gaskill (Ed.), *Counterpoint*. New York: International Universities Press, 1963. Pp. 121-153.

Bowlby, J. The nature of the child's tie to his mother. *International Journal of Psycho-Analysis*, 1958, **39**, 1-24.

Bowlby, J. Separation anxiety. *International Journal of Psycho-Analysis*, 1960, **41**, 69-113.

Bowlby, J. *Attachment and loss.* New York: Basic Books, 1969.

Bridges, K. M. B. A study of social development in early infancy. *Child Development,* 1933, 4, 36-49.

Bronson, G. W. Infants' reactions to unfamiliar persons. I. Normative patterns. Paper presented at the meeting of the Society for Research in Child Development, Minneapolis, Minn., April 1971.

Brossard, L. M., & Décarie, T. G. Comparative reinforcing effect of eight stimulations on the smiling response of infants. *Journal of Child Psychology and Psychiatry,* 1969, 9, 51-60.

Cairns, R. B. Attachment behavior of mammals. *Psychological Review,* 1966, 73, 409-426.

Carpenter, G. C., Tecce, J. J., Stechler, G., & Friedman, S. Differential visual behavior to human and humanoid faces in early infancy. *Merrill-Palmer Quarterly,* 1970, 16, 91-108.

Fairbairn, W. R. C. *Object-relations theory of the personality.* New York: Basic Books, 1954.

Fantz, R. L., & Nevis, S. Pattern preferences and perceptual-cognitive development in early infancy. *Merrill-Palmer Quarterly,* 1967, 13, 77-108.

Freud, S. Three essays on the theory of sexuality. *The standard edition of the complete psychological works of Sigmund Freud.* Vol. VII. London: Hogarth, 1953. Pp. 125-145. (Originally published: 1905.)

Freud, S. Instincts and their vicissitudes. *The standard edition of the complete psychological works of Sigmund Freud.* Vol. XX. London: Hogarth, 1962. (Originally published: 1915.)

Gesell, A., & Amatruda, C. S. *Developmental Diagnosis.* New York: Hoeber, 1947.

Gewirtz, J. L. A program of research on the dimensions and antecedents of emotional dependence. *Child Development,* 1956, 27, 205-221.

Gewirtz, J. L. A learning analysis of the effects of normal stimulation, privation and deprivation on the acquisition of social motivation and attachment. In B. M. Foss (Ed.), *Determinants of infant behaviour.* London: Methuen (New York: Wiley), 1961. Pp. 213-290.

Gewirtz, J. L. Mechanisms of social learning: Some roles of stimulation and behavior in early human development. In D. A. Goslin (Ed.), *Handbook of socialization theory and research.* Chicago: Rand-McNally, 1969. Pp. 57-212.

Griffiths, R. *The abilities of babies: A study in mental measurement.* New York: McGraw-Hill, 1954.

Heathers, G. Acquiring dependence and independence: A theoretical orientation. *Journal of Genetic Psychology,* 1955, 87, 277-291.

Klein, M. *Contributions to psychoanalysis.* London: Hogarth (New York: Anglobooks) 1952.

Maccoby, E. E., & Masters, J. C. Attachment and dependency. In P. H. Mussen (Ed.), *Carmichael's manual of child psychology.* (3rd ed.) Vol. 2. New York: Wiley, 1970. Pp. 73-158.

Mahler, M. S., & La Perriere, K. Mother-child interaction during separation-individuation. *Psychoanalytic Quarterly.* 1965, 34, 483-498.

Morgan, G. A., & Ricciuti, H. N. Infant's responses to strangers during the first year. In B. M. Foss (Ed.), *Determinants of infant behaviour IV.* London: Methuen, 1969. Pp. 252-272.

Murphy, L. B. Some aspects of the first relationship. *International Journal of Psycho-Analysis,* 1964, 45, 31-43.

Paraskevopoulos, J., & Hunt, J. McV. Object construction and imitation under differing conditions of rearing. *Journal of Genetic Psychology,* 1971, 119, 301-321.

Piaget, J. *The origins of intelligence in children.* (2nd ed.) New York: International Universities Press, 1952. (Originally published: 1936.)

Rheingold, H.L., Gewirtz, J. L., & Ross, H. W. Social conditioning of vocalizations in the infant. *Journal of Comparative and Physiological Psychology,* 1959, 52, 68-73.

Schaffer, H. R. The onset of fear of strangers and the incongruity hypothesis. *Journal of Child Psychology and Psychiatry,* 1966, **7,** 95-106.

Schaffer, H. R., & Emerson, P. E. The development of social attachments in infancy. *Monographs of the Society for Research in Child Development,* 1964, **29** (3, Serial No. 94).

Sears, R. R. A theoretical framework for personality and social behavior. *American Psychologist,* 1951, **6,** 476-483.

Sears, R. R. Dependency motivation. *Nebraska Symposium on Motivation,* 1963, **11,** 25-64.

Sears, R. R., Whiting, J. W. M., Nowlis, V., & Sears, P. S. Some child-rearing antecedents of dependency and aggression in young children. *Genetic Psychology Monographs,* 1953, **47,** 135-234.

Shirley, M. M. *The first two years: A study of twenty-five babies.* Vol. 2. *Intellectual development.* Minneapolis: University of Minnesota Press, 1933.

Spitz, R. A. Anxiety in infancy: A study of its manifestations in the first year of life. *International Journal of Psycho-Analysis,* 1950, **31,** 138-143.

Spitz, R. A. *The first year of life.* New York: International Universities Press, 1965.

Spitz, R. A., & Wolf, K. M. The smiling response: A contribution to the ontogenesis of social relations. *Genetic Psychology Monographs,* 1946, **34,** *57-125.*

Tennes, K. H., & Lampl, E. E. Stranger and separation anxiety in infancy. *Journal of Nervous and Mental Diseases,* 1964, **139,** 247-254.

Tennes, K. H., & Lampl, E. E. Some aspects of mother-child relationship pertaining to infantile separation anxiety. *Journal of Nervous and Mental Diseases,* 1966, **143,** 426-437.

Weisberg, P. Social and non-social conditioning of infant vocalization. *Child Development,* 1963, **34,** 377-388.

White, B. L., Castle, P. W., & Held, R. Observations on the development of visually directed reaching. *Child Development,* 1964, **35,** 349-364.

Yarrow, L. J. The development of object relationships during infancy and the effects of a disruption of early mother-child relationships. *American Psychologist,* 1956, **11,** 423. (Abstract).

Yarrow, L. J. Dimensions of maternal care. *Merrill-Palmer Quarterly,* 1963, **9,** 101-114.

Yarrow, L. J. Separation from parents during early childhood. In M. Hoffman & L. Hoffman (Eds.), *Review of child development research.* Vol. 1. New York: Russell Sage Foundation, 1964. Pp. 89-136.

Yarrow, L. J. The development of focused relationships during infancy. In J. Hellmuth (Ed.), *Exceptional infant: The normal infant.* Vol. 1. Seattle, Wash.: Special Child Publications, 1967. Pp. 429-442.

Yarrow, L. J., & Goodwin, M. S. The immediate impact of separation. In L. J. Stone, H. T. Smith, & L. B. Murphy (Eds.), *The competent infant: A handbook of readings.* New York: Basic Books, in press.

ATTACHMENT AND DEPENDENCY: A COMPARISON[1]

Mary D. Salter Ainsworth

Johns Hopkins University

Introduction

Attachment and dependency are concepts in terms of which systematic efforts have been made to investigate and to order certain significant aspects of social development. From a longitudinal point of view, both concepts are cast on a grand scale and are aimed to cover important behaviors throughout the life span, despite the fact that the research inspired by each concept to date has focused on a relatively narrow and early portion of that span. From a cross-sectional point of view neither concept can be comprehensive; the total range of social relations exceeds by far the scope of either. Although the connotations of attachment and dependency are by no means identical, there is substantial overlap between them. In particular, there is overlap at the point of origin of social relations. It is perhaps because each deals with origins but in divergent ways that they have been perceived as competing rather than as supplementary concepts.

[1] This chapter was prepared in conjunction with a research project on the development of infant-mother attachment, which has been supported by USPHS Grant RO1 01712, for which thanks are due. Gratitude is expressed to Silvia Bell, John Bowlby, Robert Hinde, and Robert Sears, who read the manuscript in draft, and whose suggestions, criticisms, and encouragement have been invaluable.

Gewirtz conceives that the same paradigm can account for the processes involved in both dependency and attachment. In this chapter, however, a paradigmatic distinction is proposed between the concepts. This distinction is similar to that suggested by Sears in this volume. The basic view propounded in this chapter has been identified as ethological and evolutionary, although it might equally well be described as psychobiological. It resembles that of Cairns in many respects, although the detailed review of the relevant research literature that would make clear the resemblance has been presented elsewhere (Ainsworth, in press). While we find much that is homologous in the early social relations of humans and other species, especially nonhuman primates, our emphasis coincides with Yarrow's in its viewing of the development of social relations as inextricably interlocked with the development of cognitive abilities, including those that emerge well after the relatively simple processes of the nonverbal period have been supplemented by and transformed into more sophisticated operations. Like Yarrow's, this chapter emphasizes the first "focused" relationship—the infant-mother attachment relationship—and therefore of necessity deals more with the concept of attachment, within the context of which our own research has been directed, than with the concept of dependency.

"Dependency" preceded "attachment" in the history of developmental theory and research. It would be inappropriate here to review the social-learning concept of dependency. An excellent review of the literature has been prepared by Maccoby and Masters (1970), and Sears has provided an authoritative critique of dependency theory in this volume. Suffice it to say, for our present purposes, that dependency was originally conceived as a secondary drive acquired through gratification of basic physiological drives. The origin of the infant's tie to his mother thus was hypothesized to rest upon the fact that she gratified his basic drives, and all later social-dependency relations with others were considered to come about through generalization from the initial dependency relationship with the mother figure. This was the view espoused not only by Sears and his associates (1953, 1957, 1965), but also by Beller (1955, 1957, 1959), Heathers (1955), and Stendler (1954). The secondary drive theory of the origin of the initial infant-mother relationship now seems untenable in the light of evidence reviewed not only by Bowlby (1958, 1969) and Ainsworth (1969, and in press) but also by previous proponents of this view, including Walters and Parke (1965) and Sears himself (1963, and in this volume). Meanwhile Gewirtz (1956, 1961, 1969) and Bijou and Baer (1965) shifted the theoretical focus from drive reduction to the reinforcement of operant behaviors. The account of origins of the infant's tie to his mother was thereby modified to the extent that the reinforcers operating were conceived to include not only stimuli related to biogenic drives but also other stimuli as well.

The term "attachment" was introduced into the developmental literature by John Bowlby. When, in 1958, he proposed a new theoretical approach to the origins of a child's tie to his mother, he chose the term "attachment" to refer to this tie in preference to the term "dependency" in order to avoid the connotations which "dependency" had been given by both psychoanalytic and social-learning theories. Ainsworth (1963, 1964, 1967) found Bowlby's ethologically oriented approach a useful one in her study of the development of infant-mother interaction among the Ganda, and she offered some elaborations and extensions of Bowlby's initial formulation. Bowlby (1960a, 1960b, 1961, 1963) used his new approach as a basis for understanding a child's responses to separation and loss. Nevertheless, until very recently (Bowlby, 1969; Ainsworth, 1969; Ainsworth & Bell, 1970), this approach was represented in the literature only in preliminary and fragmentary form.

The climate of opinion during the last decade has greatly favored a reexamination of the origin and development of early social relations. Despite the preliminary and incomplete formulation of the concept, "attachment" captured the interest of many, and the term has appeared with increasing frequency in theoretical discussions and in reports of research with both humans and animals. This development has coincided with unprecedented research interest in the period of infancy. It has also coincided with a renewed interest in how that which lies inside the organism contributes to organism-environment interaction. In the field of infant research, an intraorganismic emphasis has been forwarded by two main groups—cognitive psychologists who are concerned with the foundations and transformations of cognitive structures; and those who conceive of attachment as having both an inner organization and an outward behavioral manifestation, and as having an intraorganismic as well as an environmental context.

Developments in the biological sciences have had a profound effect in drawing the attention of psychologists to intraorganismic conditions for the activation, termination, and organization of behavior. One such influence has come through ethology to both developmental and comparative psychology. Darwin's evolutionary theory based on the principle of natural selection has gained new relevance, partly through ethology, but also through important advances in molecular biology and genetics. Physiological psychology has focused interest on neurophysiological, endocrine, and receptor processes that interact with environmental stimuli to activate and to terminate the activity of behavioral systems. The significant influence of Piaget on cognitive psychology may be counted as a fundamentally biological influence. Control-systems theory and computer models have also directed attention to inner "programming." All of these influences have tended to shift the attention of many developmental psychologists from an almost exclusive concern with environmental control to increased interest in what is inside the organism to start with, how this inner programming affects the response to environmental input, and how it becomes transformed as a consequence of organism-environment transactions.

The impact of these several influences on our view of the development of early social relations has led to what Kuhn (1962) terms a "paradigm change"—to a complete shift of perspective. The central feature of the new perspective, insofar as attachment theory is concerned, is viewing early social behavior in an evolutionary context. Among those who seem to have been affected by this perspective are Ambrose (1963), Caldwell (1962), Freedman (1968), Harlow (1963), Kaufman and Rosenblum (1967), Morgan and Ricciuti (1969), Robson (1967), Schaffer and Emerson (1964a), Scott (1963), and Walters and Parke (1965), to name but a few and to cite but one reference each. The recent research of these and others too numerous to mention here has influenced attachment theory substantially. Bowlby, having launched the concept of attachment in 1958, has strongly influenced this development; but his 1969 formulation is also the effect of a decade of research undertaken by many others, some working consciously within the new paradigm and some working seemingly independent of it.

The purpose of this chapter is threefold: (a) to compare the view of attachment sponsored by Bowlby and Ainsworth with the "classic" view of dependency; (b) to elucidate this concept of attachment, with particular regard for points of misunderstanding which have arisen presumably because of the lag between initial formulation and recent exposition; and (c) to discuss some directions in which further research into attachment could profitably move. It is not intended to propose a revision of the concept of dependency, as Gewirtz, Sears, and Cairns have done; such a revision is best left to those whose research has been concerned with dependency, rather than attempted by one whose research experience has been confined to attachment.

A Comparison of Attachment and Dependency

There are eight points that deserve consideration in a comparison of attachment and dependency.

Specificity. An attachment is an affectional tie or bond that one individual (person or animal) forms between himself and another specific individual. In contrast, dependency is a generalized or nonfocused response characteristic. Although their definitions of attachment and dependency differ, most of the contributors to this volume are agreed in the distinction of specific or focused versus unspecific or nonfocused.

Duration. Attachments are enduring. They may be of longer or shorter duration, but they are not transient. In contrast, a dependency transaction may be entirely transient, involving no continuing relationship between two persons. To say that attachments are enduring does not imply that there are no changes in the course of development and experience. Nor does it imply that attachments are necessarily irreversible. The bereaved child may reconcile himself to the loss of his mother and become attached to a new mother figure, just as the bereaved husband may, after a period of grief and mourning, find a new wife. Furthermore, and to modify slightly a suggestion made by Sears (this volume), early attachments usually become attenuated and to a substantial degree supplemented or supplanted by other later attachments. Nevertheless, attachments, once well consolidated, are not easily abandoned, and it seems likely that the traces of any relationship significant enough to be termed an attachment are never altogether lost. The response of a young child to separation from his mother, once he has become attached to her—and his response to subsequent reunion with her—bears witness to the enduring nature of infant-mother attachment. The fact that others may have been accepted as sources of help and nurturance during the separation does not mean necessarily that the attachment to the mother was weakened; and indeed most young children continue to give some evidence of attachment to their mothers throughout separation experiences unless these are unusually long. There is an abundance of clinical evidence that early attachments are difficult to dissolve even after they may seem to have been superseded by later attachments. Longitudinal field studies of rhesus monkeys (Sade, 1965) and chimpanzees (van Lawick-Goodall, 1968) and captive-colony studies of pigtail macaques (Rosenblum, 1971) have demonstrated that in some species attachment to the mother persists well into the juvenile period or beyond, and forms the basis for stable and continuing social groupings. Indeed it is the long-term, enduring nature of attachment relationships, and the implication that over long periods of time they have a pervasive effect on other behaviors, that make them such an important subject of research.

Level of maturity. Attachments are characteristic of all ages. Dependence, on the other hand, is the antonym of independence and implies immaturity. To be sure, Beller (1955) and Heathers (1955) pointed out that dependence and independence are not at opposite poles of the same psychological dimension and that they are learned concurrently by the young child. Nevertheless, it is popularly held that dependence should give way gradually to a substantial degree of independence. To describe an adult as dependent implies an undesirable trait; to identify him as independent is to praise him. Attachments, in contrast, do not necessarily imply the immaturity and helplessness that dependency connotes. To describe an adult as attached to one or a few other persons implies a normal state of affairs; to characterize him as incapable of attachment connotes pathology.

Research attention has been focused especially on the first attachment—the attachment of an infant to his mother—but there are or can be other significant attachments in the life span: husband to wife, wife to husband, parent to child, and close friend to close friend, to name a few. After the first half-year of life there is no age at which attachments cannot occur, but obviously the quality of the relationship is influenced substantially by the relative levels of maturity of the persons concerned. The quality of the attachment of a 1-year-old to his mother clearly differs from—and may be designated as immature in contrast with—the attachment to each other of partners in marriage. Bowlby (1969) suggests that with increasing maturity the person tends gradually to lose the egocentrism (Piaget, 1924) which has previously hampered him from entering into a thoroughly "goal-corrected partnership."

Affective implications. Attachments imply strong affect, and in this sense also—as well as because they are enduring and pervasively influential—they are significant relationships. Sears uses the strong word "passion" to apply to attachments—and restricts the term to relationships as intense as those between a young child and his parents and between marriage partners, with the possibility of one or two pseudo attachments in intervening years. Beyond these obviously affect-laden relationships, however, there seem others significant enough to be termed attachments—among some siblings, and between close friends, for example—for which the term "passion" is perhaps too strong. It does not seem too strong, however, to use the word "love" to characterize any attachment relationship. Not all companions are attachment figures. A young child is not necessarily attached to his playmates, nor a businessman to his everyday associates. Where the positive affect is too weak to be described as love, it seems ill-advised to speak of attachment.

Although strong positive affect is considered characteristic of attachment relationships, intense affect is not limited to the positive emotions. Intense anxiety is likely to be aroused by the threat of loss of or injury to a person to whom one is attached, and grief is likely to follow the realization of loss. Angry feelings may be intense if one is prevented from gaining proximity, contact, or interaction with an attachment figure, and anger may be directed to that figure if it is he who prevents attachment behavior from having its desired outcome. Jealousy may be aroused if the attachment figure is perceived as giving to another the proximity, contact, or interaction that one wishes for oneself.

In contrast, the affective implications of dependency, as traditionally conceived, have not been featured.

Proximity-seeking and contact-maintaining behavior. The behavioral hallmark of attachment is the seeking of proximity to or contact with the attachment figure. The traditional concept of dependency also includes these behaviors, but without the implication that they are directed toward any specific person or persons. Dependency as traditionally viewed goes further to include behaviors peripheral to attachment, namely, attention-seeking, approval-seeking, and help-seeking.

Even though proximity seeking is characteristic of attachment behavior, the degree of proximity sought varies from situation to situation. Sometimes all that is required is proximity close enough for intermittent interaction or communication across some distance; sometimes nothing but physical contact will do. (More comprehensive discussion of proximity and contact-seeking will follow in other sections of this chapter.)

Learning. That attachments are learned, we will all agree. The newborn is not attached to his mother, nor to anyone else. Although he may be genetically biased toward becoming attached to *some* person if he is given the opportunity to do so, it is obviously not predetermined to whom he will become attached. In contrast to precocial birds, which form attachments very quickly soon after hatching (for reviews of imprinting, see Bateson, 1966, and Sluckin, 1965), the human cannot form an attachment before a certain essential amount of cognitive development has taken place—development in which learning is clearly implicated. Furthermore, the human infant cannot become attached without having experienced a substantial number of previous transactions with the attachment figure. Just how many and what kind of transactions are required is an empirical question yet to be answered, and further research is required to elucidate the processes through which attachments are formed.

Gewirtz (1961, 1969, and in this volume) proposes that the same paradigm can account for the processes involved in dependency and attachment. Sears (this volume) implies that the learning paradigm fits the acquisition of dependency, but is not entirely applicable to the formation of an attachment. Nevertheless, it is clear that discrimination-learning is implicated in attachment, for a specific figure must be discriminated from other figures before an attachment may be formed to it.

The role played by generalization in the formation of attachments is not clear, however. The classic view of dependency implied that dependency behaviors generalized from their initial direction toward the mother to other figures. Sears (this volume) acknowledges that response generalization is applicable to attachment behavior, in that there is considerable substitutability of segments within a total behavioral unit, and in that dependency behaviors are highly generalizable from the mother to others. He strongly doubts, however, that stimulus generalization occurs with reference to attachment. Gewirtz (this volume) does not conceive of responses under control of a specific person (attachment) as generalizing to come under control of a class of persons (dependency), but rather holds that the two classes of "functional relations" are acquired independently. Both Sears and Gewirtz thus hold that attachments are highly specific relationships and that dependency does not generalize from attachment. Clinical evidence strongly suggests, however, that having become attached to one figure subsequently facilitates becoming attached to other figures; but if such facilitation is indeed present, it is not clear whether it can be described as generalization.

Although attachment theory clearly implies learning, it does not specify in any detail the learning processes implicated in the development of attachment, nor does it deal with the functional relations between stimulus and response as, for example, Gewirtz does in this volume and elsewhere. This is in part because attachment theory has emphasized the relationship between the development of infant-mother attachment and cognitive development. Although it is self-evident that learning is implicated in cognitive development, cognitive theorists have been very casual in their occasional linking of developmental concepts to the key processes of well-established learning theories—and social learning theorists rarely, if ever, refer their constructs to cognitive development.

Piaget's (1936, 1937) account of sensorimotor development has seemed to some (e.g., Bowlby, 1958, 1969; Schaffer, 1963, 1966; Schaffer & Emerson, 1964a; Ainsworth, 1967, 1969) to offer an especially useful model for the learning of infant-mother attachment—and to me to be more congenial than the models of social-learning theories. The two models overlap, of course, and much of one can be assimilated into the other. Despite the fact that the Piagetian model was not concerned with the learning of attachments, it is especially keyed to *what* is learned as well as to how—through what processes—it is learned. Piaget's account of development is particularly concerned with the transformation of the limited repertoire of relatively uncoordinated behavioral systems characteristic of the neonate into the much more extensive repertoire of interlocking, coordinated, and interchangeable strategies characteristic of the older child. In the early stages of development, discrimination-learning is comprehended as recognitory assimilation, generalization as generalizing assimilation, reorganization of existing responses as reciprocal assimilation, and the emergence of new responses as accommodation.

At about the time that an infant may first be described as attached to his mother (that is, in Piaget's Stage 4 of development), two major acquisitions are of particular pertinence to an understanding of attachment and of attachment behavior. First, he becomes capable of distinguishing between means and ends, and his "schemata" thus become "mobile" and capable of flexible organization into new patterns of behavior to suit the exigencies of a particular situation. This mobility can account for the interchangeability of specific attachment behaviors, and fits well with Bowlby's (1969) control-systems theory and with his observation that at this stage it becomes useful to describe an infant's behavior as goal-corrected and as governed by an overall plan. Second, the infant begins to be able to search for hidden objects, and thus shows the first substantial beginning of the concept of an object as having permanence despite its absence from his perceptual field. As several have already suggested (e.g., Escalona, 1953; Bowlby, 1958, 1969; Schaffer & Emerson, 1964a; Décarie, 1965; Ainsworth, 1967; S. M. Bell, 1970; and Yarrow, this volume), the acquisition of "object-permanence" marks a momentous shift in the nature of infant-mother relations and, indeed, may be seen as a necessary condition for attachment. It is not until a child is cognitively capable of conceiving of his mother as existing while not actually present perceptually that his behavior can have the time- and space-bridging qualities that distinguish attachments from other transactions.

Finally, Piaget's (1936, 1937) account of sensorimotor development culminates in the acquisition of "inner representation" and thus in the ability to operate symbolically in Stage 6—an acquisition which he suggests may be completed at about 18 months of age, but which surely begins earlier, even at the end of the first year of life, in some infants. Although this acquisition may thus come while a child is still preverbal—and indeed may not be unique to the human species—it marks the beginning of the "distinctively human capabilities" of which Cairns (this volume) speaks. Attachment theory, which is designed to comprehend attachment relationships throughout the life span, requires a view of learning which readily comprehends symbolic representation—and is by no means limited to child-mother relations during the preverbal period.

Thus, although attachment theory is geared to a learning paradigm other than those utilized by social-learning views of dependency (and also, more recently, of attachment too), it is nonetheless fully cognizant of the significance of learning. With increasing evidence of the effect of environmental influences on maturational processes, it has become exceedingly difficult sharply to differentiate maturation from learning. Nevertheless, our view of the development of attachment is not primarily a "maturational" view.

Biological function. Central to present-day biological sciences—and particularly to genetics and ethology—is the Darwinian principle that structures and behavioral systems characteristic of the species, and the genotypes that underlie them, are represented in the population because they gave survival advantage in the environment of evolutionary adaptedness—that is, in the environment in which the species first evolved and continues to evolve. The biological function of a behavioral system is that outcome of the system that originally gave it survival advantage, and that outcome is to be distinguished from all the other usual outcomes or correlates of the system. This concept of biological function is crucial to an ethologically oriented theory of attachment, and distinguishes it from other theoretical approaches to attachment or dependency. Bowlby (1969) conceives the primary function of attachment, and of reciprocal maternal behavior, to be protection of the infant.

The biological function of a behavioral system may or may not give special advantage in one or another of the various environments in which a species now lives—and this principle is obviously relevant to the human case, and to the behavioral systems implicated in human attachment behavior. Nevertheless, genetic programming continues to bias the infant to behave in ways adapted to the original environment of evolutionary adaptedness; and although the dangers of his contemporary environment may differ from those that threatened infants in that original environment, there is good reason to believe that the protective function of attachment behavior is still advantageous.

Implications for personality development and for psychopathology. There seems little doubt that the psychological significance attributed both to dependency and to attachment derived originally from the central role imputed by psychoanalytic theory to object relations both in personality development and in the etiology of psychopathology. Sears and his associates (1943, 1953, 1957, 1963, 1965) drew many of their principles from psychoanalytic theory, as did Beller (1955, 1957, 1959); and Dollard and Miller (1950) explicitly attempted to translate psychoanalytic theory into terms compatible with Hullian learning theory. Of those who have espoused the concept of attachment in preference to that of dependency, it is no accident that Bowlby, Ainsworth, and Schaffer—and indeed also Yarrow (1967, and in this volume), whose concept of "focused relationship" resembles the concept of attachment—came to investigate the development of infant-mother relationship after having been concerned with the anomalous and sometimes psychopathological outcomes of deprivation of the opportunity to form an attachment with the mother (maternal deprivation) and of interruption of the tie once formed (mother-child separation). Although Bowlby (1969) has been much influenced by ethology and control-systems theory, he presents his formulation of attachment theory within the context of psychoanalysis; he offers it as a contribution to psychoanalytic theory and is clearly alert to the psychopathological implications of anomalies of development. It is probably accurate to state that investigators who find the concept of attachment a useful one in the study of human behavior are not so much concerned with exploring the development of attachment for its own sake as with using it as a conceptual tool in the course of fine-grain studies of early intrapersonal interactions and their effect on personality development. If the concept of dependency is to be redefined, as other contributors to this volume propose, it is worth considering the implications of the proposed redefinitions for a study of personality development and of the etiology of psychopathology.

The Development of Child-Mother Attachment

Within the limits of this chapter, there can be no extensive exposition of the theory of attachment advanced by Bowlby and Ainsworth. It seems desirable, however, to describe the development of child-mother attachment as it proceeds through four main phases. Whatever further differentiation, extension, or subdivision of phases of development of attachment may seem needed in the light of future research, there is already substantial evidence (see reviews by Bowlby, 1969, and Ainsworth, in press) and considerable agreement that three main stages of development occur, under normal circumstances, in the first year of life. These are: (a) the initial preattachment phase, during which there are precursors of attachment in the form of various proximity-promoting behaviors, but before these become effectively discriminating; (b) a phase during which attachment may be described as "in the making," during which discriminations are learned, preferences are formed, and attachment behavior becomes differentially focused on one or a few specific persons—usually the mother (or substitute mother), and perhaps other members of the household who have significant interaction with the baby; and (c) a phase after unmistakable attachments have been formed with the mother and/or other specific figures. Finally, Bowlby has distinguished a later phase (d) characterized by the formation of a "goal-corrected partnership."

THE INITIAL PREATTACHMENT PHASE

This phase begins at birth and occupies the first few weeks of life. From the very beginning, the infant is disposed to respond more readily to stimuli within certain ranges than to others, and there is much evidence to support the proposition that the stimuli to which he is most responsive tend to be those most likely to emanate from other members of the species, and perhaps especially from adult females (Bowlby, 1969; Wolff, 1963, 1969). Also, from the very beginning, the infant's repertoire includes behaviors which promote proximity and/or contact with conspecifics, and most usually with the mother. Some of these behaviors have the usual outcome of attracting the adult into proximity with him. In many species these behaviors include species-characteristic vocalizations. Soon, only in the human, smiling emerges to supplement crying and other proximity-promoting behaviors. Other behaviors are more directly and actively proximity-promoting, rather than being merely signaling behaviors like the cry or smile. These more active behaviors are at first limited to rooting, sucking, grasping, following with the eyes, and perhaps a few other primitive and prototypical attachment behaviors.

Whether functional at birth or only after some weeks of development, proximity-promoting behaviors such as these can easily be described as species-characteristic, and these are later supplemented by a number of other behaviors which also seem to be species-characteristic. Whether functional at birth or emerging later, these proximity-promoting behaviors, as far as can be ascertained, are well-nigh universal in the species, appearing in all cultures and following a reasonably predictable and regular schedule of emergence in development, despite indications that environmental variations have considerable influence.

These initial behaviors together with later behaviors that promote proximity and/or contact of infant to mother (or to other significant adult) have been labeled "attachment behaviors." In this early stage, they are precursor behaviors in the sense that they are undiscriminating and nondifferential, and therefore one cannot speak of attachment to specific figures during the earliest months. Nevertheless these behavioral systems, implicated from the very beginning in promoting proximity, later and without great transformation clearly mediate attachment; therefore the label of "attachment behavior" is not inappropriate even in this first "precursor" phase.

THE PHASE OF ATTACHMENT-IN-THE-MAKING

The beginning of the phase is indeterminate, because discriminations emerge through some modalities before others. Long before he can discriminate through the visual modality, the baby can differentiate by auditory means, and it seems very likely that he can differentiate even earlier in terms of various somesthetic receptors. The end of the phase is, however, fairly sharp. There is general agreement that the end of the period—the point at which the child can be described as clearly attached to a specific figure—occurs in the second half of the first year of life, with 7 months as the milestone for many babies (cf. Schaffer, 1958; Schaffer & Callender, 1959).

During this phase the various proximity-promoting behaviors—attachment behaviors—become discriminating and differential. Take smiling, for example. Smiling can at first be elicited by any adult who presents the baby with an effective stimulus. Although the effective stimulus is at first auditory (cf. Wolff, 1963), it soon becomes visual—full face-to-face confrontation at an optimal distance—and the visual stimulus is even more effective if enhanced by movement and by vocalization. In this second phase, however, smiles to unfamiliar figures become infrequent, even though these figures may offer an optimal stimulus, while smiles to the mother and perhaps to a few other familiar figures occur more readily, frequently, and fully, even under conditions when the preferred figure does not offer an optimal stimulus.

In this second phase discrimination-learning is obviously implicated, and perhaps generalization as well. The organization of behaviors does not seem to exceed in complexity the model of stimulus-response chaining. At the end of this phase the various original proximity-promoting behaviors have become clearly differential, and new multipurpose behaviors, such as reaching and the beginnings of locomotion, are being accommodated to proximity-seeking as well as to other ends. As Piaget would say, the behaviors gradually become "mobile" as the child begins to learn to distinguish means from ends.

THE PHASE OF CLEAR-CUT ATTACHMENT

Very soon after discriminating and differential behavior has become established—and when it can operate effectively not only in close encounters but also on the basis of more distant cues—comes a phase in which there is a great increase of active proximity-seeking behavior which partly, but certainly not wholly, replaces the discriminative signaling behavior conspicuous in the second phase. This is especially noteworthy with the onset of locomotion. As soon as the baby can crawl, locomotion can serve to bring him into proximity to the figure or figures to whom he is becoming attached—although obviously locomotion can serve as means to other ends also, and indeed, especially at this time of life, it may often be an end in itself. As mentioned earlier, the child at this time also begins to search for objects after they have been hidden from view and begins to have a concept of his attachment figures as existing even though they are not present to perception. It is roughly coincident with the emergence of his ability actively to seek proximity and to conceive of absent objects as existing that a baby can be judged to have become attached to specific persons.

In regard to his attachment figure, the infant sometimes behaves in such a way as to maximize proximity and contact. The same kinds of behaviors are implicated as in previous phases, although they are supplemented by new acquisitions. On the other hand, proximity-seeking is by no means the sole and constant aim of a child, no matter how strongly and contingently it may have been rewarded by a responsive mother. All children have aims that compete with proximity-seeking, and some of the same behaviors that are implicated sometimes in proximity-seeking are implicated at other times as means to other ends—of which one of the most conspicuous is exploring the properties of the physical environment and, indeed, those of the social environment as well. All of the behavioral systems implicated in attachment must be viewed in balance with those which have aims incompatible with proximity-seeking.

Although Bowlby (1969) acknowledged that S-R chaining might account for the organization of attachment in earlier phases of development, he turned to a control-systems model as appropriate for organization in this and subsequent phases of development—a model such as that proposed by Miller, Galanter, and Pribram (1960). He suggested that behavior becomes organized hierarchically in terms of an overall plan, and that within the context of this plan behavioral systems are to a greater or lesser extent interchangeable. In regard to attachment behavior this implies much flexibility. The "set-goal" may at any one moment be "set" for a certain degree of proximity, but there may be a variety of alternative behavioral systems through which a child may attempt to approximate that set-goal.

Thus the specificity of each sort of behavior becomes much less important than previously, and it becomes difficult to draw up a comprehensive and yet nonredundant catalogue of attachment behaviors. Consider locomotor approach, for example. Is this one behavior or several? A baby may approach his mother as a haven of safety when he is alarmed; he may approach her in greeting after a brief period of separation; or he may approach her in pure and simple proximity-seeking, perhaps as a brief diversion during exploration, when there is no hint of alarm or separation anxiety. On the other hand, a given interpersonal situation may evoke a response which may be mediated by a variety of attachment behaviors—together or as alternatives. An example is the greeting situation. The greeting response at first seems to involve smiling and general bodily excitement which may be accompanied by vocalization. Later a child may not only smile, jiggle, or vocalize, or all three together, but also may reach toward the returning loved person. Still later locomotor approach may be added to the constellation of behaviors—or, indeed, a baby may greet his mother by crying. Are these to be classified as one, three, or more distinct attachment behaviors? The essential issue is that the set-goal of proximity and/or contact often overrides the significance of discrete behavioral systems. Once a child is cognitively capable of having a plan, the component behavioral systems, which had heretofore seemed individually significant, lose much of their individual distinctiveness.

Both Bowlby (1969) and Ainsworth (1969) have been quite explicit in their statements that at any one moment the set-goal is situationally determined. A child, playing in a park with his mother seated on a bench nearby, can be conceived as having a certain set-goal of proximity maintenance—although this, of course, may differ from child to child. For any single child-mother pair, the set-goal operative in a situation can be inferred from empirical observation (Anderson, 1972). Let us say that it is 100 feet. The child moves away from his mother to explore or to play. In the course of his wanderings he tends not to go beyond 100 feet. Instead he turns, without any evident stimulus, to go back toward his mother. He may go the whole way back and make contact with her, or he may merely return to some point within the 100-foot radius before resuming his play.

If there is some occasion for alarm, the set-goal may immediately shift to another setting. Perhaps under these circumstances the set-goal will be changed to a distance not exceeding 5 feet; or perhaps the set-goal will be the closest possible, namely, physical contact. Furthermore, the attachment behavior may also change, either in kind or in degree or in both, when the set-goal is changed. Casually slow locomotion with pauses may change to the most rapid locomotion of which a child is capable. A child previously silent may call or cry. When he reaches his mother he may clamber up and cling tightly, whereas before the alarm his contact behavior, if any, might well have been limited to a hand placed briefly on his mother's knee before he once again moved off.

Because of the situational shiftings of the set-goal, it is not altogether satisfactory to measure the strength of proximity-seeking behavior—let alone the strength of attachment—in terms either of the mean distance maintained between an infant and his mother or of the time spent within a span of distance arbitrarily identified as indicating "proximity." The latency, speed, and degree of active initiative in proximity-seeking are relevant factors also.

THE PHASE OF A GOAL-CORRECTED PARTNERSHIP

Although in the third phase the child gradually became able to adapt his plans and set-goals to his mother's behavior, he could accomplish this only empirically, for he was still too limited by "egocentrism" to be able to infer what his mother's set-goals and plans might be that influence her behavior. Now, however, (beginning no earlier than his second birthday) he may gradually become capable of seeing things from her point of view and of gaining some insight into her feelings and motives. To be sure, this increasing understanding is imperfect for many months or years; probably it is not until he becomes adult that he can fully appreciate another's plans and set-goals—if then. Nevertheless, with even an imperfect understanding, he can go beyond a mere accommodation of his behavior to hers, and can begin to attempt to change her plans and set-goals and thus to influence her behavior. To the extent that this is so, a child develops a much more complex relationship with his mother than previously—a relationship which Bowlby called a partnership. This phase of development has not been studied systematically as yet. To do so should prove rewarding, for the goal-corrected partnership may be presumed to characterize mature, nonpathological attachment.

It is obvious that a partnership of this kind presumes "inner representations"—imagination and empathy at a level that is distinctively human. It is equally obvious that a substantial amount of cognitive development is necessary before a child is capable of partnership. On the other hand, it is likely that social experiences with a normally sensitive mother who is willing to reciprocate in a partnership will strongly promote relevant aspects of his cognitive development.

Further Issues in Attachment Theory

Let us now turn to a consideration of several issues pertinent to attachment theory in regard to which there has been controversy or misunderstanding or both. All of these issues center upon a distinction between attachment and attachment behavior. They include questions of criteria of attachment, of conditions of activation and termination of attachment behavior, of strength of attachment, and of quality of an attachment relationship.

CRITERIA OF ATTACHMENT

The question of criteria of attachment emerged first in a developmental context. When can a child be described as having become attached to a specific figure? Through what behaviors does he show that he has become attached? The implication is that it is a developmental milestone to have become attached.

It may be of practical or diagnostic significance to be able to ascertain whether an infant or young child has become attached to a mother figure. For example, practices relating to adoption or to removing a child from home (or from a foster home) may be influenced by an assessment of his attachment status. An assessment of the presence or absence of an attachment relationship may be of moment in diagnosing pathological conditions such as infantile autism, or in evaluating the effects on an individual child of prolonged deprivation experiences or of prolonged or repeated separation experiences. Furthermore, an assessment of attachment even in the simple "milestone" sense may be of significance for research. Such an assessment might be a focal dependent variable in comparative investigations of cultural or subcultural groups differing in infant-care practices. Finally, any investigation of the development of early social relations may well require an assessment of attachment as a baseline for evaluating the influence of different situations on attachment behavior, or for ascertaining the relationship of attachment to other variables.

The concept of a clear-cut age of onset of attachment itself stemmed from studies of the responses of infants to a definitive separation from the mother figure (Spitz & Wolf, 1946; Schaffer, 1958; Schaffer & Callender, 1959; Yarrow, 1967). Responses differ strikingly with age. The dividing point can be fairly clearly located at 7 months plus or minus a month or so. Infants older than this are clearly distressed by separation; infants younger than this critical age-point are not. The term "definitive separation" is used to distinguish brief, everyday absences of the mother in a familiar environment perhaps containing familiar substitute figures, from longer, perhaps even permanent, separations, and especially from those which involve frightening features, unfamiliar figures, and a strange environment. The latter longer and more severe separations are termed "definitive." Faced by such a separation, an infant younger than 6 or 7 months may indeed show some distress or disturbance. It seems very likely that this is attributable to unaccustomed handling and routines (Burlingham & Freud,

1944), and it tends to be short-lived. Whatever distress is manifested tends to be diffuse and undirected, and the infant adapts himself fairly readily to mother substitutes. If, however, this very young separated infant is placed in an environment in which there is insufficient opportunity for interaction with or stimulation by substitute figures, he does not so much show distress as sink into apathy; and, according to Schaffer (1958), he regresses into a less frequently alert and more undifferentiated state.

Infants older than 7 or 8 months behave quite differently. Their distress is more intense, more long-lasting, more clearly directed toward recovery of the mother figure, and not readily alleviated by attention from substitute caretakers. Within the limits of his repertoire the child attempts to regain his mother— through crying, calling, or searching—and with increasing age (c.f. Bowlby, 1953, 1960b, 1961; Robertson & Bowlby, 1952) these efforts become increasingly coordinated and directed. The empirical findings are open to the interpretation that the younger infant may be briefly disorganized and distressed by the disruption of his usual routines, but that the older infant or young child is distressed chiefly by the absence of the figure or figures to whom he has become attached.

It is reasonable to assume that the critical criterion of whether a child has become attached to a specific figure is his unequivocal distress when he is definitively separated from that figure. It is obviously neither desirable nor feasible to engineer such major separation experiences for the purposes of diagnosis or research assessment. Are there dependable criteria of attachment other than distress in a major separation situation?

It is plausible to suppose that one such criterion might be a child's distress in a minor separation situation. Spitz (e.g., 1959) proposed the phenomenon of "8-month anxiety" as a criterion of the attainment of "true" object relations. This anxiety was shown by mother-reared infants in a penal institution at about 8 months of age (but with a range of individual differences in age) when approached by a stranger in the absence of the mother. Although at first glance the infant's distress might be attributed to fear of strangers, Spitz conceived it to be a manifestation of separation anxiety. Schaffer and Emerson (1964a), in a pioneer study of the development of attachment among Glasgow infants, used separation protest in minor, everyday situations as the criterion in terms of which they judged age of onset of attachments. Ainsworth (1963, 1967), in another pioneer study of the development of attachment in Ganda infants, used multiple criteria of attachment, including separation protest. These three studies, despite differences in criteria, agree essentially in placing the mean age of onset of attachment in the third quarter of the first year. Nevertheless Ainsworth doubted the validity of distress in minor separation situations as the sole criterion of attachment when she observed that some infants in her Ganda sample, who appeared to be clearly attached, failed to show consistent distress in everyday separation situations in the home environment.

A variety of attachment behaviors has been identified (Ainsworth, 1963, 1964, 1967) as relevant to an assessment of whether an infant has or has not become attached. These include: crying and/or following when the mother leaves the room; greeting responses of several kinds; active contact behaviors such as "scrambling" over the mother, exploring her person, burying the face in her lap, and affectionate behaviors such as embracing, hugging, and kissing; approach through locomotion; the use of the mother as a secure base from which to explore; flight to the mother as a haven of safety; and clinging. In order to be considered criteria of attachment, it is assumed that these behaviors must be manifested in a discriminating and differential way. Differential smiling, crying, and vocalization[2] were also observed to be characteristic of attached infants. These specific differential behaviors, however, develop earlier than either separation distress or the more active behaviors listed above. If they were to be used as criteria of having become attached, infants as young as 2 or 3 months might be considered to have reached this milestone. Although it has been pointed out (Ainsworth, 1967; Yarrow, 1967; Bowlby, 1969) that it is an arbitrary matter, depending on choice of criteria, at what developmental stage an infant may be labeled as "attached," it is our preference to so label him when he manifests the active proximity-seeking and contact behaviors listed above, which emerge very soon after he first shows his ability to discriminate his mother at a distance by crying when she leaves the room and/or by greeting her when she enters. It is assumed that an infant who has become attached according to these criteria would also demonstrate his attachment through clear-cut distress in a major separation situation.

Because the mean age of onset of distress in both major and minor separation situations coincides essentially with the mean age of onset of the other criterion behaviors listed above, it may seem a matter of little moment which behaviors are chosen as criteria of attachment. It matters, however, when one is concerned with the individual case, whether one's assessment is for diagnostic or research purposes. Ainsworth's first report (1963) of the development of attachment among Ganda infants recommended multiple criteria because of observed individual differences in the way attachment behavior was organized and manifested—differences that seemed to be related to differences among mothers in their infant-care practices.

This initial impression has been well confirmed by later studies with an American sample (Ainsworth & Wittig, 1969; Ainsworth, Bell, & Stayton, 1971, 1972). Some infants were minimally disturbed by minor separations but, in

---

[2] Visual-motor orientation was also included in this list. As a criterion of attachment it was specified as an orientation of the eyes and a tense orientation of the whole body of the infant toward the mother, when he was being held by someone else and at some distance from the mother. Under other circumstances the frequency or duration of looking at the mother (at least by the second half of the first year) would be misleading as a criterion. Thus, for example, when both the mother and a stranger are present in our strange situation, infants look significantly more frequently at the stranger than at the mother.

ordinary interaction with their mother, seemed clearly attached. They greeted the mother enthusiastically when she returned after a brief everyday absence; they were intermittently active in seeking proximity and contact with her; they enjoyed physical contact and displayed active contact behavior. When separated briefly from her in a strange situation, however, they tended to be distressed, but especially they showed greatly heightened proximity-seeking and contact-maintaining behavior when she returned. Other infants showed relatively frequent and intense distress in ordinary separation situations at home. These infants tended to be those who cried relatively frequently when their mothers were also present; they tended also to greet their mothers with a fuss, and to be ambivalent about physical contact with her, perhaps responding negatively to contact, but in any event lacking active contact behavior. It was these infants who tended to fuss when put down, however, while those who responded positively to contact were cheerful about being put down after being held, and turned readily to exploratory activity. Some of those who cried frequently at home and who there showed frequent separation distress did not cry when the mother left them in a strange situation, although they tended to show their attachment by strongly searching for her; and yet when the mother returned they did not seek proximity or contact.

It is findings such as these that have led us not only to emphasize the importance of multiple criteria for judging that an infant is attached, but also to stress the desirability of assessing the quality of the attachment relationship. By one set of criteria or another, all of the infants in the sample mentioned above were attached, despite striking qualitative differences in their attachments. One of the dimensions in terms of which qualitative differences may be assessed is security-insecurity, a dimension that has also been identified in the case of Ganda subjects (Ainsworth, 1963, 1967). It is because infants who might be described as securely attached were distinguished chiefly by positive behavioral criteria (happy greetings, active approach, and active contact behavior) rather than by negative behavioral criteria (crying and separation anxiety in the home environment) that we have placed stress on "positive" indices of attachment to supplement the criterion of separation distress.

Gewirtz and Cairns (both in this volume) have also distinguished the "positive" indices from other indices of attachment. They characterize the behavior activated by separation as disorganized, whether because of the emotional component contingent upon the frustration of separation or because of the disruption of other ongoing behavioral sequences. They prefer as indices of attachment "positive" behaviors that demonstrate that an attachment figure has stimulus control over an infant or provides him with significant behavioral support. Although we would probably agree in our identification of behaviors to be labeled "positive," and although we attach significance to these behaviors as indices of attachment, we do so for different reasons, as is apparent from the preceding discussion.

If one believes that attachment behavior has the important biological function of protection, behavior activated by a separation situation cannot be characterized as altogether disorganized. Under such circumstances it is adaptive for behavioral systems such as exploration to be disrupted and to give way to heightened proximity-promoting behavior. In the "ordinary expectable environment," crying may well have the outcome of recalling the mother, and search behavior may well succeed in locating her. Heightened emotion may well lend strength to these endeavors. Furthermore, if one adopts an evolutionary viewpoint, one cannot bypass the occurrence of separation distress as a significant index of attachment. In recommending multiple criteria for the assessment of attachment, it is not intended to omit such indices as crying when the mother leaves or attempting to follow her; it is merely intended to draw attention to other supplementary criteria which may be of significance in the case of infants and young children whose attachment relationship is secure enough that they may not consistently display either distress or anxious search under conditions of accustomed or relatively minor and nonstressful separation situations.

Much of the research undertaken to date on attachment behavior manifest at home or in relatively nonstressful laboratory situations (as distinct from behavior in major separation situations) has been concerned with infants in the first 18 months of life. Research with older subjects may well lead to new or modified sets of criteria for assessing attachment. It is reasonable to suppose that separation distress may become less significant as a criterion as a child becomes better able to sustain attachments *in absentia,* and that close proximity and contact may to some extent be supplanted by communication and interaction across a distance. Meanwhile research employing multiple behavioral criteria affords the best possibility of tracing the developmental relationship between earlier and later manifestations of attachment.

ACTIVATION AND TERMINATION OF ATTACHMENT BEHAVIOR

Despite its variety and despite the variations that greater maturity may bring, all attachment behavior may be viewed as proximity-promoting behavior. Once an infant has become attached to his mother, active proximity-seeking behavior organized on a goal-corrected basis becomes increasingly conspicuous. The distance from the mother which serves to activate attachment behavior, as well as the kind, degree, and duration of proximity that is required to terminate it, depends at least in part on the current setting of the "set-goal." (See pages 109 to 110). Either internal or external conditions or both may, however, change the set-goal to one of much closer proximity, perhaps to one of the closest physical contact. The intensity of activation of attachment behavior may be viewed as depending upon at least three sets of related conditions: (*a*) the extent to which the set degree of proximity has been exceeded, (*b*) the extent to which the set-goal shifts, and (*c*) the abruptness of the change of the set-goal.

There are a number of conditions that are likely to change the "set" of the set-goal to one of much closer proximity and thus to increase the intensity of activation of attachment behavior beyond the degree of activation provided merely by having exceeded the current "set". These include situations that are painful or alarming, actual or threatened separation from an attachment figure, return of an attachment figure after a period of absence, rebuff by the attachment figure, and certain states of the child including hunger, fatigue, or illness. Some of these conditions require further comment. Although stimulus situations that are merely unfamiliar may be alarming, they may, on the contrary, elicit exploratory behavior; much depends on the degree of unfamiliarity to the particular individual in question and perhaps also on the extent of his experience in facing and coping with the unfamiliar. Mere decrease of proximity to or separation from an attachment figure does not in itself intensely activate attachment behavior. A child can move away from his mother on his own initiative with equanimity (and up to the limits of his current set-goal), but his set-goal may change abruptly and his attachment behavior is likely to be sharply activated if she moves away from him, and especially if she departs under unexpected circumstances. Separations in familiar environments can be tolerated increasingly if the child's experience has led him to build up expectations about where he can find his mother when he wants her or when she is likely to return. It is the enforced separation under unexpected or unfamiliar circumstances that tends greatly to shift the set-goal and to heighten attachment behavior—or the realization that the mother is not where the child expected to find her or that she did not return when expected. Furthermore, the set-goal may be shifted to one of closer proximity by an antecedent separation experience, so that an actual or threatened separation which follows on its heels may activate attachment behavior more sharply and intensely than did the earlier experience initially.

The more intensely it is activated, the stronger the attachment behavior is likely to be. Approach is rapid rather than slow or interrupted. Close proximity is sought, rather than mere sight or sound of an attachment figure across a distance; or close physical contact may be sought and maintained through clinging and resisting release. Specific attachment behaviors may increase in strength, speed, or duration; and one behavior may be replaced by another "stronger" behavior that is more appropriate to a shrunken set-goal distance, or several behaviors may be simultaneously activated. Thus, for example, an undisturbed child may clamber up and briefly place his hand on his mother's knee, whereas a frightened child may seek to cling tightly. Or, a child who ordinarily follows his mother slowly and with pauses for exploration when she leaves the room may, under more intense conditions of activation, scream while following her as quickly as he can.

Under extreme conditions of activation, paradoxes may appear. A child who is intensely upset (as in the strange-situation experiment of Rheingold, 1969a) may cling tightly even to a stranger if his mother is not nearby. Thus the ordinarily high degree of specificity of the figure toward whom attachment behavior is directed may break down under stress. Furthermore, if it is the mother herself whose behavior provides the conditions of high-intensity activation, as, for example, Harlow's surrogate mothers that emitted alarming airblasts (1961), or his motherless mothers who were extremely rejecting and punitive (1963), the infant is likely to direct greatly heightened attachment behavior toward her, despite the fact that it brings alarming or painful consequences.

Most attachment behaviors are terminated, or at least reduced in intensity, when the set-goal of proximity or contact to the mother has been achieved. When, however, the mother's behavior is itself responsible for the activation, the infant's attachment behavior, although directed toward her as the attachment figure, tends not to terminate but rather to continue at high intensity.

ATTACHMENT BEHAVIOR AND ITS RELATION
TO SOME OTHER BEHAVIORAL SYSTEMS

Attachment behavior is but one of a number of behavioral systems. Often enough when one behavioral system is activated, the ensuing behavior is incompatible with that of another system. Considerable attention has been given to exploratory behavior as competing with attachment behavior. The stimuli activating exploration tend to draw the child away from his mother, whereas the stimuli activating attachment behavior tend to draw him to her. When attachment behavior is strongly activated, for example, under conditions of alarm, separation, or threat of separation, exploratory behavior disappears even in the presence of stimulus objects which might otherwise evoke exploration. In a familiar situation, such as that provided by the home environment, an infant's exploratory behavior may be activated even in the absence of his mother, especially if he has built up expectations about her whereabouts or return. In an unfamiliar situation, however, the mother's presence is, for most infants, a necessary condition for the activation of exploratory behavior, as demonstrated by studies of behavior in strange situations (e.g., Arsenian, 1943; Rosenthal, 1967; Cox & Campbell, 1968; Rheingold, 1969a; Ainsworth & Wittig, 1969; Ainsworth & Bell, 1970). Since the mother's presence is conceived as raising the child's threshold for fear of the unfamiliar and as holding the activation of attachment behavior at a low level, the child may be described as using her as a secure base from which to explore. "Secure" implies the absence of fear, not the presence of fear. The child can leave his mother on his own initiative, even going out of sight in his exploratory forays, with no sign of fear. On the other hand, if she left him in the same unfamiliar environment, his attachment behavior would be heightened, his exploratory behavior would be overridden, and he might well show marked distress (Ainsworth, 1963, 1967; Rheingold & Eckerman, 1970).

The fact that attachment behavior may be kept for extended periods at a low level of activation and may be overridden by exploratory behavior may be viewed as itself having a significant adaptive function, for a child through his exploratory behavior can learn about his environment and the properties of objects in it. At the same time, if he is to explore away from his mother, it is of obvious survival value for his attachment behavior to be promptly activated by any alarming stimulus or by any sign that the mother is about to move off. The dynamic equilibrium between these two behavioral systems is of even more significance for development (and for survival) than either in isolation.

Whereas any pair of behavioral systems may be incompatible in a given situation merely because the behavior implicit in one cannot occur when the other is more strongly activated, there is one behavioral system—proximity-avoiding—which is intrinsically incompatible with attachment behavior. We first noted proximity-avoiding behavior in conjunction with our use of a strange situation as a setting in which to observe attachment behavior (Ainsworth & Bell, 1970; Ainsworth et al., 1971). In this situation a substantial minority of 1-year-olds ignored the mother, or looked away from her, or turned or moved away under circumstances (especially upon reunion after brief separation) when most infants display heightened proximity- and contact-seeking behavior. Proximity-avoiding behavior is, of course, compatible with exploratory behavior, although few of our subjects explored constructively while avoiding proximity. The rest tended either to move about hyperactively, or to alternate proximity-avoiding with proximity-seeking behavior. That proximity-avoiding is distinct from exploratory behavior was also suggested by the fact that it occurred most conspicuously when the mother was actively attempting to elicit approach behavior.

Elsewhere (Ainsworth & Bell, 1970) we drew attention to the similarity of proximity-avoiding behavior in the strange situation and failure to "recognize" the mother upon reunion after major separations—a distanciation from the mother which Bowlby (1960b) has termed "detachment." We also observed that similar looking-away behavior occurred during the extinction period of conditioning experiments on precursor attachment behaviors such as smiling and babbling (Brackbill, 1958; Rheingold, Gewirtz, & Ross, 1959). It was hypothesized that such looking-away (proximity-avoiding) behavior was detachment-in-the-making—a primitive kind of defense against the distress consequent upon the failure of an actual or potential attachment figure to respond appropriately to attachment behavior. It seems entirely appropriate to identify defensive proximity-avoiding behavior as signifying an extinction process—but clearly one in which there is an active process of blocking attachment behavior by another antithetical behavior which has, often temporarily, gained the greater strength. That the blocking may be temporary is shown by the fact that proximity-avoiding behavior both in the strange situation and, more significantly, upon return home after major separations often gives way to greatly heightened attachment behavior.

We further hypothesized (Ainsworth et al., 1971) that those 1-year-olds who respond with proximity-avoiding behavior to the return of their mothers after very brief separations in a strange situation must already have formed such a defensive reaction in response to their mothers' rebuffs of attachment behavior in the course of mother-infant interaction at home. Support for this hypothesis was found in the fact that all infants whose mothers obtained above-average ratings on rejection displayed proximity-avoiding behavior in the strange situation.

Exploratory behavior and proximity-avoiding behavior both compete with attachment behavior and are incompatible with it in the sense that when one of these behavioral systems is activated strongly the other tends to be temporarily overridden. There is still another behavioral system which, although competing with attachment behavior, does not necessarily block it out. This may be identified as aggressive or angry behavior, which appears conspicuously in some infants in the form of contact-resisting behavior. Both in the strange situation and at home (Ainsworth et al., 1971, 1972), some infants are highly ambivalent. They seek to gain and to maintain contact, and they also resist it. They seek to be picked up by the mother, but then hit, kick, or push away from her; if put down they tend to resist release and struggle to gain contact again. Ambivalent responses of this sort are common in young children returning home after separations (Heinicke & Westheimer, 1965). Separation tends to heighten aggressive behavior of this kind, as well as attachment behavior. Similar behavior has been observed in infant monkeys, both after separation (Spencer-Booth & Hinde, 1966) and after weaning (e.g., DeVore, 1963).

STRENGTH AND QUALITY OF ATTACHMENT

It is evident from the foregoing discussion that attachment behavior may be absent in situations in which it is either not activated or less intensely activated than are other competing behavioral systems which are incompatible with it. When it is activated it may be relatively weakly activated, as for example when the proximity set-goal is slightly exceeded; or it may be intensely activated, as for example under conditions of alarm or threat of separation. Under conditions of weak activation, attachment behavior is both quantitatively and qualitatively different from what it is under conditions of intense activation. Since the intensity of activation of attachment behavior is dependent upon the situation of the moment, it is unsatisfactory to assess strength of *attachment* in terms of the strength of *attachment behavior* in any given situation. Indeed, it is unsatisfactory to assess strength of attachment thus even over a variety of situations, unless one is willing to equate it with the degree of insecurity and the frequency of fear, for there is no doubt that the strongest attachment behavior occurs when the infant or young child is intensely alarmed, intensely apprehensive that his mother may leave him, or intensely distressed because he has in fact been separated from her. To equate strength of attachment with strength of attachment behavior under ordinary nonstressful circumstances would lead to the conclusion that an infant who explores his environment when his mother is present is necessarily less attached than one who constantly seeks proximity to his mother, whereas, in fact, his freedom to explore away from her may well reflect the healthy security provided by a harmonious attachment relationship.

Furthermore, it is by no means evident that strength of attachment is an especially useful dimension, despite the fact that it seems of crucial significance to ascertain whether a child is or is not attached. If an infant has insufficient interaction with any one figure, he may not become attached to anyone. Nearly all family-reared infants, however, have sufficient interaction with their mothers to become attached, however widely the quality of the interaction may differ from one infant-mother pair to another. There is to date no empirical evidence which suggests that differing strengths of attachment are associated with different qualitative outcomes, or which enables us to identify conditions (whether environmental or intraorganismic) associated with differing strengths of attachment. On the other hand, both accumulated clinical evidence and more recent research findings (e.g., Ainsworth & Wittig, 1969; Ainsworth & Bell, 1969; Ainsworth et al., 1971, 1972; S. M. Bell, 1970; Stayton, Hogan, & Ainsworth, 1971) strongly suggest that qualitative differences in infant-mother attachment relationships are associated both with qualitative differences in antecedent maternal behaviors and with different behavioral outcomes in the case of the child. Therefore, although it seems fruitless in the present state of our knowledge to attempt to assess strength of attachment, it seems useful to evaluate the *quality* of the attachment relationship.

The dimensions of an infant's behavior that seem pertinent to an assessment of the quality of his attachment to his mother include the following: a dimension of security-insecurity (see page 114); the characteristic balance between attachment behavior and defensive proximity-avoiding behavior; the characteristic degree of ambivalence in seeking proximity or contact with the mother; and activity-passivity both in proximity-seeking and in other behaviors. Dimensions of maternal behavior that have emerged as related significantly to qualitative differences in the infant-mother attachment relationships—and which have been given explicit behavioral definition despite the "global" tags used to label them—are: sensitivity-insensitivity, acceptance-rejection, cooperation-interference, and accessibility-ignoring.

Let us very briefly review some of the findings that lead us to emphasize the utility of qualitative assessments of the infant-mother attachment relationship. Mothers who are sensitively responsive to their infants' signals and communications tend also to be accepting rather than rejecting, cooperative rather than interfering, and accessible rather than ignoring and neglecting. This sensitive responsiveness to signals was found to have a high degree of continuity from the first 3 months of life in which it was observed specifically in the feeding situation (Ainsworth & Bell, 1969) to the last quarter of the first year in which it was observed more generally (Ainsworth et al., 1971, 1972). At both times it was found to be related to infant behavior in a controlled strange situation at the end of the first year—to ability to use the mother as a secure base from which to explore a strange environment in the relatively nonstressful episodes of the situation, and to heightened proximity-seeking and contact-maintaining behaviors in the episodes of reunion after brief separation, with a minimum of defensive proximity-avoiding or ambivalent contact-resisting behaviors. This constellation of strange-situation behaviors was found to be associated with an optimum balance and smooth transition between attachment and exploratory behaviors at home, with a minimum of anxiety in minor everyday separation situations, and with positive response to contact and minimal ambivalence in contact- and proximity-seeking. This same constellation of strange-situation behaviors was found to be characteristic of infants who had developed a concept of the permanence of persons more readily than a concept of the permanence of inanimate objects—and who indeed were generally advanced in the development of the "concept of the object" (S. M. Bell, 1970). Sensitive maternal responsiveness was found to be associated with a marked decrease of infant crying behavior in the course of the first year (S. M. Bell, 1971; Ainsworth et al., 1972) and with a clear-cut tendency for an infant to comply with his mother's verbal commands at the end of the first year (Stayton et al., 1971).

Maternal insensitivity to infant signals was found, conversely, to be associated with relatively frequent and prolonged infant crying in the course of the first year, with a relative retardation in the development of the concept of object permanence (and especially the concept of persons as permanent), and, in association with maternal rejection of the infant, was linked to failure to comply with maternal commands. Space does not permit a comprehensive summary of the various patterns of infant behaviors linked with varying patterns of insensitive maternal behavior. Let us be content with a few examples. Infants whose mothers were both insensitive and rejecting showed conspicuous proximity-avoiding behavior in the reunion episodes of the strange situation at the end of the first year; those whose mothers were also inaccessible and frequently ignoring tended also to display marked proximity-avoiding behavior and concomitant independence in exploration at home. Those whose mothers were insensitive and inaccessible, although neither rejecting nor interfering, tended to be passive both at home and in a strange situation, showing relatively little of both active proximity-seeking and defensive proximity-avoiding, but showing (especially in response to the stresses of the strange situation) substantial ambivalence in regard to contact with the mother.

Throughout this series of analyses no convincing evidence emerged that any of these family-reared infants lacked attachment to the mother, or that any one was more strongly attached than another. On the other hand the variations in their behaviors strongly suggested that the ways in which attachment behaviors were organized represented qualitatively different organizations of the infant-mother attachment relationship.

ATTACHMENT AS DISTINGUISHED FROM
ATTACHMENT BEHAVIOR

The entire trend of the foregoing discussion points to the importance of differentiating between attachment and attachment behavior. Let us recapitulate.

We have seen that attachment behaviors—behaviors that promote proximity and/or contact—are manifest during the earliest months before the infant can be described as attached to anyone. Even after he has become attached he does not manifest attachment behavior continuously. Under some circumstances his attachment behavior is more strongly activated than under other circumstances, and sometimes it is wholly or partially overridden by other competing behavioral systems. Attachment behavior may be strongly activated during the absence of the attachment figure, and continues to be proximity-promoting in intent rather than disorganized—despite the fact that the intensity of its activation may disrupt other behavioral systems.

In the previous discussion of separation (pages 111 to 114), no reference was made to responses other than the initial responses of distress. As separation continues, distress tends to diminish. If substitute mother figures are available, there is no doubt that an infant or young child will avail himself eventually of the comfort and nurturance offered by them, and, in proportion to their accessibility as figures with whom he can interact, he may become attached to them. Indeed, as the fostering studies of the Robertsons (e.g., 1968a, 1968b, and for comparison, 1969) demonstrate, separation distress may be greatly alleviated by sensitive foster parents who encourage the development of an attachment relationship. Nevertheless these same studies strongly suggest that such sensitive foster care does not diminish a child's attachment to his own parents, and facilitates rather than hampers the reestablishment of harmonious and secure relations upon reunion.

Distress also eventually diminishes in separation environments in which there are no adequate substitute mother figures; attempts to recover the mother may disappear altogether, and because attachment behavior is not in evidence, it may seem that a child is no longer attached. Characteristic responses to reunion, however, make it clear that attachment has survived. There may, to be sure, be some delay before a child manifests attachment behavior after reunion—and the younger the child, the longer the separation, and the more depriving the experience, the longer the delay is likely to be. But when attachment behavior is reactivated, it is very common for it to be more intensely activated than it was prior to separation. A child is likely to manifest "separation anxiety"; he tends to follow his mother everywhere she goes, wants physical contact with her more frequently than before, and is very sensitive to any threat of another separation. It appears as though separation has not weakened the attachment; it has merely made it more insecure. Behavior during the period of delay is itself interesting. A child may treat his mother as a stranger, or may fail to recognize her, or may recoil from her or reject her. Bowlby (e.g., 1960b) identifies such behavior as reflecting a defensive process of "detachment." As implied earlier (page 118) such behavior seems actively to block attachment behavior. Sometimes, in instances of unusually long, depriving separations which begin at a particularly vulnerable age, the block may last indefinitely. Much more commonly, however, it gives way suddenly to greatly heightened attachment behavior.

Thus, despite striking vicissitudes of attachment behavior, attachments may be seen to bridge time and distance. They cannot be conceived as being present or absent (or varying in intensity) from moment to moment. We infer the existence of an attachment from a stable propensity over time to seek proximity and contact with a specific figure, even though attachment behavior may appear only intermittently, or—in the case of major separations—may be absent for long periods. The term "attachment" refers to the propensity, whereas the term "attachment behavior" refers to the class of diverse behaviors which promote proximity and contact, at first without discrimination of figure, but later with increasing specificity in regard to the figure(s) to whom the child is or is becoming attached.

It is further suggested that it is useful to view attachment—as a construct—as an inner organization of behavioral systems which not only controls the "stable propensity" to seek proximity to an attachment figure, but also is responsible for the distinctive quality of the organization of the specific attachment behaviors through which a given individual promotes proximity with a specific attachment figure. Such an hypothesis implies some kind of stable intraorganismic basis for individual differences in the organization of attachment behaviors. Such a relatively stable inner organization must be conceived as interacting with environmental conditions and other "situational" intraorganismic conditions—neurophysiological, hormonal, and receptor processes—to activate, terminate, and direct attachment behavior in any specific situation. It is conceived as a hierarchical organization that permits more or less interchangeable behaviors to be directed by any one of several general plans or strategies that may be specifically tailored to fit the requirements of different situations. A hierarchical organization of this kind suggests internal structure—"structure" in much the same sense that Piagetians use the term to refer to the inner organization of "schemata" and later "representations" that underlies first the organization of "means-ends" relationships and later the network of strategies that constitute "operations." The concept of attachment as propensity or structure is of the same order as "mediating process," "intervening variable," "hypothetical construct," or "higher level construct" (as proposed by Sears in this volume).

Other constructs that have had an honorable place in the history of the psychology of personality development are "drive" and "trait." The concept of attachment as propensity or structure is to be distinguished from these constructs. As a first consideration, "attachment" is not a "general" construct— neither like a generalized drive nor like a generalized trait. It refers to a specific relationship between one individual and a specific other. Thus, in a sense, it is not conceived as a characteristic that an individual carries around with him as a part-determiner of his response to a wide variety of interpersonal situations; it is specific to his relations with the attachment figure in question.

Attachment has motivational implications, however, despite the fact that our attachment theory makes it seem unhelpful to conceive of an attachment drive. As Hinde (1966) implies, the basic issue of motivation is to determine the conditions under which a given behavioral system is activated and terminated. In addition to the environmental stimuli and contextual circumstances that are more or less obvious conditions for activation or termination, there are intraorganismic conditions including neurophysiological, receptor, and hormonic processes. Insofar as these intraorganismic processes may be distinguished to have a stable organization over time, they are in essence what we mean by "structure." In this sense motivation may be conceived as implicit in structure, as indeed it may be conceived to be implicit in a behavioral system itself. Behavior systems, or indeed "drive systems," may be subject to investigation in rich and minute detail in order to ascertain the various environmental and intraorganismic conditions of activation and termination and how they interact together. The construct "drive" seems likely to have its major utility prior to detailed investigation of the way its component behavioral systems are controlled. It does not seem likely to contribute to research into the conditions of activation and termination of attachment behavior to invoke a concept of drive.

Dependency research (cf. Maccoby & Masters, 1970) has been directed in large part by a concept of dependency as a unitary drive or trait. In this context it was hypothesized that the various behaviors taken as indicative of dependency (contact-seeking, proximity-seeking, attention-seeking, help-seeking, approval-seeking, and the like) should be positively correlated with each other to a significant degree. It has sometimes been suggested that the validity of the attachment construct should rest similarly upon a demonstration of significant positive correlations among attachment behaviors. This suggestion would be pertinent only if individual differences in attachment were conceived to be primarily differences in strength of some general drive or trait of attachment. If, however, attachment is conceived as a mode of relating to a specific figure, and individual differences are conceived as being chiefly qualitative differences in the way attachment behaviors are organized, there is no reason to expect that there should be substantial positive correlations between all component attachment behaviors in any random population of cases. On the contrary, one might expect that different patterns of correlations of classes of attachment behavior might well be grounds for distinguishing qualitative differences in the organization of attachment relationships. That this latter is the case is demonstrated by evidence summarized on pages 120-121.

Attachment is to be distinguished from attachment behavior, and has a distinctively different relationship to it than dependency has been conceived to have to dependency behavior. The paradigms are basically different. It would be a disservice to both concepts, if, in an attempt to seek common ground, the paradigmatic distinction became blurred.

Directions of Future Research into Attachment

First, the concept of attachment may be viewed as giving a useful "direction marker" to research into mother-infant interaction. It provides cues directing attention to infant behaviors that may be particularly profitable to observe. Thus, for example, despite the fact that emphasis has been recently given (e.g., Caldwell, 1962; Rheingold, 1963; Walters & Parke, 1965) to the role of the distance receptors in mother-infant interaction, and despite the fact that recent research into the infant's visual behavior has much enriched our knowledge of his repertoire, attachment theory would prompt us not to neglect study of the infant's contact-seeking behavior and of his behavior when in physical contact with his mother. Our own research into the behavior of infants in a strange situation points toward contact-maintaining behavior in episodes of reunion after brief separations as being a key behavioral variable in elucidating individual differences, and this is true also of contact-resisting behaviors (Ainsworth & Bell, 1970; Ainsworth et al., 1971). In regard to behavior in the familiar home situation, physical-contact behavior emerges again as crucial as an index of individual differences in the whole study of mother-infant interaction (Ainsworth et al., 1972). The more general point is, however, this: since attachment itself cannot be directly observed, and since attachment behavior must be observed in its situational context, research into attachment and its development should be set up as research into the processes of interpersonal interaction—and, as Cairns and Sears have emphasized, in the context of dyadic synchronization.

Second, and related to the issue of research into processes of interaction, is the question of how fine-grained the research should be. Both Gewirtz and Cairns (this volume) have emphasized the desirability of collecting and analyzing data in a way that preserves the detail of contingencies in mother-infant interaction so that the dynamic interplay of dyadic interaction is not swallowed up in summary constructs. Indeed this emphasis upon rich detail is a conspicuous characteristic of contemporary research into infant behavior, both in studies of mother-infant interaction and in studies of cognitive development.

Our own present research is a very intensive and detailed longitudinal study of mother-infant interaction throughout the first year of life, in which an emphasis is placed on sequences of interaction, and in which an important aim is to trace how such characteristic sequences affect the eventual quality of the infant-mother attachment relationship. Analysis of the data has been only partially completed. Nevertheless, we have been concerned not only with identification of general trends in the way infant-mother attachment affects behavior, but also with individual differences. An analysis of patterns of infant-mother interaction relevant to feeding during the first 3 months of life (Ainsworth & Bell, 1969) demonstrates a concern with the preservation of considerable detail in the description of dyadic interaction as well as an interest in the ways in which early patterns of behavior relate to later behavior at the end of the first year. Our analysis of the relation between maternal responsiveness and infant crying (S. M. Bell, 1971; Ainsworth et al., 1972) was based upon detailed coding of every episode of infant crying that occurred during approximately 72 hours of observation for each infant, spread over the whole of the infant's first year of life. Similarly detailed coding was the basis for the findings on everyday separation responses and physical contact behavior to which reference has already been made.

On the other hand, we share Cairns' reservation in regard to the useful limits of detailed analysis, and Sears' dissatisfaction with halting a conceptualization of interaction with an emphasis on the unique and idiosyncratic transactions of each infant-mother pair. Both reservations call for compromises with the ideal of fine-grain research into the individual dyad.

Since detailed longitudinal research into the processes of interpersonal interaction is so extremely time-consuming, there is inescapable pressure to compromise in planning and conducting such research. The more intensive the research—the more frequent and the longer the observational sessions—the fewer the subjects that can be included in the sample, and the shorter the longitudinal time-span that can be encompassed. The more comprehensive the aims of the study, the greater the number of "variables" to be taken into account, the more difficult it is to insure precision of observation of behavior relevant to any one variable. To focus on a few variables—as in the case with coded time-sampled observations—may enable one to observe these more precisely, but this is at risk of losing the relevant context of the behaviors in question and also of losing the process "flow" of interpersonal interaction. All of this refers merely to naturalistic research; the introduction of experimental controls raises a host of other issues, some advantageous and some not.

In any one study there is no one solution which is entirely satisfactory. In terms of his problem, theoretical orientation, resources, opportunities, and personal style, each investigator chooses his own set of compromises. The interests of science seem likely to be best served in this context by a multiplicity of studies, each with its own compromises, which yet may in aggregate answer the questions that no single study can answer crucially at the present time.

Third, further research is needed into those conditions that activate, terminate, and reinforce precursors. A substantial amount of research has already been directed toward identifying the stimuli which most effectively activate and terminate the behavioral systems in question. According to ethological studies, specific environmental stimuli are implicated. Less attention has been paid to the terminators of the precursor attachment behaviors than to their activators. Nevertheless, there is some pertinent research, such as that by Gordon and Foss (1966), Kessen and Leutzendorff (1963), and Wolff (1969), on the terminators of crying. To be sure, crying which stems from a specific source such as hunger or pain is most effectively terminated by dealing with the source, but crying for other reasons may be terminated (and even hunger or pain crying may be arrested for substantial time periods) by certain kinds and degrees of auditory stimulation, by nonnutritive sucking, or by picking up and/or rocking.

The conditions which reinforce attachment behaviors have been studied almost not at all. Here the term "reinforcer" is used to refer to a stimulus occurring contingent upon a response, which strengthens the response and thus makes it more likely to recur. Or, to rephrase the definition in language more consistent with that of attachment theory, a reinforcer is an outcome or consequence of a behavior which makes it more likely to be activated (or more strongly activated) at some future time, even though other conditions of activation are essentially similar or perhaps even weaker. Although this usage may not coincide in all precise particulars with all the connotations of reinforcement as specified by Gewirtz (e.g., 1961, 1969) or by other learning theorists, it is hoped that no essential distortion is implicit in our usage. "Reinforcement" and "reinforcer" are convenient terms that have gained wide circulation among many behavioral scientists, many of whom do not use them precisely as originally defined. The core meaning of "reinforcer" is so widely understood that it seems preferable to use it here rather than to coin another term specific to attachment theory.

Activators and terminators have, unfortunately, been confused with reinforcers. Thus, for example, the human face, full face, smiling or in movement, has been found repeatedly to be an effective activator of infant smiling. If, each time an infant smiles, he is rewarded by an adult smile, and if this results in repeated infant smiles, then is the result because the smiling response was strengthened by the contingent smiles of the adult, or is it because the adult's smile merely evoked another infant smile? This question does not imply that an activator cannot also be a reinforcer, but it cannot be assumed to be so, and especially it cannot be assumed to be the most effective reinforcer. This is a matter for empirical exploration.

Similarly, environmental conditions that terminate an attachment behavior have sometimes been assumed to be reinforcing. Thus it has been assumed by many (cf. U. S. Children's Bureau *Infant Care* publications, 1922, 1938, 1940) that picking up a baby when he cries will strengthen crying behavior and make it more likely to occur again; in fact it has been assumed that a baby will become "spoiled" as a result of such a practice. Although it seems established that to pick up a crying baby—and to feed him if he is hungry—is likely to *terminate* crying behavior (e.g., Ainsworth et al., 1972), it has not been established that what terminates the cry is a reinforcer. Although the terminating stimulus is contingent upon the cry, it may not therefore be assumed that it tends either to increase the rate of crying or to make crying more likely to recur. Ainsworth (1963, 1967) and Gordon and Foss (1966) have presented some evidence to the contrary, and many clinicians believe the traditional view to be the opposite of what ordinarily occurs. The most convincing evidence that has come to our attention, however, stems from our own current data (S. M. Bell, 1971;

Ainsworth et al., 1972) which demonstrate that maternal unresponsiveness to crying in any of the first three quarters of the first year is significantly associated with a relative *increase* in the amount of crying in the *next* quarter, whereas maternal responsiveness is conversely associated with a relative decrease in crying in the next quarter, so that by the last 3 months of the first year those babies who cry the most are those who have been the least frequently and contingently responded to, while those who cry the least are those who have been the most contingently responded to. These findings demonstrate that the stimuli that terminate a cry tend not to reinforce it—at least not in the first year of life.

Similarly, it has been suggested that infants who protest most strongly in separation situations are likely to be those whose mothers have most efficiently reinforced their usual crying behaviors presumably by responding promptly and consistently to them. Our data (Stayton, 1971; Ainsworth et al., 1972) show that infants who cry most frequently in minor everyday separation situations are those whose mothers have been relatively unresponsive to cries, either delaying in responding to them or ignoring them altogether. (There is no reason to suppose that these findings would hold for infants or young children confronted with definitive separation situations; in these it could not be anticipated that more intense protest would be shown by those who cried more at home.)

On the other hand, maternal responsiveness to infant crying was found to be positively and strongly correlated (S. M. Bell, 1971; Ainsworth et al., 1972) with the variety, subtlety, and clarity of infant communication—facial expression, gestures, and noncrying vocalizations—during the last quarter of the first year. Our analyses could not deal in detail with maternal responsiveness to these noncrying communications, but our clear impression is that those mothers who were most contingently responsive to them were also most promptly responsive to crying signals. Thus, it appears that responsiveness to infant signals of all kinds facilitates the development of other modes of communication while at the same time weakening the tendency to signal through crying. The finding of the experimental study conducted on two babies by Etzel and Gewirtz (1967) may be viewed as congruent with this position. During the period of the experiment the adult responded to the infant's smiles and glances but did not respond to his cries; as a consequence of this treatment crying diminished. In conjunction with our findings, it seems reasonable that adult responsiveness to other signals may well have been more effective than unresponsiveness to crying in diminishing (extinguishing) crying. The crucial experiment would be one in which one treatment was like that utilized by Etzel and Gewirtz, and the other treatment was one in which the adult responded promptly (as our sensitive mothers tended to do) to all kinds of signals including crying.

There has been very little experimental research into the relative efficacy of different environmental stimuli as reinforcers for specific behaviors. The only example with which we are familiar is a study by Brossard and Décarie (1969) on the reinforcement of the smiling response—and this can be considered merely a promising beginning because the sample was too small to yield significant differences except between the two most extreme of eight experimental conditions.

Such research is very much needed. The issue of reinforcers has perhaps more immediate relevance than other issues to practical applications of research and theory. The literature on "parent education" is full of pronouncements about what parents should do in rearing their children, but these pronouncements have tended to be extrapolations from theory—both psychoanalytic and learning theories—without adequate empirical evidence that the extrapolations are valid. Extrapolations about "reinforcers"—particularly those to be avoided when attempting to socialize a child—have been conspicuous in such pronouncements. Despite the fact that both Hullian and Skinnerian learning theories imply that a stimulus can be identified as reinforcing only after it has been found to make a response upon which it is contingent more likely to recur, it has been easy for many to assume that what appears to be rewarding must be reinforcing, or that a stimulus that has been found to reinforce one behavior will serve to reinforce other behaviors.

There is considerable evidence (e.g., Sevenster, 1968) that reinforcers are not effective in all contexts. It seems reasonable to hypothesize (as Gewirtz, 1967, 1972, has stated) that a specific behavior may be more effectively reinforced by one stimulus than by another and, indeed, that there may be a gradient of effectiveness of reinforcement among several relevant stimuli. Research is essential, and when it is a question of reinforcement of attachment behaviors, it seems likely that experimental research must be supplemented by short-term longitudinal research with human subjects in a natural setting. Since it is clear that attachment behaviors are much subject to purely situational strengthening or heightening, a substantial span of time seems required to disentangle these situational effects from the effects of true reinforcers.

Fourth—important as an understanding of the component behaviors may be, it is surely more important to investigate the infant-mother attachment itself and its relation to other aspects of development. This relationship has been viewed as especially significant because of its pervasive effect on many aspects of behavior, especially exploration and fear; therefore, attachment should be studied not in isolation, but rather in a naturalistic context. There are several significant issues related to the infant-mother relationship in regard to which attachment theory seems to hold high promise of utility.

One such question is: what is the effect of infant-mother attachment upon other attachments and upon other interpersonal interactions in which the child is engaged now or in the future? Ever since Freud (1938) characterized the infant-mother relationship as the prototype of all future relationships, it has been widely accepted that this early relationship has a profound and pervasive influence on other interpersonal relations. And yet research has had little to say in regard to *how* it is that infant-mother relations affect other interpersonal relations. Ainsworth (1963, 1967) and Schaffer and Emerson (1964a) have pointed out that attachments to one or a few other figures may emerge simultaneously, soon after, or even in advance of an infant-mother attachment relationship. It is plausible to expect that an attachment relationship with one figure (perhaps especially a secure attachment relationship) may facilitate relations with others. To have experienced security, trust, interest, and gratification in relations with one figure may predispose a child to expect these desiderata in relations with other figures, and the behaviors which he has come characteristically to display in interaction with an attachment figure may, when displayed in interaction with other figures, evoke behavior from them which continues to support his optimistic expectations. And yet attachments are clearly specific. An infant does not become attached to all figures with whom he has interaction. On some basis he chooses a few preferred figures. Ainsworth (1967) and Schaffer and Emerson (1964a) suggest that his choice is based on the amount and nature of the interaction he experiences with each of the figures familiar enough to be candidates for attachment figures. Much more research is yet required before we understand attachments in infancy. Even more is required before we understand the influence these early attachments have upon later interpersonal relations, and through what processes facilitating influences may operate. Research is required also to clarify distinctions between different later relationships. Which may be best understood as attachments, which may be better characterized as playmate relationships, and which may be manifestations of "dependency" or "affiliative" tendencies?

Another question: what is the relationship of infant-mother attachment to other behavioral systems and to other lines of development? The relationship of attachment and attachment behavior to exploratory behavior has already been discussed; although research has already been done in this area, more is obviously needed. Similarly, some mention has already been made of the relationship of attachment and attachment behavior to fear. In addition, Morgan and Ricciuti (1969) showed that the presence and proximity of the mother reduce an infant's fearful response to strangers—although this effect varies with the age of the age of the infant. Wanda Bronson (1971a, 1971b) is investigating the relationships between attachment behavior, exploratory behavior, fear of the strange, and "effectance." Stayton et al. (1971) report evidence that individual differences in the infant-mother attachment relationship are related not only to the extent to which an infant obeys his mother's verbal commands and prohibitions, but also to the infant's IQ in the first year of life. S. M. Bell's (1970) findings provide striking evidence that the qualities of mother-infant interaction that facilitate the development of a secure attachment also facilitate at least one aspect of cognitive development, the development of the concept of the object. These analyses reflect only a few of the possible significant correlates of an infant's early attachment relationship with his mother, and suggest only a few of the promising directions in which research stimulated by attachment theory might move.

Furthermore, there is the question of how infant-mother attachment affects behavior, interpersonal and otherwise, at ages later than infancy and early childhood. A large body of clinical evidence suggest that significant relationships exist, but this issue remains largely unexplored by direct, detailed observational methods.

Finally, there is the significant general question of how the interaction between an infant and his mother figure shapes the quality of the first attachment relationship. In attempting to answer this question the contribution the infant makes to the interaction must not be ignored, as Rheingold (1969b), R. Q. Bell (1968), and Yarrow (1963) have argued. Some progress has been made in identifying constitutional differences between infants that influence their behavior from the beginning. Thomas, Chess, Birch, Hertzig, & Korn (e.g., 1963), Brazelton (1970), and Freedman (e.g., 1964) have concerned themselves with a large variety of constitutional differences. R. Q. Bell (e.g., 1971) and Schaffer and Emerson (1964b) have addressed themselves specifically to tactual sensitivity and response to physical contact. G. W. Bronson (1968, 1970, 1971) is exploring constitutional components of fearfulness. It may be assumed that such constitutional differences are reflected in the course of mother-infant interaction, although research into this problem has scarcely begun.

More attention has been paid to the mother's contribution to mother-infant interaction, and to the question of how variations in maternal behaviors affect the development of attachment, both the pacing of this development and the quality of the attachment relationship that ensues. Of considerable practical interest are studies of the effects of infant-care practices. Despite the fact that previous studies of the effects of infant-care practices have yielded equivocal findings (cf. Caldwell, 1964), there is good reason to expect that direct and fine-grain observational studies would demonstrate clear-cut effects of maternal practices upon the organization of an infant's attachment behavior—as suggested by the Ainsworth and Bell (1969) study of interaction in the feeding situation. It is expected, however, that detailed studies of infant-care practices will highlight the significance of more general aspects of maternal behavior, such as responsiveness to infant signals and behavior in respect to physical contact, reported by Ainsworth et al. (1972).

Cross-cultural studies provide a promising approach to an understanding of the influence of maternal behavior on infants' social development. For example, Gewirtz and Gewirtz (1965) have reported differences in the course of the development of smiling behavior in four Israeli caretaking environments. Caudill and Weinstein (1969) reported significant differences between middle-class Japanese and American mothers with concomitant differences in infant behavior. Ainsworth (1967) suggested that differences between Ganda and American infants in regard to the organization of attachment behavior stem at least in part from differences in infant-care practices. Studies such as these represent only the slightest of beginnings of exploration of the effect of cultural and subcultural differences in infant-care practices on the development of infant-mother attachment.

These are very significant issues. Despite their complexity and magnitude they are researchable issues. In addressing ourselves to them it is obviously necessary to go beyond an attempt to ascertain the nature of species-characteristic patterns that make for similarities within and across cultures. It is necessary to explore individual differences, to attempt to discover regularities in the relationships between patterns of mother-infant interaction and patterns of organization of the child's attachment behavior, and further to investigate how these individual differences arise and how they are related to individual differences in other behavioral systems both concurrently and developmentally.

REFERENCES

Ainsworth, M. D. The development of infant-mother interaction among the Ganda. In B. M. Foss (Ed.), *Determinants of infant behaviour II.* London: Methuen (New York: Wiley), 1963. Pp. 67-112.

Ainsworth, M. D. Patterns of attachment behavior shown by the infant in interaction with his mother. *Merrill-Palmer Quarterly,* 1964, **10**, 51-58.

Ainsworth, M. D. S. *Infancy in Uganda: Infant care and the growth of love.* Baltimore: Johns Hopkins Press, 1967.

Ainsworth, M. D. S. Object relations, dependency, and attachment: A theoretical review of the infant-mother relationship. *Child Development,* 1969, **40**, 969-1025.

Ainsworth, M. D. S. The development of infant-mother attachment. In B. M. Caldwell & H. N. Ricciuti (Eds.), *Review of child development research.* Vol. 3. Chicago: University of Chicago Press, in press.

Ainsworth, M. D. S., & Bell, S. M. Some contemporary patterns of mother-infant interaction in the feeding situation. In A. Ambrose (Ed.), *Stimulation in early infancy.* London: Academic Press, 1969. Pp. 133-163.

Ainsworth, M. D. S., & Bell, S. M. Attachment, exploration, and separation: Illustrated by the behavior of one-year-olds in a strange situation. *Child Development,* 1970, **41**, 49-67.

Ainsworth, M. D. S., Bell, S. M., & Stayton, D. J. Individual differences in strange-situation behavior of one-year-olds. In H. R. Schaffer (Ed.), *The origins of human social relations.* London: Academic Press, 1971. Pp. 17-52.

Ainsworth, M. D. S., Bell, S. M. & Stayton, D. J. Individual differences in the development of some attachment behaviors. *Merrill-Palmer Quarterly,* 1972, **18**, 123-143.

Ainsworth, M. D. S., & Wittig, B. A. Attachment and exploratory behavior of one-year-olds in a strange situation. In B. M. Foss (Ed.), *Determinants of infant behaviour IV.* London: Methuen, 1969. Pp. 233-253.

Ambrose, J. A. The concept of a critical period for the development of social responsiveness in early infancy. In B. M. Foss (Ed.), *Determinants of infant behaviour II.* London: Methuen (New York: Wiley), 1963. Pp. 201-225.

Anderson, J. W. Attachment behaviour out-of-doors. In N. Blurton-Jones (Ed.), *Ethological studies of human behaviour.* Cambridge: Cambridge University Press, 1972. Pp. 199-215.

Arsenian, J. M. Young children in an insecure situation. *Journal of Abnormal and Social Psychology,* 1943, **38**, 225-249.

Bateson, P. P. G. The characteristics and context of imprinting. *Biological Review,* 1966, **41**, 177-220.

Bell, R. Q. A reinterpretation of the direction of effects in studies of socialization. *Psychological Review,* 1968, **75**, 81-95.

Bell, R. Q. Stability of individual differences and relations between measures of sleep, tactile sensitivity, and nonnutritive sucking within the newborn period. Paper read at the meeting of the Society for Research in Child Development, Minneapolis, Minn., 1971.

Bell, S. M. The development of the concept of the object and its relationship to infant-mother attachment. *Child Development*, 1970, **41**, 291-312.

Bell, S. M. The effectiveness of various maternal responses as terminators of crying: Some developmental changes and theoretical implications. Paper read at the meeting of the Society for Research in Child Development, Minneapolis, Minn., 1971.

Beller, E. K. Dependency and independence in young children. *Journal of Genetic Psychology*, 1955, **87**, 25-35.

Beller, E. K. Dependency and autonomous achievement striving related to orality and anality in early childhood. *Child Development*, 1957, **28**, 287-314.

Beller, E. K. Exploratory studies of dependency. *Transactions of the New York Academy of Sciences*, 1959, **21**, 414-426.

Bijou, S. W., & Baer, D. M. *Child development*. Vol. 2. *Universal stage of infancy*. New York: Appleton-Century-Crofts, 1965.

Bowlby, J. Some pathological processes set in train by early mother-child separation. *Journal of Mental Science*, 1953, **99**, 265-272.

Bowlby, J. The nature of the child's tie to his mother. *International Journal of Psycho-Analysis*, 1958, **39**, 350-373.

Bowlby, J. Grief and mourning in infancy and early childhood. *Psychoanalytic Study of the Child*, 1960, **15**, 9-52.(a)

Bowlby, J. Separation anxiety. *International Journal of Psycho-Analysis*, 1960, **41**, 89-113.(b)

Bowlby, J. Processes of mourning. *International Journal of Psycho-Analysis*, 1961, **42**, 317-340.

Bowlby, J. Pathological mourning and childhood mourning. *Journal of the American Psychoanalytic Association*, 1963, **11**, 500-541.

Bowlby, J. *Attachment and loss*. Vol. 1. *Attachment*. London: Hogarth (New York: Basic Books), 1969.

Brackbill, Y. Extinction of the smiling response in infants as a function of reinforcement schedule. *Child Development*, 1958, **29**, 115-124.

Brazelton, T. B. *Infants and mothers*. New York: Delacorte Press, 1970.

Bronson, G. W. The development of fear in man and other animals. *Child Development*, 1968, **39**, 409-431.

Bronson, G. W. Fear of visual novelty: Developmental patterns in males and females. *Developmental Psychology*, 1970, **2**, 33-40.

Bronson, G. W. Fear of the unfamiliar in human infants. In H. R. Schaffer (Ed.), *The origins of human social relations*. London: Academic Press, 1971. Pp. 59-64.

Bronson, W. Exploratory behavior of fifteen-month-old infants in a novel situation. Paper read at the meeting of the Society for Research in Child Development, Minneapolis, Minn., 1971.(a)

Bronson, W. The growth of competence: Issues of conceptualization and measurement. In H. R. Schaffer (Ed.), *The origins of human social relations*. London: Academic Press, 1971. Pp. 269-277.(b)

Brossard, L. M., & Décarie, T. G. Comparative reinforcing effect of eight stimulations on the smiling response of infants. *Journal of Child Psychology and Psychiatry*, 1969, **9**, 51-60.

Burlingham, D., & Freud, A. *Infants without families*. London: Allen & Unwin, 1944.

Caldwell, B. M. The usefulness of the critical period hypothesis in the study of filiative behavior. *Merrill-Palmer Quarterly*, 1962, **8**, 229-242.

Caldwell, B. M. The effects of infant care. In M. L. Hoffman & L. W. Hoffman (Eds.), *Review of child development research*. Vol. I. New York: Russell Sage Foundation, 1964. Pp. 9-88.

Caudill, W., & Weinstein, H. Maternal care and infant behavior in Japan and America. *Psychiatry,* 1969, **32,** 12-43.

Cox, F. M., & Campbell, D. Young children in a new situation with and without their mothers. *Child Development,* 1968, **39,** 123-132.

Décarie, T. G. *Intelligence and affectivity in early childhood.* New York: International Universities Press, 1965.

DeVore, I. Mother-infant relations in free-ranging baboons. In H. L. Rheingold (Ed.), *Maternal behavior in mammals.* New York: Wiley, 1963. Pp. 305-335.

Dollard, J., & Miller, N. E. *Personality and psychotherapy.* New York: McGraw-Hill, 1950.

Escalona, S. Emotional development in the first year of life. In M. J. E. Senn (Ed.), *Problems of infancy and childhood: Transactions of the sixth conference.* New York: Josiah Macey Jr. Foundation, 1953. Pp. 11-92.

Etzel, B. C., & Gewirtz, J. L. Experimental modification of caretaker-maintained high rate operant crying in a 6- and a 20-week-old infant (*Infans tyrannotearus*): Extinction of crying with reinforcement of eye contact and smiling. *Journal of Experimental Child Psychology,* 1967, **5,** 303-317.

Freedman, D. G. Smiling in blind infants and the issue of innate vs. acquired. *Journal of Child Psychology and Psychiatry,* 1964, **5,** 171-184.

Freedman, D. G. Personality development in infancy: A biological approach. S. L. Washburn & P. C. Jay (Eds.), *Perspectives in human evolution.* New York: Holt, Rinehart, & Winston, 1968. Pp. 258-287.

Freud, S. *An outline of psychoanalysis.* London: Hogarth, 1938.

Gewirtz, J. L. A program of research on the dimensions and antecedents of emotional dependence. *Child Development,* 1956, **27,** 205-221.

Gewirtz, J. L. A learning analysis of the effects of normal stimulation, privation, and deprivation on the acquisition of social motivation and attachment. In B. M. Foss (Ed.), *Determinants of infant behavior.* London: Methuen (New York: Wiley), 1961. Pp. 213-299.

Gewirtz, J. L. Deprivation and satiation of social stimuli as determinants of their reinforcing efficacy. In J. P. Hill (Ed.), *Minnesota symposia on child psychology.* Vol. 1. Minneapolis: University of Minnesota Press, 1967. Pp. 3-56.

Gewirtz, J. L. Mechanisms of social learning: Some roles of stimulation and behavior in early human development. In D. A. Goslin (Ed.), *Handbook of socialization theory and research.* Chicago: Rand McNally, 1969. Pp. 57-212.

Gewirtz, J. L. Some contextual determinants of stimulus potency. In R. D. Parke (Ed.), *Recent trends in social learning theory.* New York: Academic Press, 1972. Pp. 7-33.

Gewirtz, J. L., & Gewirtz, H. B. Stimulus conditions, infant behaviors, and social learning in four Israeli child-rearing environments: A preliminary report illustrating differences in environment and behavior between the 'only' and the 'youngest' child. In B. M. Foss (Ed.), *Determinants of infant behaviour III.* London: Methuen (New York: Wiley), 1965. Pp. 161-180.

Gordon, T., & Foss, B. M. The role of stimulation in the delay of onset of crying in the newborn infant. *Quarterly Journal of Experimental Psychology,* 1966, **18,** 79-81.

Harlow, H. F. The development of affectional patterns in infant monkeys. In B. M. Foss (Ed.), *Determinants of infant behaviour.* London: Methuen (New York: Wiley), 1961. Pp. 75-97.

Harlow, H. F. The maternal affectional system. In B. M. Foss (Ed.), *Determinants of infant behaviour II.* London: Methuen (New York: Wiley), 1963. Pp. 3-34.

Heathers, G. Emotional dependence and independence in nursery school play. *Journal of Genetic Psychology,* 1955, **87,** 37-57.

Heinicke, C. M., & Westheimer, I. *Brief separations.* New York: International Universities Press, 1965.

Hinde, R. A. *Animal behaviour: A synthesis of ethology and comparative psychology.* New York: McGraw-Hill, 1966.

Kaufman, I. C., & Rosenblum, L. A. Depression in infant monkeys separated from their mothers. *Science,* 1967, **155**, 1030-1031.

Kessen, W., & Leutzendorff, A.-M. The effect of non-nutritive sucking on movement in the human newborn. *Journal of Comparative and Physiological Psychology,* 1963, **56**, 69-72.

Kuhn, T. S. *The structure of scientific revolutions.* Chicago: University of Chicago Press, 1962.

Maccoby, E. E., & Masters, J. C. Attachment and dependency. In P. H. Mussen (Ed.), *Carmichael's manual of child psychology.* (3rd ed.) Vol. 2. New York: Wiley, 1970. Pp. 73-158.

Miller, G. A., Galanter, E., & Pribram, K. H. *Plans and the structure of behavior.* New York: Holt, Rinehart, & Winston, 1960.

Morgan, G. A., & Ricciuti, H. N. Infants' responses to strangers during the first year. In B. M. Foss (Ed.), *Determinants of infant behaviour IV.* London: Methuen, 1969. Pp. 253-272.

Piaget, J. *The language and thought of the child.* New York: Harcourt Brace, 1926. (Originally published: 1924.)

Piaget, J. *The origins of intelligence in children.* (2nd ed.) New York: International Universities Press, 1952. (Originally published: 1936.)

Piaget, J. *The construction of reality in the child.* New York: Basic Books, 1954. (Originally published: 1937.)

Rheingold, H. L. Controlling the infant's exploratory behavior. In B. M. Foss (Ed.), *Determinants of infant behaviour II.* London: Methuen (New York: Wiley), 1963. Pp. 143-178.

Rheingold, H. L. The effect of a strange environment on the behavior of infants. In B. M. Foss (Ed.), *Determinants of infant behaviour IV.* London: Methuen, 1969, Pp. 137-166.(a)

Rheingold, H. L. The social and socializing infant. In D. A. Goslin (Ed.), *Handbook of socialization theory and research.* Chicago: Rand McNally, 1969. Pp. 779-790.(b)

Rheingold, H. L., & Eckerman, C. O. The infant separates himself from his mother. *Science,* 1970, **168**, 78-83.

Rheingold, H. L., Gewirtz, J. L., & Ross, H. W. Social conditioning of vocalizations in the infant. *Journal of Comparative and Physiological Psychology,* 1959, **52**, 68-73.

Robertson, J., & Bowlby, J. Responses of young children to separation from their mother. II. Observations of the sequences of response of children aged 16 to 24 months during the course of separation. *Courrier, Centre International de l'Enfance,* 1952, **2**, 131-142.

Robertson, J., & Robertson, J. *Young children in brief separation. Film No. 1; Kate, aged 2 years 5 months, in foster-care for 27 days.* London: Tavistock Institute of Human Relations, 1968.(a) (New York: New York University Film Library.)

Robertson, J., & Robertson, J. *Young children in brief separation. Film No. 2: Jane, 17 months, in foster-care for 10 days.* London: Tavistock Child Development Research Unit, 1968. (b) (New York: New York University Film Library.)

Robertson, J., & Robertson, J. *Young children in brief separation. Film No. 3, John, 17 months, 9 days in a residential nursery.* London: Tavistock Child Development Research Unit, 1969. (New York: New York University Film Library.)

Robson, K. S. The role of eye-to-eye contact in maternal-infant attachment. *Journal of Child Psychology and Psychiatry,* 1967, **8**, 13-25.

Rosenblum, L. A. Polymatric rearing and infant attachment in monkeys. In H. R. Schaffer (Ed.), *The origins of human social relations.* London: Academic Press, 1971. Pp. 85-109.

Rosenthal, M. K. Effects of a novel situation and of anxiety on two groups of dependency behaviors. *British Journal of Psychology,* 1967, **58**, 357-364.

Sade, D. S., Some aspects of parent-offspring and sibling relations in a group of rhesus monkeys, with a discussion of grooming. *American Journal of Physical Anthropology,* 1965, **23**, 1-18.

Schaffer, H. R. Objective observations of personality development in early infancy. *British Journal of Medical Psychology,* 1958, **31**, 174-183.

Schaffer, H. R. Some issues for research in the study of attachment behavior. In B. M. Foss (Ed.), *Determinants of infant behaviour II.* London: Methuen (New York: Wiley), 1963. Pp. 179-199.

Schaffer, H. R. The onset of fear of strangers and the incongruity hypothesis. *Journal of Child Psychology and Psychiatry,* 1966, **7**, 95-106.

Schaffer, H. R., & Callender, W. M. Psychological effects of hospitalization in infancy. *Pediatrics,* 1959, **24**, 528-539.

Schaffer, H. R., & Emerson, P. E. The development of social attachments in infancy. *Monographs of the Society for Research in Child Development,* 1964, **29** (3, Serial No. 94).(a)

Schaffer, H. R., & Emerson, P. E. Patterns of response to physical contact in early human development. *Journal of Child Psychology and Psychiatry,* 1964, **5**, 1-13.(b)

Scott, J. P. The process of primary socialization in canine and human infants. *Monographs of the Society for Research in Child Development,* 1963, **28** (1, Serial No. 85).

Sears, R. R. *A survey of objective studies of psychoanalytic concepts.* New York: Social Science Research Council, Bulletin 51, 1943.

Sears, R. R. Dependency motivation. *Nebraska Symposium on Motivation,* 1963, **11**, 25-64.

Sears, R. R., Maccoby, E. E., & Levin, H. *Patterns of child rearing.* Evanston, Ill.: Row, Peterson, 1957.

Sears, R. R., Rau, L., & Alpert, R. *Identification and child rearing.* Stanford, Calif.: Stanford University Press, 1965.

Sears, R. R., Whiting, J. W. M., Nowlis, V., & Sears, P. S. Some child rearing antecedents of dependency and aggression in young children. *Genetic Psychology Monographs,* 1953, **47**, 135-234.

Sevenster, P. Motivation and learning in sticklebacks. In D. Ingle (Ed.), *The central nervous sytem and fish behavior.* Chicago: University of Chicago Press, 1968. Pp. 233-245.

Sluckin, W. *Imprinting and early learning.* Chicago: Aldine, 1965.

Spencer-Booth, Y., & Hinde, R. A. The effects of separating rhesus monkey infants from their mothers for six days. *Journal of Child Psychology and Psychiatry,* 1966, **7**, 179-198.

Spitz, R. A. *A genetic field theory of ego formation.* New York: International Universities Press, 1959.

Spitz, R. A., & Wolf, K. M. Anaclitic depression. *Psychoanalytic Study of the Child,* 1946, **2**, 313-342.

Stayton, D. J. Infants' responses to brief everyday separations: Distress, pursuit, and greeting. Paper presented at the meeting of the Society for Research in Child Development, Minneapolis, Minn., 1971.

Stayton, D. J., Hogan, R., & Ainsworth, M. D. S. Infant obedience and maternal behavior: The origins of socialization reconsidered. *Child Development,* 1971, **42**, 1057-1069.

Stendler, C. B. Possible causes of overdependency in young children. *Child Development,* 1954, **25**, 125-146.

Thomas, A., Chess, S., Birch, H. G., Hertzig, M. E., & Korn, S. *Behavioral individuality in early childhood.* New York: New York University Press, 1963.

U. S. Children's Bureau. *Infant care.* Care of Children Series No. 2. Bureau Publication No. 8 (Revised), 1922.

U. S. Children's Bureau. *Infant care.* Care of Children Series No. 2. Bureau Publication No. 8 (Revised), 1938.

U. S. Children's Bureau. *Infant care.* Care of Children Series No. 2. Bureau Publication No. 8 (Revised), 1940.

van Lawick-Goodall, J. The behaviour of free-living chimpanzees in the Gombe Stream Reserve. *Animal Behaviour Monograph,* 1968, **1** (3), 165-311.

Walters, R. H., & Parke, R. D. The role of the distance receptors in the development of social responsiveness. In L. P. Lipsitt & C. C. Spiker (Eds.), *Advances in child development and behavior.* Vol. 2. New York: Academic Press, 1965. Pp. 59-96.

Wolff, P. H. Observations on the early development of smiling. In B. M. Foss (Ed.), *Determinants of infant behaviour II.* London: Metheun (New York: Wiley) 1963. Pp. 113-138.

Wolff, P. H. The natural history of crying and vocalization in early infancy. In B. M. Foss (Ed.), *Determinants of infant behaviour IV.* London: Methuen, 1969. Pp. 81-110.

Yarrow, L. J. Research in dimensions of early maternal care. *Merrill-Palmer Quarterly,* 1963, **9,** 101-114.

Yarrow, L. J. The development of focused relationships during infancy. In J. Hellmuth (Ed.), *Exceptional infant: the normal infant.* Vol. 1. Seattle, Wash.: Special Child Publications, 1967. Pp. 428-442.

ATTACHMENT, DEPENDENCE, AND A DISTINCTION IN TERMS OF STIMULUS CONTROL

Jacob L. Gewirtz

National Institute of Mental Health

Introduction

The metaphoric concepts "attachment" ("bond," "affectional tie," "object relationship") and "dependence" ("dependency," "socio-emotional" or "affectional" dependence) have been approached in varied ways that often overlap. These abstract molar terms for object relations have been employed to label a broaα area of scientific interest. They have also served to label aspects of the (sometimes reciprocal) reliance of one individual upon another—mother and child, teacher and pupil, lover and loved one—expressed in many responses, stimulus situations, and contextual conditions. Therefore, these concepts have been applied to cases where, in many situations, one person's behaviors rely intimately upon (that is, are under the control of stimuli provided by) the appearance and behaviors of another or others. More specifically, these terms have served to label a complex of child behavior systems cued and maintained primarily by adult (and occasionally by peer) behaviors, as well as concurrent reflections of that control process (for instance, differential preferences for those adults).

The patterned social behavior systems comprising the child's involvement in such a two-sided interaction process have often comprised the arena in which researchers have sought to identify the effects of early experience on social behavior, including experience in routine as well as deficient or disrupted environments. Because the S-R functions involved in dyadic interchanges are pervasive, and can become highly disorganized (with the display of concurrent intense emotional responses) if interfered with, the broad concepts of attachment or dependence have often served as central foci of diverse theories of social development. They have served also as bases for environmental engineering prescriptions (with evaluative adjectives—good or bad, warm or hostile— occasionally added to differentiate among the experiential patterns involved). Even so, there is as yet little detailed information about the origins, nature, and course of human social development generally, much less about the phenomena classified specifically under the two terms. There is even less information available about the reciprocal influence of the child's characteristics and behaviors on the behaviors of the adults involved, in dyadic interchanges.

Though they share some of the same origins, the attachment and dependence concepts have evolved in somewhat divergent ways, in part insulated from each other. Yet they have often been employed interchangeably and inexplicitly. Moreover, each of these terms has sometimes been used to label: (a) a developmental *process,* (b) *outcomes* or end points of that process (like a child beginning to walk unsupported), or (c) process *and* outcome simultaneously, possibly also with a value implied in the usage. And the work carried out under the attachment and dependence terms has often centered around different (a) purposes and problems, (b) research procedures, (c) behavior systems, and (d) species and age spans of experimental subjects. Further, the criterion indices used for these concepts (particularly for attachment) have often differed among investigators. Concomitantly (or perhaps as a result), the body of theory that has evolved to organize the stimulus-response functions these terms encompass has not gone beyond an early phase. In addition, under these headings for object relations, disagreements between theoretical approaches which may seem fundamental can often be traced simply to theorists' preferences for alternative paradigms. Hence, even when focused on the very same events, alternative conceptual approaches may appear aimed at organizing very different phenomena.

Accordingly, my posture in this chapter (and the next) is to treat the attachment and dependence terms as abstractions that are often useful in labeling, organizing, or summarizing classes of stimulus-response functions within a wide range, when the receptor and effector capacities of the child that are involved will go through sequential (i.e., developmental) changes. There are conceptual purposes for which these terms may be particularly useful, as in ordering apparently different phenotypic stimulus-response functions (or their sequential changes in time) under the same process model. For other purposes, these terms may be entirely unnecessary. In this frame, I have routinely suggested that exploration of the underlying phenomena can proceed efficiently through use of concepts that are closely tied to observable events.

As with such other abstract concepts as intelligence, some concerns involved in the study of attachment and dependence have simultaneously had relevance for broad, traditional issues in psychology. For instance, these would include identifying: (a) behaviors that occur naturally in early life (some of which could be species-specific); (b) changes in the topography of behaviors and in the organization of behavior patterns at successive developmental points; (c) unconditioned (releasing) stimuli and their roles in conditioning; and (d) early attentional processes and setting factors that determine momentary stimulus efficacy.

In the conceptual context outlined, a comparison between attachment and dependence—in terms of the assumed modes of acquisition and operation of the cued behaviors they encompass—could be catalytic for theory and research. Moreover, an examination of the historical context in which the two terms have evolved, of the research literature, and of selected aspects of the instrumental-conditioning paradigm has suggested that a heuristic distinction between those concepts is warranted. It can organize diverse phenomena under the two concepts and can suggest some new research directions. Therefore, in this chapter I develop further such a distinction, which evolved in several of my earlier analyses. The behaviors involved, in and of themselves, are assumed to play no differential role in the proposed distinction. Rather, the distinction is made solely in terms of a difference in features of the stimuli controlling these behaviors—whether they stem from a particular person (attachment) or from a person who belongs to a discriminable class of persons (dependence). Some implications of the distinction and its utility are illustrated in a discussion of the acquisition and maintenance of the apparently different stimulus-response systems that connote attachment and dependence. At the same time, this chapter updates several earlier analyses of how conditioning processes could be involved in this acquisition and maintenance process (Gewirtz, 1961b, 1969a, 1969b).

In the social-learning analysis that follows, the development of, and systematic changes in, response systems connoting dependence or attachment are explored primarily in terms of relations between behaviors of the initially helpless child and stimuli provided by one or more people (mostly adults) in his environment. This is done in a frame where (*a*) the relevant receptor capacities and behaviors of the child will often change with development, and (*b*) the degree to which particular behavior systems could be affected by environmental conditions is often unknown. Nevertheless, the dyadic attachment and dependence functions are conceived as not limited to any particular age range or interaction partner. That is, while the focus of this chapter is the young child and his earliest relationships, attachment and dependence may refer to behavior systems connoting reciprocal, dyadic patterns between *any* two people (child and adult, children, or adults). Within this frame, the analysis can also account, at any point in life, for some effects of separation and for the development of new or substitute attachment or dependence behavior configurations when a pattern is broken (for instance, by death of a parent or mate or by divorce).

Let me conclude this introduction with some comments about the features of the functional approach and the conditioning paradigm I emphasize in the heuristic analysis that follows. Many conceptions have evolved to provide a basis for interpreting how recurring environmental events acquire systematic control over behaviors. These are typically grouped under the open-ended heading of *learning*. In this context, this chapter emphasizes the paradigm of instrumental or operant conditioning (for my purposes, they are treated as a single paradigm), which I have found useful for various heuristic purposes. That learning paradigm specifically stresses controlling cue (discriminative) stimuli, overt responses, and stimulus consequences that constitute extrinsic reinforcement (when their presentation contingent upon responses systematically affects the rate of those responses). Under this conception, behaviors and stimuli are assumed to be codetermined with the stimulus-response (S-R) unit serving as the functional unit of analysis. In this frame, a response can be any movement of the organism that is under stimulus control. Reciprocally, any environmental event which affects a response is considered a stimulus. This functional framework therefore requires that one specify, in parallel detail, both the child's behaviors and their stimulus determinants (Gewirtz, 1969a). Children are conceived to acquire behaviors in relation to controlling stimuli, and not to acquire behaviors in the abstract. In such a conceptual analysis, these S-R systems are considered to be the essential products of development.[1]

---

[1] A behavioral approach like the one I use is open to grouping the functional relations between children's responses and their controlling stimuli by the type of control process, content, or some other relevant principle. Organized patterns of S-R relations may thus be identified under a learning approach and labeled to represent a higher order of classification, or levels or phases of an ordered sequence in time, should that seem useful. These patterns may encompass some of the events and S-R relations that underlie the cognitive concepts invoked by other theoretical approaches. One might occasionally find it useful to assign to some such organized patterns of S-R relations descriptive labels (e.g., "schema" as in the "schema of mother").

In this chapter, I emphasize mainly conditioning concepts for positive stimulus control over social behaviors. For heuristic simplicity, I avoid the use of fear-, anxiety-, and conflict-based concepts that have occasionally served in approaches to dependence (e.g., Sears, Whiting, Nowlis, Sears, & collaborators, 1953; Cairns, 1961; Beller, 1971). Insofar as the paradigms underlying those concepts depend on the acquisition and maintenance of approach responses that preclude noxious stimulation, they would be compatible with those I emphasize in this chapter, though some may be more complex. This emphasis mainly on positive stimulus control simplifies the analysis and seems to result in the loss of little explanatory power or scope. At the same time, it permits me to make a more complete treatment of the key theoretical and procedural issues.

The issues I deal with in this chapter are conceived to be generic for all theories of social development and the origins of object relations, regardless of their orientations, their heuristic flavor, their degree of formality, or how systematically they approach those issues. At the same time, my emphasis on the operant paradigm would not preclude the use of other learning models (e.g., that of Pavlovian conditioning which overlaps it at some key points) or different theoretical approaches (e.g., those emphasizing diverse cognitive, connative, or affective responses) to order behavior phenomena grouped under the rubrics of attachment or dependence. Neither would it preclude the integration of some of those alternative views with the one advanced here. The important consideration for my present purpose is that the instrumental-conditioning paradigm has shown its utility in the efficient and parsimonious ordering of both simple and seemingly complex behavior systems (Gewirtz, 1969b, 1971a, 1971c). Thus, it promises to provide a fruitful basis for describing how learning factors can operate in similar situations involving dyadic interchanges.

The Historical Perspective

The concepts of attachment and dependence, and their precursors, have been approached in a number of ways over the years. Psychoanalysis and its derivatives have considered the phenomena connoting attachment (and perhaps also dependence) in terms of cathexis, object formation, and object relations [the "object" being the instrumental person, typically the mother, through whom the "instinctual aim" is satisfied (Freud, 1905, 1914, 1926, 1931, 1938)]. In this frame, Freud (1926) at one point considered a child's anxiety about separation from his mother to be an indication of an object relation.

ATTACHMENT

Approaches to comparative animal behavior have emphasized observations of gregariousness, imprinting, and the ties developed between humans and animals of some species (Spalding, 1873; Lorenz, 1935; Harlow, 1958, 1966; Scott, 1960, 1967; Sluckin, 1965; Salzen, 1967). Recently, the work of Bowlby (1953,

1958, 1960a, 1960b, 1968, 1969) has provided the impetus for combining selected psychoanalytic assumptions with ethological and, to a degree, cognitive conceptions [in particular those of Piaget (1936, 1937) and of Miller, Galanter, & Pribram (1960)] . In this frame, Bowlby has used the term "attachment" to label a child's "affectional tie," particularly to his mother-figure. Following Bowlby's lead, Ainsworth (1963 et seq.), Schaffer and Emerson (1964), and others have used the term similarly. In the context of the disruption of early mother-child relationships, Yarrow (1956, 1964, 1967) first used the term "object relationship" and later the term "focused [individualized] relationship" to label what seem to be the same behavior systems of the human infant toward his mother-figure.

In a parallel vein, Harlow and his associates have used the terms "affectional attachment" (Harlow & Zimmermann, 1959) and "affectional system" [which passes through a "comfort and attachment" stage (Harlow & Harlow, 1965, 1966)] to label behavior systems that "bind" the macaque infant first to his mother and then to others in the course of his development. In a similar way, Mason (1970) has used the term attachment (apparently synonymously with the term emotional dependence–p. 53) to order the clinging behavior pattern of infrahuman primates. As does Harlow, Scott (e.g., 1960, 1967) has conceived of a "primary social relationship," "primary bond," or "social attachment" to order the patterned behaviors of organisms with regard to another (or others). He has assumed it develops in animals (including humans) independent of environmental stimulation, requiring only prolonged "contact" with the mother or others during the "critical period" for the species. In this general context, Cairns (1966) has proposed that social attachment in mammals is acquired as a function of association (learning) with an object in a given context, but also of the object's cue weight; and I have used the attachment term to summarize the mostly positive stimulus control (assumed acquired via instrumental learning) over a variety of the child's orienting and approach responses made in connection with his mother-figure or some other individual (Gewirtz, 1961b).

DEPENDENCE

In contrast to the use of the term "attachment," the term "dependence" (dependency) has been used primarily in the framework of learning theories and only occasionally in psychoanalytic or ethological frames. In conditioning-oriented approaches of the past quarter century, dependence has usually served to encompass the diverse, presumably learned, trait-like social "motive" systems of post-Watsonian behaviorism (e.g., Shaffer, 1936)–which had evolved to reflect the shift in emphasis to experience from earlier postulated "instincts" (e.g., McDougall, 1908, 1923). Such usage of the term dependence has stressed mainly some implications (for social behavior outcomes of child rearing) of the conception of conditioned, secondary reinforcement (e.g., Whiting, 1944; Sears, 1951, 1963; Sears et al., 1953; Gewirtz, 1954, 1956b, 1961b, 1969b; Beller, 1955,

1959; Heathers, 1955a; Sears, Maccoby, & Levin, 1957). That conditioned-reinforcement conception is central to laboratory research on instrumental conditioning. At times, it has been qualified by a postulated conflict or anxiety "motive" based upon occasional nonreward (frustration) or even punishment of dependent overtures (Sears et al., 1953; Cairns, 1961; Beller, 1971). Also, there have been recent attempts to reconcile the assumptions of various learning approaches with the concepts and findings of comparative animal behavior studies (e.g., see Gewirtz, 1961b; Cairns, 1966, this volume).

DIFFERENTIAL USES OF THE CONCEPTS

Reviews of the literature on attachment and dependence have been characterized by a lack of emphasis on an explicit distinction between the concepts, much less the selection for use of one over the other [e.g., see the comprehensive reviews of Hartup (1963) and Maccoby and Masters (1970)]. The two sets of terms may be used interchangeably in many such reviews, or the tendency may be to employ the term that happened to be used by whichever theorist or researcher is being reviewed. Further, as reviews have tended not to emphasize a distinction between the terms, there has been little need to group or evaluate relevant studies (on acquisition, effects of separation, and the like) that, according to criteria touched upon in this paper, possibly have differential implications for the concepts of attachment and dependence.

I noted earlier that the psychoanalytic theory of object relations seems to have been a starting point of approaches to both attachment and dependence. And there are instances where theorists have related situational determinants to the behaviors connoting each concept. Thus, external frustration conditions have been related to dependence behaviors (Whiting, 1944), and a mother's preparations to depart or her being reunited with her infant have been related to attachment behaviors (Bowlby, 1960a, 1960b). However, most often conceptualizations of attachment and dependence have been variable and the definitions of the terms inexplicit and sometimes overlapping. In this context, there are many instances where arbitrary conditions seem to have set the tone in considering topics grouped under the two terms. Thus, matters which might relate to both concepts have sometimes been considered relevant to only one or the other concept but not to both. Moreover, it has been rare for such distinctions to be explicit. However, one explicit distinction is the equation of the dependence term with an immature (even psychopathological) relationship or one reliant on situational requirements, and the equation of the attachment term with a more mature, enduring relationship (Ainsworth, 1969, this volume; Bowlby, 1969).

Typically, however, considerations that might apply equally to the two concepts have been applied to one only. Thus, theorists have taken account of issues, concepts, and data stemming from the ethological tradition in connection with attachment (Bowlby, 1958, 1960a, 1960b, 1968; Scott, 1967), but ethological concepts have seldom been considered in relation to dependence, for which conditioning concepts have been employed almost exclusively (e.g., Sears, 1951, 1963; Sears et al., 1953, 1957; Gewirtz, 1956b). Another tendency has been to employ the term attachment in research related to social behavior systems of both human and animal infants, while reserving the term dependence almost exclusively for research on human social behaviors, particularly of nursery-school-age children. There is also a remarkable instance where the attachment term has been used as a broad label for both the extent and the intensity of the overall pattern of a child's interaction with his mother, while terms normally used at the same level of analysis, namely social- and instrumental-dependence and affiliation, have served as overlapping labels for behavior attributes defining attachment (e.g., Caldwell, Wright, Honig, & Tannenbaum, 1970).

There are additional matters that could be relevant to both attachment and dependence that have been taken up more under one concept than under the other. Topics considered more in connection with attachment than with dependence include: comparative and developmental changes in response topography; critical periods (Scott, 1967); attachment as a precondition for, or sometimes a result of, identification [as was discussed by Gewirtz and Stingle (1968) and by Gewirtz (1969b)]; and a mutuality of interaction effects. With respect to mutual interaction effects, the "attachment" of the parent-caretaker to his child is often given emphasis together with the child's attachment behavior pattern. This is in contrast to the usual child-oriented, unidirectional emphasis of the dependence conception under which typically only the child and not his interacting parent-caretaker is scored for dependence. (Even so, the latter person may be scored for "nurturance" or similar attributes, though these are conceived more as assessments of antecedents than as assessments of outcomes.)

On the other hand, several matters that might apply equally to the attachment and the dependence concept have been more characteristic of earlier work on dependence. These include: a greater amount of systematic research; attempts to relate dependence to antecedent variables, and to other concurrent behavior systems (e.g., Sears et al., 1953); investigation of the behavior-control effects of social reinforcing stimuli—e.g., the spoken word *good* (Gewirtz & Baer, 1958a, 1958b; Cairns, 1961; Cairns & Lewis, 1962; Gewirtz, 1969c); and examination of interrelations among response indices (e.g., Sears et al., 1953; Gewirtz, 1954, 1956a; Beller, 1955, 1959; Sears, 1963; Rosenthal, 1967a, 1967b).

Researchers and theorists of dependence, most of whom have operated in the learning tradition, have not emphasized a distinction between attachment and dependence, much less one between the behavior patterns focused on an individual and those focused on any one of a class of individuals (e.g., Whiting, 1944; Sears, 1951, 1963; Sears et al., 1953, 1957; Whiting & Child, 1953; Gewirtz, 1954, 1956b; Beller, 1955, 1957, 1959; Heathers, 1955a, 1955b; Kagan & Moss, 1962; Bandura & Walters, 1963; Hartup, 1963). (In retrospect, it was probably unwise of me to term this latter pattern "nonfocused" in some earlier papers.) Even so, there have been instances in which children's dependence behaviors have been scored with reference to the category of recipients of initiations (i.e., objects) or the degree of the recipients' availability. However, this was done in contexts where, for the most part, a theoretical distinction between dependence acts to the mother and such acts to others was not emphasized (e.g., Sears et al., 1953; Sears, Rau, & Alpert, 1965). In this frame, Sears' (e.g., 1963) and some others' approaches to a child's dependence behavior have sometimes seemed to imply an object-person focus like that at the core of the attachment concept.

In an approach which, on this issue, does not seem to have changed since 1958, Bowlby (1958, 1960a, 1960b, 1968, 1969) has emphasized explicitly that the dependence term should be avoided. He has held that it connotes disparagement and is derived from a secondary drive theory "... that is almost certainly false [Bowlby, 1969, p. 228]." The arbitrary bases for this distinction notwithstanding, viewed in terms of the distinctions I have stressed (Gewirtz, 1961b, 1969b) and will touch upon in the next section, Bowlby's conclusion is drawn in a framework differentiating only between instrumental dependence on, and attachment to, the mother-figure. In making this distinction exclusively, Bowlby has bypassed some implications of the socio-emotional dependence concept.[2] Consequently, researchers and theorists of attachment who have followed Bowlby's lead (e.g., Ainsworth, 1963, 1964, 1967; Schaffer, 1963; Schaffer & Emerson, 1964) up to now have tended to devote little attention to socio-emotional dependence and/or implicitly to equate it with attachment. For example, Schaffer and Emerson (1964) appear to have used the term attachment (qualified by adjectives like "indiscriminate" or "breadth") to connote some

---

[2] Bowlby (1969) has referenced the critique (Gewirtz, 1961b) which (a) emphasized the relevance, to his differentiation, of the distinction between instrumental and socio-emotional dependence, and (b) questioned his conception that the "secondary drive" (conditioning) approach to the acquisition of attachment was limited exclusively to those reinforcing events provided directly through caretaking that have direct organismic implications (i.e., food, water, and the removal of noxious stimulation). Indeed, Bowlby (1961) even replied to my critique as a whole. My analysis there [and earlier ones (e.g., Gewirtz, 1956b)] has noted specifically that it was unnecessarily limiting to equate the functioning of a limited set of organismically relevant reinforcing stimuli with a contemporary conditioning approach (that provides a broader basis for the "secondary drive theory"). This equation is particularly regrettable in a context where a functional learning approach (such as the one I outlined in 1961 and detail here) remains entirely open with respect to the identities of the behaviors and the cue and reinforcing stimuli (the latter including, but not limited to, organismically relevant stimuli) involved in the acquisition and maintenance of the S-R complexes connoting attachment at different points in early human development. My analysis stresses—as Bowlby also does—the reciprocal interaction between infant and mother-figure.) However, Bowlby has not yet commented directly on these questions of his theoretical analysis that I raised in my 1961 critique and subsequently (Gewirtz, 1969b). He has not dealt directly with the issue in his most recent statement (Bowlby, 1969).

features of what others have termed "dependence" on shared stimuli from a class of persons (e.g., Gewirtz, 1969b).

A Distinction between Attachment and Dependence with Some Implications

I have noted that the concepts of attachment and dependence have often been used in variable, inexplicit, and idiosyncratic ways. Their definitions have sometimes overlapped, been complementary, or been mutually exclusive. Thus, an attempt to delineate their meanings (at least grossly) has seemed warranted. The distinction between attachment and dependence that I develop further in this chapter is made in terms of selected aspects of the instrumental-conditioning paradigm my functional learning approach emphasizes. In this and in a subsequent section, I consider some implications of this heuristic distinction for organizing the social-relations phenomena implied by the two terms. At the very least, this tack could stimulate advances in theory and research under the attachment and dependence headings.

AN ATTACHMENT-DEPENDENCE DISTINCTION

In a functional learning frame, it has seemed reasonable to conceive of dependence and attachment as abstractions for sets of relations among variables in which there is (mostly) positive stimulus control over a wide variety of an individual's orienting, approach, and other responses made to or in connection with a recipient. These responses are under the control of discriminative (cue) and reinforcing stimuli either from any one of a *class* of persons—dependence— or from a *particular* person—attachment (Gewirtz, 1961b, 1969a, 1969b). Specifically, in dependence, an individual's behavior systems come to be controlled by cue and reinforcing stimuli which stem from any member of a *class* of persons who share certain discriminative stimulus characteristics (e.g., as those involved in gender, race, age, or caretaking routine) and who also can provide the same stimuli for a child's behaviors. In contrast, in attachment, the efficacy of cue and reinforcing stimuli in controlling an individual's behavior systems comes to rely upon the unique physical and/or behavioral characteristics of a *particular* "object-person" (e.g., his facial features, tactile characteristics). In terms of this distinction, both dependence and attachment are assumed to be acquired and maintained as orthogonal systems. The behaviors involved in each case can be termed focused with regard to object—dependence on a specific class of persons, and attachment on one person.[3]

---

[3] The behaviors denoting dependence are conceived to be focused on stimuli from any one of a class of object-persons. I regret having termed them "*non*focused" in an earlier analysis (Gewirtz, 1969b), for that label implies, incorrectly, that the behaviors involved are *not* focused on stimuli from a class of persons.

Patterns of differential control over sets of child behaviors by stimuli involving unique features of a particular individual must not be confused with dependence under the proposed distinction. For, in dependence, the stimuli that acquire positive control over certain approach behaviors of the child may be provided by any member of a discriminable class of persons, and are conceived to be independent of the unique features of the particular class members. As a corollary to this conception, dependence focused on stimuli from (any member of) a class of persons is *not* the generalization of a focused attachment. (The reasoning involved is detailed later in this section.)

In a subsequent section, I shall detail some assumptions about the differential development of S-R patterns connoting attachment and dependence, particularly as to the stimuli, behaviors, and contingencies involved. Even so, because a few illustrations of how I think the proposed distinction bears on the acquisition of the response systems involved can be helpful at this juncture, I sketch these in briefly.

In the frame outlined, it is conceivable that a child could acquire several dependence patterns, involving mostly different sets of interactive responses, with each such set under the control of stimuli provided by different categories of persons. In attachment, however, certain of his behaviors could come under the positive control of stimuli provided by the *unique* characteristics of one person. And other of his behaviors (and even some of the same behaviors) could come to be controlled by *different* stimuli involving the unique characteristics of another person. Hence, under this conception a child could acquire (primary) attachments to more than one person. [These persons collectively would not represent a class of stimulus sources (object-persons), as is conceived for dependence. However, where identical behaviors of the child are controlled by stimuli from two or more attachment objects, there is potentially the basis for establishing a class of object-persons as in dependence.] Finally, an individual could acquire these attachment patterns concurrently or at different life points. On these last bases, this conception of attachment diverges from the traditional one which appears to hold that, early in life, a child will ordinarily acquire a pervasive, primary attachment to one person (typically his mother).

This distinction between the different foci of socio-emotional dependence and attachment points up the differences between the two sets of phenomena and their antecedents. However, it also implies some similarities. And, even though I assume that the processes underlying the acquisition of attachment and dependence behavior patterns involve the very same principles, I conceive that the two systems can be independent. Further, I assume that these independent processes may be acquired and manifested either concurrently or sequentially. Consider an example of concurrently acquired attachment and dependence patterns. A child may spend part of his day in each of two different environments, such as the family home and a day-care center. He may acquire an attachment pattern that is focused on the single mother-figure—the primary person who interacts with and cares for him at home. At the same time, and quite independently, he may acquire a dependence pattern that is focused upon the class of persons who care for and interact with him at the day-care center.

Thus, the context in which the behavior systems summarized by these concepts will be acquired and exhibited is pertinent to the distinction between attachment and dependence that is proposed here. When an infant is in the care of a single, ever-present caretaker (as is often the case in an intact urban middle-class family that has only one child), it is plausible that his initial social behavior systems will connote an attachment pattern rather than a dependence pattern. For in this case there is conceived to be a single, prepotent, other person who mediates many of the environmental stimuli impinging upon the infant, including those that function as reinforcers for his behaviors vis-à-vis this individual. Consequently, the behaviors and appearance of this individual should readily acquire distinctive cue value for the infant's behaviors. Conversely, when an infant is cared for by a number of caretakers (as is often the case in institutional environments), his behaviors toward them are likely to reflect a dependence pattern insofar as they are controlled by stimuli from that class of persons.[4] Thus, the pattern initially acquired is conceived to depend on conditions in the caretaking environment, including the discriminability of the unique cues provided by the single caregiver on the one hand, or of the common cues from the group of caregivers on the other.

THE ATTACHMENT-DEPENDENCE DISTINCTION AND STIMULUS GENERALIZATION

It is recalled that I assumed the discriminative (cue) and/or reinforcing stimuli involved in the conditioning of a dependence pattern are those provided not uniquely by a single person (as in attachment) but by members of a class of persons who share certain stimulus characteristics. The provision of common stimuli by any member of this object class is thus assumed to be equally effective for the infant. In contrast, for the attachment case I assumed that the efficacy of stimuli is a function of their being provided uniquely by a single person. Thus, I have conceived that: (a) the difference between the two distinct behavior systems can be expressed in terms of what is learned, i.e., in the stimuli controlling the responses and provided by the persons involved; and (b) the acquisition and functioning of these two patterns are independent but governed by the very same principles.

---

[4] In this last connection, it has been shown that, in family settings, the greater the number of persons who routinely interact with a child (within or without caretaking), the greater the number of his "attachment objects" at 18 months [the language is that of Schaffer and Emerson (1964, p. 58)]. I noted earlier that, as the attachment term is used in this example, it converges on a conception of dependence. Therefore, this finding is compatible with my notion of the acquisition of dependence in such places as institutions, and can further illustrate the overlap if not also the ambiguity of current attachment and dependence usage.

Nevertheless, there are contexts in which dependence behaviors to common stimuli from a class of persons may not seem to be the result of an acquisition process that is orthogonal to that of attachment, but rather simply to be the *generalization* of attachment behaviors that are controlled by (focused on) the unique stimuli from a particular person, *to* similar yet different stimuli from another person or persons. In terms of what is understood of the process of stimulus generalization, the distinction between what is learned in the two systems is the key for my conception that dependence is *not* the generalization of an attachment.

Let me begin by taking up the most direct implication of the concept of stimulus generalization. Consider a child who has acquired an attachment pattern with reference to stimuli from one object-person, and who is then shifted to a situation containing only unfamiliar (potential object-) persons. The events provided by the strangers in the new setting will vary from the stimuli offered by the attachment object-person. In such cases, stimulus generalization may occur initially in the new situation: discriminated responses, acquired, cued, and maintained by stimuli in the earlier environment, may be displayed (i.e., "generalized") to stimuli from the person or persons present in the new setting. That is, the child may not, as it were, "discriminate" between stimuli ("S^Ds") provided by the attachment-object and those provided by the new person(s). (The latter events would not have an acquired discriminative function for the child's responses, even though he may earlier have been exposed to some of them.) As the earlier-conditioned responses would not be emitted in the presence of their controlling cue stimuli ("attachment S^Ds") in the new setting, nor reinforced there when they occur, their rate will decrease rapidly and soon drop out altogether. Therefore, the stimulus-generalization effect will ordinarily be fleeting.

However, stimulus generalization can provide the initial basis for entirely *new,* even *rapid* learning, directly following a major environmental shift for a child. Thus, when the response patterns that in the earlier setting connoted attachment are initially generalized, and then conditioned, to stimuli provided by one person in the newly entered situation, the newly conditioned outcome there may resemble the simple maintenance of attachment behaviors via stimulus generalization. To those for whom the newly acquired object-person implies an expansion via generalization of the object class (to include two persons), this outcome might connote not a new attachment pattern but only the transformation of (an) attachment into dependence. Further, when the initial generalization and rapid learning in the novel setting involves a class of persons, the outcome might suggest, to some, only that dependence behaviors were being maintained there via the generalization of attachment behaviors. Nevertheless, in each case the resemblance of the outcome to the maintenance of attachment behaviors via stimulus generalization would only be superficial. This is because, when responses that denote stimulus generalization are initially displayed to stimuli in a novel situation, new learning can result if those responses are reinforced there. Those responses will come under the control of *new* cues. In this way, a new set of cued responses (S^D-Rs) can be acquired, often rapidly, in connection with the distinctive stimuli provided by the person or persons available in the new setting.

In summary, the construct of stimulus generalization can account for (i.e., support) the initial occurrences of earlier-conditioned behaviors connoting dependence or attachment only for a brief initial period in a new situation. But during that brief time, responses generalized on that basis can provide the frame for, and hence facilitate, new learning: when reinforced in the novel situation, control over these responses can be acquired by the cue stimuli provided there. These cues can be provided uniquely by a person who is initially a stranger (connoting a new attachment pattern) or by the common stimuli from a group of persons, initially strangers (connoting a new dependence pattern).

SITUATIONAL DETERMINANTS AND TRANSFORMATIONS

Another consideration that bears on the proposed distinction is that current situational and ecological factors which define behavior and reinforcement possibilities are often likely to determine the limits within which behavior patterns are acquired and exhibited. I explore the implications of these factors for my distinction, assuming that the child's reinforcement history is held constant. Specifically, situational factors could determine whether a child will display those cued behaviors that connote attachment or those that connote dependence. I shall try to make my point here with some examples.

In a nursery school or day-care setting, several adult teachers or caregivers may be available to the child simultaneously and may share the responsibility for him. Thus, despite apparent differences in their appearance and behavior, these adults are conceived to have common features that cue and reinforce the child's behaviors and that comprise their part of the interaction dyad with him. In this frame, if a "desired" stimulus is not provided by one adult contingent on the child's initiation in such situations, the child could often make his initiation to another adult. Hence, several equally effective potential sources of stimuli may be available to maintain his behaviors. And regardless of whether or not a child exhibits an attachment pattern to his mother-figure in his home, when he enters a day-care or nursery school setting in which there are several adults (who share the stimulus characteristics involved in caretaking or in other reinforcing routines), his behaviors there will very likely be directed to common features of the adults as a *class*. In that sense, his initiations will connote dependence. (Similarly, in a nursery school in which there are several children and but one teacher, it is conceivable that many of the teacher's behaviors will be under the stimulus control of, and directed to, the children as a class, and thus could be said to reflect the teacher's dependence on them.)

Conversely, an individual may be placed in a *total* environment with only *one* other person who was not previously an attachment-object for him. This could be the case when individuals are isolated together (e.g., marooned on a desert island, or when a child is alone for an extended period with a babysitter). As each individual will then be the *only* source of social stimuli for the other, their appearance and behavior characteristics would have unique stimulus value for the other's behaviors. Therefore, the functional relations describing their behavior systems to one another could connote attachment. [Moreover, one would expect interference with response sequences to the other person that initially connoted dependence—"frustration"—to be followed frequently by intense emotional responses, when there is no other person available either to dispense the desired stimulus or to remove the interference. These responses could be the same as, or sometimes even could be more intense than, those that follow the frustration of initiations to an attachment-object in "nonmarooned" situations (as will be discussed).]

Before moving on to several more general implications of the attachment-dependence distinction, I shall digress briefly to outline a conditioning approach to the development of the behavior systems that connote attachment and dependence. At the same time, I shall also list some empirical questions that are involved.

Some Assumptions about the Development of Behavior Patterns Connoting Attachment or Dependence

THE "SECONDARY DRIVE" THEORY

Through roughly the first half of this century, the theory of "acquired" or "secondary drive" was generally held to explain the acquisition of social motivation and object relations, including dependence and attachment (particularly the child's bond to his mother). The central feature of this theory was that conditioned cue and reinforcing stimuli (provided by caretaker appearance and behavior characteristics) acquire and maintain their value by association with a limited set of apparently unconditioned reinforcing stimuli (in particular, food, water, and the removal of noxious stimuli) conventionally thought to reduce "physiological needs." The behaviors controlled by the conditioned stimuli received little emphasis under this conception. By implication, these could be orienting, approach, and interactive behaviors of almost any type (including those connoting attachment or dependence). This appealingly simple secondary drive conception was at the core both of Freud's theory of cathexis and object formation (e.g., Freud, 1938; Fenichel, 1945; A. Freud, 1954) and of the earlier conditioning approaches to acquired motivation (e.g., Miller & Dollard, 1941; Mowrer & Kluckhohn, 1944; Dollard & Miller, 1950; Sears, 1951, 1963).

In the past two decades, the adequacy of the "secondary drive theory" has been questioned on at least three grounds:

1. The possibly important role of species-specific and other seemingly unconditioned S-R patterns in the organization, at successive developmental

points, of the cued-behavior systems connoting dependence and attachment [based on (a) ethological investigations of unconditioned and species-specific behavior patterns and (b) conditioning studies of response topography].

2. Findings that the seemingly unconditioned reinforcers able to control behaviors of the developing infant appear to represent a much wider range than those, like food and water, that tradition has labeled organismically relevant (based on conditioning and performance research).

3. A realization that the term "drive", which is at the core of this formulation, has neither provided distinct explanatory leverage upon the functional relationships involved nor helped to engineer changes in the child's behavior or in the environment. Instead, "drive" appears to be a gratuitous term within this theoretical framework, as the behaviors once assumed to be determined by an infant's "secondary drive" can be accounted for entirely in terms of conditioned discriminative and/or reinforcing stimulus control.

The three considerations listed here have provided the bases for attempts to account for the acquisition and maintenance of the behavior classes connoting attachment and dependence in functional terms.

SOME ASSUMPTIONS ABOUT LEARNING PROCESSES IN THE CHILD

The emphasis of a learning approach is on the diverse ways in which recurring conditions of the environment can have a systematic impact on the behaviors of an organism. In this frame, progress toward understanding dependence and attachment phenomena would seem to require the close examination and clear specification of the empirical relationships among environmental events and behaviors encompassed by these abstract terms. Under the conditioning model outlined, this requires discovering, in their developmental sequence contexts, which (physical and/or behavioral) aspects of object persons can (a) be discriminative for a variety of the child's approach, smile, and other behaviors, and (b) reinforce and subsequently maintain those child behaviors. It will also be most useful to discover which contextual factors determine the efficacy of those stimuli for the child's behaviors.

From this viewpoint, it is important to determine the sequential and timing relationships of stimuli from object-persons to the child's responses. Some of these patterns could constitute opportunities for the behaviors to be conditioned according to the Pavlovian, the operant, or some other paradigm. It is also important to identify the conditions under which the removal (e.g., through temporary or long-term separation) of the particular supporting stimuli for the child's behavior systems ordinarily provided by an object-person might lead to an "ardent" search for the attachment-object, to "aimlessness," to disorganization, "sadness," "crying," and to "bitter distress"; and the conditions under which reunion results in "ultimate joy" (to paraphrase Sears, this volume).

In this overall frame, a conditioning approach necessarily remains open to, and where relevant takes account of, issues that have been raised in developmental and ethological theories about biogenic makeup, structural changes, genetic determinants, and the like. Thus, it recognizes that, in early life, a child's responses will differ in their initial probabilities of occurrence. Some of his responses will be prepotent, while diverse others will enter his behavioral repertoire at different sequential points. Further, at various points in the child's (physical and social) development, changes will occur in the topography of repertoire responses based on increased capacity of his effector systems and on the particular effector elements or compounds the caretaker-mother will reinforce. Based on increasing receptor capacity, changes will also occur in the discriminative and reinforcing value of stimuli, with some stimuli superseding others in terms of their efficacy for the child's behaviors. Hence, there will be developmental, sequential (although not necessarily ordered) changes in both the stimuli and responses involved in the functional relations characterizing attachment and dependence.

Under a functional learning approach, I assume that diverse classes of events (in addition to the limited number thought to relate directly to organismic survival) can come to function as evocative, discriminative, and/or reinforcing stimuli for the acquisition and maintenance of child behaviors. I assume that the variety and complexity of these behaviors will increase with development. Connoting either attachment or dependence (or both), these behaviors include visual-facial orienting, fixating, and tracking, eye-contacting, approaching, touching and clinging, smiling, and vocalizing. The variety of environmental events that may function as unconditioned stimuli in early life, or that may come to acquire conditioned value, include: *proximal* stimuli from sources near the child, such as are provided through the infant's being touched, held, caressed, and raised in the air; and *distal* stimuli from sources more remote from the child, such as visual events provided by the sight of people (for example, their size, hair color, facial features, and characteristic behaviors like gait and successive movements in space), auditory events provided by approaches and other movements and by speech, and olfactory events. [That some stimuli for infant approach behaviors in the preceding list have seeming unconditioned ("releasing") value, and that other stimuli have seeming conditioned value, is incidental to the main assumptions of the present social-learning analysis of the acquisition of S-R patterns connoting attachment or dependence.]

Therefore, in this conceptual context I see the acquisition of the stimulus-response patterns connoting dependence or attachment as involving two intimately correlated facets of the same process. These begin when the infant is helpless and relatively immobile. The first facet is the conditioning of the physical and behavioral characteristics shared by a class of persons (dependence) or of a particular person (attachment) as discriminative and/or reinforcing stimuli for the child's behaviors. The second is the acquisition and maintenance of a variety of the child's behavior systems (the complexity of which increase with his developing capacities) on the basis of being cued and reinforced by the diverse stimuli provided by the person(s). These interdependent conditioning processes can account for the development of progressively longer and more intricate S-R interaction chains between the infant and his caretaking environment. Some stimuli and responses will occur in one or very few chains. Others will occur in many different chains and, on that basis, will acquire generalized value (Gewirtz, 1961b, 1969b; Cairns, 1966).

Straightforward stimulus-control principles can also account for many of the effects of *separation* from, and *reunion* with, the attachment object (or dependence object in those unlikely contexts in which no alternative member of the object class is available to dispense the stimuli). That is, the cessation of, or marked decrease in, behaviors denoting attachment (or dependence) following temporary or long-term separation from the attachment- (or a dependence-) object can be explained as due to the removal of the stimuli which had been supporting those behaviors. When the cue stimuli are again presented during a reunion with the attachment- (or a dependence-) object, it is expected that the attachment (or dependence) behaviors to that person will again be displayed—provided that at reunion there are present no conditions making the emission of such behaviors impossible (Gewirtz, 1961b).[5]

---

[5] This discriminative-control axiom of a conditioning analysis bears directly on the correlated issues of (a) "where has the attachment gone during separation" and (b) the requirement for a concept of "inner structure" as the basis for attachments. There are theoretical approaches for which differences in response patterns prior to, and during, separation from an attachment-object, and at subsequent reunion with that object, have constituted important evidence for attachments having an "inner structure" (e.g., Ainsworth, 1969). In such approaches, this "inner structure" is required to account for the "enduring" nature of attachments, and specifically for their surviving periods of the object's absence undiminished in strength despite a diminution in the incidence of attachment behaviors during that separation. In this discussion, I shall pass over the axiomatic notion that, in some sense, all behavior systems must have "under-the-skin" correlates. I shall emphasize, instead, the conditioned-stimulus control conception here discussed, to explain why a conditioning approach will routinely expect responses that are under close stimulus control (a) not to occur in the absence of their controlling stimuli, and (b) to reoccur when their controlling stimuli reappear. This (or other) conditioning assumptions provide bases for understanding some types of delays occasionally noted at reunion after separation before attachment behaviors are again exhibited to the reunited attachment-object: the controlling cue stimuli may not yet have been appropriately presented so as to be effective. Alternatively, emotional ("frustration," etc.) responses may be displayed at reunion (e.g., turning-away from or ignoring the object-person) which would be incompatible (until habituated) with responses connoting attachment. [Delays before attachment behaviors are exhibited following reunion, and/or emotional responses displayed then, are among the behavior patterns that have connoted "detachment" (Bowlby, 1960b).] In this heuristic frame, one can understand how the behaviors under close stimulus control that connote attachment "survive" undiminished in "strength" in the absence of the attachment-object while attachment behaviors have diminished in incidence.

RECIPROCAL LEARNING PROCESSES OF CHILDREN AND ADULTS

In the approach I have been outlining, attachment and dependence are each conceived to imply a mutual learning process (Gewirtz, 1961b). Yet, until recent years, the literature has given scant attention to the child as conditioner (socializer) of his caretaker(s), and specifically to the possibility of acquisition by adults of attachment or dependence behavior patterns vis-à-vis the child (or children). I shall therefore sketch in some features of this reciprocal learning process that I assume takes place for the object-person(s).

At the same time that the attachment or dependence behavior systems of the child are assumed to be initially acquired or subsequently maintained by the process just outlined, through a parallel process the behaviors of an object-person could come rapidly under the control of discriminative and reinforcing stimuli provided by the child's (children's) appearance and behavior. That is, the behavior systems of the caretaker-mother could reflect the acquisition of an "attachment" to (or "dependence" upon) the stimuli provided by her charge (or class of charges) in a way similar to the child's becoming "attached" to her (or showing "dependence" upon her when she is a member of a class of caretakers). Specifically, when an infant appears to exhibit differential responses to the caretaker-mother in the case of attachment (or to members of a class of persons in the case of dependence), *his* responses and appearance can come to provide salient discriminative cues and reinforcers to control an increasing range of *her* behaviors with reference to him. [Incidentally, the caretaker(s) may often interpret this differential pattern of her charge as an indication of his special relationship to, and "love" for, her.] Thus, attachment and dependence are conceived to entail a reciprocal learning process which, in this view, can encompass and serve as one explanation of many of the diverse S-R phenomena commonly termed "love."

ON TYPES OF POSITIVE STIMULUS CONTROL

I have assumed that a wide range of the infant's behaviors will come under the acquired control of cues from object-person(s) (e.g., a mother) who are present in his vicinity. I also assume that far fewer of his behaviors will come under the control of (*a*) cues implying the imminent departure (and absence) of object-persons *or* (*b*) cues from the conditions of their absence. As a consequence, I would expect most of the infant's behaviors that connote attachment or dependence to be cued more readily and more frequently in the actual physical presence of object-persons rather than either at their departure or in their absence. Nevertheless, control over an infant's behaviors by the latter two sets of cues can also indicate positive stimulus control in the conditioning model I emphasize in this chapter, and hence will also connote attachment or dependence.

Let me illustrate the cases of positive stimulus control when object-persons are about to depart or are absent. An infant's "protests" [or other responses that can imply "distress" (e.g., see Ainsworth & Wittig, 1969)] can become conditioned to cues from his mother's preparations for departures (and the short- or long-term separations that would ensue), when the mother would have responded frequently and rapidly to those responses of the infant. (Such situations, and the representativeness of the criterion indices they can provide, will be discussed extensively in the next chapter.) Thus, also, an infant's ("plaintive") responses can become conditioned to cues from the object-person's absence, when those responses would frequently have effected her return to his vicinity. In such cases, the infant's reinforced responses will typically have had to bridge physical and/or distance barriers to affect the absent object-person. Therefore, his responses that come to be cued by that person's absence will often be lengthy in duration and/or intense. (This is not to say that positive stimulus control bases are necessarily the only ones underlying the infant's responding in the object-person's absence.) In connection with the infant's behavior after separation from his mother, we recall that some theorists (e.g., Bowlby, 1969) have conceived that an infant's "attachment" may be "activated" when his mother moves away from him or disappears from his view.

A DISTINCTION BETWEEN INSTRUMENTAL AND SOCIO-EMOTIONAL DEPENDENCE

At this point, I examine in passing the distinction between "socio-emotional" dependence (which I have been using synonymously with the term "dependence" in this chapter) and "instrumental" or "task-oriented" dependence (e.g., see Sears et al., 1953, 1957; Heathers, 1955a; Gewirtz, 1956b, 1961b; Kagan & Moss, 1962; Bandura & Walters, 1963). This distinction emphasizes behavior capacity and selected reinforcing consequences in the instrumental case and only reinforcing consequences (though usually in a wider range) in the socio-emotional case. The distinction comprises a focus upon the acquisitions of dependence and attachment behavior patterns which differs somewhat from that used earlier in this section, and may be relevant more to (learning) conceptions of dependence than of attachment. However, a consideration of this dependence distinction may provide some additional leverage upon theory pertaining to the acquisitions of attachment and dependence. In particular, it could supply an historical context for the ways in which the acquisition of one or both these behavior systems have been conceived by learning approaches.

The essence of the concept of instrumental dependence is that some (helping) response of another person is required to provide the individual child with a stimulus (such as food or the removal of noxious stimulation). Learning conceptions have assumed that this stimulus provision can reinforce the requester's response on which it is contingent, independent of the characteristics of either the helper's response (e.g., her attention) or appearance (e.g., her smile). The instrumental-dependence frame would make it possible for the appearance and behavior aspects of a single helper or multiple helpers to acquire cue and reinforcing value for a child's behaviors. It therefore constitutes another way of looking at the context for the acquisition of attachment or dependence, as detailed earlier in the present section.[6]

I have noted that the distinction between socio-emotional and instrumental dependence is made by identifying the maintaining (reinforcing) stimulus. For instance, the distinction depends on whether it is: (*a*) an object from a high shelf, physically impossible for the child to reach, which he has asked his teacher to get for him and which he clearly requires for a structured ongoing activity (instrumental dependence); or (*b*) the attention he receives from his teacher as she gets an object that, at other times, he has been known to reach himself (socio emotional dependence). The neglect of this distinction between instrumental dependence and socio-emotional dependence has seemed to accompany the assumption that dependence and attachment are synonymous in early life, or the assumption that dependence is (and attachment is not) associated with immaturity or some other less-than-admirable condition (e.g., Bowlby, 1969). It is likely that behaviors directly connoting instrumental dependence are less prevalent at later developmental points when the child is better able to manipulate and control his physical environment, but this need not be the case for behaviors connoting socio-emotional dependence (or attachment). However, the latter behaviors might also be influenced by changes in the behavioral capacities of the child and, concurrently, in the rules used by environmental agencies for reinforcement of the child's behaviors (based on the increasing "expectations" of those agencies). The functional distinction between attachment

[6] Before leaving this topic, I emphasize once again that the labels one applies to phenomena, and the phenomena emphasized, depend entirely on one's theoretical model. Thus, Beller (1955) has grouped what I have termed "instrumental dependence" and "socio-emotional dependence" together under the term "dependency"; and he has grouped taking initiative, overcoming obstacles, persistence, just wanting to do something and wanting to do it by oneself under the orthogonal term "independence". Thus, also some behaviors not included in my analysis above have sometimes been termed "instrumental independence" ("instrumental self-reliance"); and other behaviors that include self-assertion and reinforcement provided by task mastery have been termed "emotional independence" or "emotional self-reliance" (Heathers, 1955a). Further, under theoretical models with still other emphases, reinforcing stimulus attributes such as "approval" for meeting achievement standards might be termed "socio-emotional independence" rather than dependence. Finally, one could conceive of theoretical models under which the acquisition of certain behavior patterns maintained by attention, or by attention and approval, are considered to be not dependence, but rather the first phases in the acquisition by the infant of "socio-emotional independence" or instrumental or interpersonal "competence." As a consideration of such conceptual options is peripheral to my present purpose, I mention them here only in passing to provide a context for my points in this chapter and the next about concept label usage.

and dependence that I outline in this chapter may help to delineate the uses of these concepts, and the role that development plays in them.

ON ASSESSING ATTACHMENT OR DEPENDENCE

The next chapter will deal with the selection and use of attachment and dependence indicators. However, some comments on the issues involved can be useful in the context of the discussion here.

There are many ways in which the process and outcomes of attachment or dependence that have been described might be grouped, depending upon the purposes of particular analyses. For those analyses in which an overall summary statement would be desired by a researcher, the "strength" or pervasiveness of a dependence or attachment behavior pattern could be conceived to be a positive function of some or all of the following approach behavior parameters: (a) the range and/or number of behavior systems of the child under the stimulus control of a class of persons or of a particular person; (b) that range and/or number relative to the range/number of behaviors under the stimulus control of others; (c) the degree of positive control by a person or class of persons over each behavior system; and (d) the number of stimulus settings in which the control process operates. For different conceptual purposes, one might emphasize only particular behavior systems, organized patterns of behavior, or stimulus control conditions. Further, one might employ only selected subsets of these approach behaviors to define levels or subvarieties of dependence or attachment [for instance, "secure-insecure" or "mature-immature," as Ainsworth (1963, 1967) has done]. However, for the didactic purposes of the social-learning analysis I make in this chapter, such distinctions are premature. (Some issues relevant to such grouping, as well as to the use of indices based on disorganization- and emotional-behaviors, are considered in the next chapter.)

One last point about assessment should be mentioned. Analyses whose purposes have been served by gross summary variables have necessarily ignored the moment-to-moment impact on, and control of, behaviors by both preceding and consequent stimuli. These stimuli have mostly been provided by the behaviors of caretaker-parents. The sequential meshing and interweaving of such stimuli with child behaviors comprises the essence of the interaction process. Hence, as I note in the next chapter, summary variables will be inappropriate for many analyses of such interchanges.

Some General Implications of the Proposed Attachment-Dependence Distinction

The distinction I have drawn is between the control over a child's behaviors by stimuli from any one of a class of persons (connoting dependence) and the control over his behaviors by stimuli from a particular individual (connoting attachment). That distinction, made under a single theoretical model, has some general implications for the conceptualization of the phenomena subsumed under those terms, in addition to those I have enumerated earlier. In particular, in the sections that follow I shall apply some corollaries of my distinction to the issue of whether attachment and dependence phenomena might best be conceived as involving a single process or two different processes.

IS A QUALITATIVE DISTINCTION BETWEEN ATTACHMENT AND DEPENDENCE WARRANTED?

Several implications of the proposed distinction may, under a single theoretical model, help to account for some of the features that seemingly differentiate dependence and attachment. Those features have led several theorists (including Ainsworth and Sears in this volume) in varying ways to conclude that dependence and attachment phenomena are qualitatively different and operate by entirely different principles. One basis for this conclusion that attachment and dependence may involve different processes pertains to features of the acquisition of the behaviors connoting attachment and dependence. Specifically, compared to dependence, attachment behavior systems can often appear to enter a child's repertory with dramatic *speed* in early life. In addition, attachment behavior systems can appear more *pervasive* than dependence systems. Finally, the child's seemingly very different reaction patterns to conditions that *interfere* with attachment and dependence behavior patterns ("frustration") also appear to be a factor. That is, the blocking of attachment behaviors often seems to lead to more intense reactions. Considerations such as these have led the theorists mentioned to seek an explanation of the attachment process by principles other than those that pertain exclusively to learning. I shall in the sections that follow discuss several of these considerations in terms of the heuristic distinction between attachment and dependence that I develop in this chapter.

The seemingly more rapid acquisition of attachment than dependence behavior systems. The often dramatic sudden appearance of cued behaviors connoting attachment may simply be the result of environmental conditions conducive to a child's behaviors becoming rapidly focused under the mostly positive control of stimuli provided by a single object-person. For instance, these conditions might include the consistent presence of a single, intensely interacting caretaker. Specifically, in contexts that facilitate attachment behavior patterns in connection with a single object-person, the provision of discriminative cues and the reinforcement contingencies involved may conceivably be more discriminable, more frequent, and/or more consistent than those provided in contexts that generate dependence patterns upon the stimuli shared by a class of object-persons. In addition, in such situations conducive to the rapid acquisition of attachment behavior patterns, it is conceivable that response definitions for reinforcement may be more consistent and that response consequences constituting reinforcement may be provided more rapidly. Based on such assumptions as these, about possible differences in stimulus provision and response definition between environments, the functional relations that connote attachment could often appear to be acquired rapidly, even suddenly, and early in life.[7] On reciprocal bases, the functional relations involving stimuli from a class of persons that connote dependence could appear to be acquired relatively less rapidly and perhaps also later in life.

In this frame, such social response systems as "active recognition" of, and differential preference for, the caretaker-mother, "active differentiation of strangers," and "stranger anxiety" (discussed in the next chapter as possible indices of attachment or dependence) may well be more likely to occur under conditions that lead to single-object rather than to object-class formation, and at an earlier age. These social-response patterns are among those that would connote an attachment to some theorists and, to others, different "levels of object relationship" (e.g., see Yarrow, 1967). To still other theorists, some of these responses may suggest an "intensity" of attachment or less "transient" and more "mature" attachments (e.g., see Ainsworth, this volume). More definitive research on the issues raised here could help to dispel some of the confusion that seems to have resulted from the different and limited age ranges studied for each of the two concepts, and to some extent also from unrecognized ecological facilitators or constraints that may have operated in some investigations.

Differential reaction patterns to interference with attachment and dependence behavior systems. Interference with behavior sequences connoting attachment or dependence, and the rather different reaction patterns that could result, apparently constitute another basis for the contention that two qualitatively different processes may be involved. Such interference conditions may involve actual physical blocks or simply the removal or unavailability of the cue stimuli upon which the sequences of attachment or dependence behaviors depend. (They have sometimes been termed "frustration," to suggest an "emotional state" of the organism.) Interference conditions like these have often seemed to evoke different reaction patterns depending upon whether the interfered-with behavior sequences were directed to a single object-person (in attachment) or to a member of a class of object-persons (in dependence). Thus, the implied assumption has been that interference with response sequences connoting dependence may lead to routine adaptive responses of low or moderate intensity, but that interference with those behavior chains that are uniquely oriented to one object-person (as through *separation* from that individual) may

---

[7] In some recent analyses of observational-learning patterns that have seemed present in very young organisms, I have suggested how such phenomena could be conceived to be (*a*) derivatives of experience under conventional learning paradigms and (*b*) rapid learning early in life. A few of the salient learning assumptions of those analyses are considered here. More extensive treatments of such factors can be found in two recent papers (Gewirtz, 1971a, 1971b).

often evoke an extremely persevering, trial-and-error response pattern. When unsuccessful, the latter pattern may continue maladaptively with great ("emotional") intensity ("affect"). [See Yarrow (1964) for a useful survey of the effects on child behavior of various types of separations from parents.]

The latter outcome of interference with *attachment* behavior sequences can often suggest to an onlooker that what is at issue for the child is a response pattern involving a most important "goal." Further, prolonged interference-frustration conditions for the child (as during a lengthy separation from, or rejection by, an object-person) may result in emotional patterns of high amplitude involving such responses as intense crying, rage, or undirected violence. (An ultimate result of such prolonged conditions may even be behavior patterns characterized by an unresponsiveness to environmental events connoting "despair" and/or "apathy.") Often termed "emotional" or "affect-full," such patterns of intense responding can also be the initial reaction of some children to almost any interference with attachment behavior sequences. Similarly, these behavior patterns may be initial or prolonged reactions of adults to frustration conditions resulting from separation, divorce, or death. In these cases, also, the ultimate result may be prolonged despair or apathy. Such response patterns as these will often be incompatible with behaviors that could be directed to possible attachment substitutes [and hence, also, with the possibility of acquiring new attachment patterns (Gewirtz, 1961b)].

Separation constitutes a sudden, extreme *shift* in the conditions of stimulus control, from a context in which the child's behaviors have been under close control to a context in which they are not. On this basis, the child's initial response pattern in the new situation may often be characterized as weakened or deteriorated. His responses there may even have ceased to occur entirely (leading to labels like "apathy"). In particular, the controlling stimuli from the object-person will no longer be available at all (much less in their sequential contexts). Hence, the behaviors (and behavior sequences) exhibited by the child in the new context (insofar as they are even emitted at all) may be less complex, and more primitive (in the sense that behavior sequences may not occur in their entirety) than those that were exhibited under the close control of stimuli in the previous context.

In contrast, the short- or long-term blocking of *dependence* responses (and sequences) has been assumed to be far less likely to lead to the perseveration of seemingly intense emotional responses (and ultimately deep "despair") often reported to result from interference with attachment responses (and sequences). Under the conceptual distinction I have been emphasizing, dependence behaviors may be oriented to any member of the object class. Therefore, these more benign outcomes may be conceived as often resulting simply from the fact that most situations provide alternative members of that class to whom the individual whose behaviors are blocked can turn, and from whom the relevant cue and reinforcing stimuli will be equally appropriate. Even so, in those contexts in which *no* member of the dependence-object class is available to dispense the relevant stimuli, the effect of blocking dependence initiations could be similar to that of blocking attachment initiations to a single object-person. As such, that interference should result in response outcomes of similar (*a*) intensity and/or (*b*) characteristics of disorganization.

Considerations about the differential development of attachment and dependence. Another basis for the conclusion that attachment and dependence are qualitatively different may be provided by considerations about their differential development. The proposed distinction between attachment and dependence may be theoretically more meaningful when applied at some developmental points than at others, or in some ecological contexts than in others. For instance, the distinction may be more applicable in later infancy after the child has been exposed to a variety of environmental conditions that provide the basis for his acquiring both dependence and attachment behavior patterns, than in earlier infancy when only an initial behavior system may be acquired within a single environmental condition. Indeed, part of the confusion regarding the distinction between attachment and dependence and such questions as whether or not attachment is a precursor of dependence, may have resulted from the fact that each of the two systems has generally been studied in subjects of different ages, attachment in infants and dependence in older children of nursery-school age. But this fact does not mean that dependence cannot be acquired until nursery-school age or that the acquisition of an attachment is limited to early infancy. I have already noted that, even in early infancy, the pattern of stimulus control over an infant's behaviors could connote dependence rather than attachment. This would be so if that infant were in an institutional or family setting, where there are many people who share caretaking responsibilities for him and interact with him. I have also suggested earlier that there are conceivable circumstances under which the infant may acquire orthogonal attachment patterns to more than one individual.

A summary of my case pertaining to the need for a qualitative distinction between attachment and dependence. Let me now restate the main points made so far in this and earlier sections, which follow from the functional distinction I have drawn between attachment and dependence. Holding reinforcement history constant, I have noted that whether a behavior pattern connoting attachment or one connoting dependence is exhibited by an individual can often depend entirely on situational constraints. Further, I have used the instrumental conditioning paradigm to suggest some acquisition and performance bases of those cued behavior patterns. When comparing attachment to dependence behavior systems, these bases could account for: (*a*) the dramatic suddenness with which attachment behavior systems often seem to enter the child's repertory; (*b*) their apparent pervasiveness; (*c*) the seeming intensity with which attachment behaviors are displayed; and (*d*) the intense emotional reactions ("passion," "affect") and/or disorganization that seem often to follow interference with attachment behavior sequences. These features seem to be accounted for reasonably well by the conditioning model I have emphasized and by its implications. However, these same features have led some theorists, who use different theoretical models, to conclude that the phenomena of attachment and dependence are qualitatively different, reflecting separate processes and thus derived from different principles.

For instance, Ainsworth (this volume) has assumed that strong positive "affect," or "love," is involved in attachment but not in dependence, and that attachment and dependence operate according to qualitatively different principles. Such phenomena also seem to have provided the basis for Sears' (this volume) similar conclusion that "passion" (passionate "love," "ardor") is involved in attachment and not in dependence. Sears has assumed further that dependence behavior patterns are learned according to routine conditioning principles (operating, for instance, through reinforcers from the caretaker), but that attachment patterns may involve a "genetically determined propensity" for their development (although the necessary conditions for establishing the primary attachment are unknown). (It is not critical for my case here that neither Ainsworth nor Sears has as yet specified denotative operations for the concepts "passion," "love," or "affect.")

My analysis has suggested that the implications of a functional distinction between the concepts under the paradigm of instrumental conditioning can provide a basis for explaining the phenomena parsimoniously. Therefore, under such a conditioning model there appears to be no need to postulate separate paradigms to account for the assumed differences in performance characteristics. That is, the acquisition, maintenance, and extinction of both attachment and dependence behavior systems can be ordered efficiently by common principles of acquired stimulus control over behavior, and of performance, operating upon the child's biogenic makeup.

Identification and *imitation* are terms from another conceptual area where a somewhat similar line of reasoning has been used to support the contention of a qualitative distinction between them. It can be instructive to examine the considerations raised in connection with the issue in that area, for they could bear on the qualitative distinction between attachment and dependence that has been discussed here. Bronfenbrenner (1960) has assumed that the identification concept could not be reduced to a notion like imitation, on the basis that such a reduction might lose Freud's view of identification as a "sweeping and powerful phenomenon" that involved the child's taking on a total pattern of the parent-model's behavior with an emotional intensity that implied a powerful "motive in the child to become like the parent [p. 27]." Here, identification, but not imitation, is said to involve emotional intensity (similar to the passion that is said to be involved in attachment but not in dependence). I prepared an analysis of identification-imitation parallel to the one of attachment-dependence discussed in this chapter (Gewirtz, 1969b; Gewirtz & Stingle, 1968). In those papers, I emphasized observable phenomena, holding constant what appeared to be irrelevant issues that have been involved with the broadly specified identification concept, but not with the more narrowly delineated imitation concept that has been oriented to matched behaviors. (These irrelevant matters included the involvement of motivation, the unconsciousness of the phenomena, and their acquisition through unconventional learning modes.)

In this framework, I developed the case that the phenomena of identification could be reduced parsimoniously to the concept of conditional responding, with imitation a functional matching-response class comprised of diverse responses matched to a demonstrator-model's behaviors. I noted also that the acquisition and the maintenance of that matching-response class were readily explained in terms of simple instrumental-conditioning principles. [This analysis has recently been updated (Gewirtz, 1971a).] On this basis, both identification and imitation phenomena would be explicable in terms of the very same set of assumptions, with neither concept requiring the (gratuitous) postulate of an underlying "motivational state." This thesis is not identical to the heuristic case I have advanced in this chapter. However, it parallels my case here insofar as (a) the functional S-R relations connoting attachment and dependence can both be ordered by the same basic conditioning principles (operating upon the biogenic makeup of the child) and (b) the utility of postulating an underlying affective state is similarly questioned.

DEFICIENCY CONDITIONS OF STIMULATION AND ATTACHMENT-DEPENDENCE

In this section, I shall consider briefly some implications of deficiency conditions of stimulation for attachment and dependence behavior patterns. These deficiency conditions are not infrequently tied conceptually to attachment or dependence. Indeed, Sears (this volume) has discussed such a relationship in his analysis. In this frame, an examination is warranted of just how such deficiency conditions could affect social behavior systems like attachment or dependence. I treat the modes of operation of deficiency conditions as qualifiers of the conditioning factors I have outlined.

Privation and deprivation, attachment and dependence. Several of the attachment- or dependence-frustration outcome patterns that have been described are like those which this writer has discussed elsewhere as resulting from *deficiency conditions of stimulation* termed *privation* and *deprivation* (Gewirtz, 1961a, 1961b, 1968a, 1968b, 1969b, 1972a). These deficiency conditions need not depend solely on the availability of potential stimuli: potential stimuli may be abundant but nonfunctional because of inappropriate contextual-setting conditions or an inept mode of provision (e.g., noncontingent rather than contingent on behavior). In this conceptual frame, I have used the term stimulus *privation* to refer to the paucity of all, or of particular classes of, functional stimuli through lengthy time spans, usually during the early phases of a child's life, the very time when such stimuli would support basic learnings. In such cases of stimulus paucity, I would expect neither behavior patterns connoting attachment nor those connoting dependence (nor, for that matter, many others) to be acquired by children.

I have applied the term stimulus *deprivation* to conditions involving gross shifts in the maintaining environment brought about by the removal, or the decreased availability, of stimuli that have had functional significance for key behavior systems of the child (for instance, those from S-R chains that characterize routine interaction patterns with object-persons and that connote attachment or dependence). As a result of downward shifts in functional stimulus availability (deprivation), there may be a severe decline in the rate of the attachment or dependence behaviors those stimuli control. Decreased functional stimulation may result from: (*a*) a reduction in the accustomed level or rate of stimulation; (*b*) a change in some relevant stimulus features effected by a change in their source; (*c*) a removal of contextual (setting) conditions that can enhance or have been enhancing the efficacy of key stimuli; or (*d*) a blocking of responses to such stimuli by direct interference.

Separation from an object-person (touched upon briefly in the preceding section) or related frustration situations (such as "rejection" by that object-person) may be considered exemplars of several of these conditions that result in downward shifts in stimulus availability. As such, those stimulus conditions and their (attachment or dependence) behavior effects can be ordered within a conditioning framework. Separation is a broad term which may be conceived in myriad ways. Its definition would depend on at least three sets of differential conditions. These are: (*a*) the routine stimulus conditions (provided by the object-person) that had been maintaining the child's (attachment or dependence) behaviors in his usual environment; (*b*) the conditions under which the departure and absence of the object-person is effected and maintained; and (*c*) the conditions prevailing in the child's environment after the separation has occurred (for instance, the stimuli present there and whether provided by some person). Thus far, there have been few attempts to break down the conditions of separation and absence into such terms [for an exception on longer-term separations, see Yarrow (1964)]. [In this discussion, I touch only in passing on the fact that an infant may himself initiate separations in situations that facilitate his exploratory behaviors (e.g., Rheingold & Eckerman, 1970).]

On the same theme, I have elsewhere explored possible conditioning bases for the acquisition of behaviors connoting substitute attachments (e.g., after separation) [in particular, see Gewirtz (1961b)]. I have also explored potential learning bases for diverse behavior outcomes connoting various attachment and dependence patterns which can result from different strategies and tactics used by environmental agencies in therapeutic settings or in deliberate attempts to create substitute relationships (Gewirtz, 1968b, 1969a, 1969b, 1972a).

On the utility of the deficiency-motivation conception for attachment and dependence. Learning concepts have evolved to order cumulatively experiential effects in time. I have elsewhere contrasted the implications of a learning analysis for the effects of privation and deprivation conditions on behavior, particularly when they operate over *lengthy* periods of time, with the homeostatic deficiency-motivation conception that apparently provides the basis for concepts like David Levy's (1937) "primary affect hunger" (Gewirtz, 1961b, 1968b, 1972a). The homeostatic deficiency conception has evolved to order, through hours (at most a very few days), an organism's periodically recurring and readily reversible (satiable) requirements for indispensible appetitive stimuli (food and water). It has implied *no* residual effects that accumulate. In this frame, the application of this conception to lingering, long-term "hungers" for such nonappetitive commodities as stimulation or affection and love was found entirely *in*adequate for: (*a*) explaining the behavioral outcomes of such childhood deficiency conditions, described by Levy (1937) as behaviors characterized by a lack of "emotional response" and by Spitz (1949) as resulting in "emotionally-starved" children; or (*b*) providing a conceptual basis by which to engineer reversals of the undesired behavior outcomes.

The predictive power of the learning analysis I offered as an alternative for ordering such phemonena derives in great part from an assumption that one must account for the circumstances under which given stimuli are made available and, in particular, for whether these stimuli are functional and enter into effective learning contingencies with the child's behaviors. In this frame, exclusive consideration of which, or of how many, stimuli are provided to a child is assumed to be inadequate. This basic assumption of the learning approach is often overlooked by proponents of a long-term deficiency conception.

At first glance, Sears' behavior-oriented treatment (in this volume) appears to depend on a deprivation conception quite similar to Levy's (1937). Insofar as this is so, his conceptual treatment may not be integrated optimally with his otherwise behavioral learning concepts. This asynchrony could constitute a difficulty in a conceptual framework where Sears has emphasized deprivation conditions and reactions to frustration as a primary basis for distinguishing between attachment and dependence.

Some Metatheoretical Assumptions Underlying the Approach of this Chapter

ASSUMPTIONS ABOUT THE USE OF THEORY

I have tried to account for many of the phenomena labeled attachment or dependence in terms of a conditioning approach and its ancillary performance concepts. At the same time, I have tried to illustrate the utility of a distinction between the terms. I recognize that the learning approach I have favored is not the only theoretical model that could serve my heuristic purpose, and that learning approaches up to now have devoted rather little energy to the theoretical enterprise required, particularly when the attachment concept has been involved. However, my model provides an efficient and plausible account of salient features of the stimulus-response systems involved, just as it has been found most useful in diverse analyses of the origins and operating modes of other complex social behavior systems, for instance, such as are involved in cases of observational, imitative learning. In this context, a review of some working assumptions underlying my approach to theory and of some metatheoretical assumptions ["protopostulates" (Kantor, 1959)] that are involved (Gewirtz, 1969a) could help fit my analysis into perspective with some of the other contributions to this volume.

Underlying the use of my theoretical model is the assumption that what have been called "central, mediating, cognitive" terms are unnecessary for ordering S-R relations collected under a conditioning approach. In a conditioning frame, routine descriptive instrumental-conditioning concepts can provide an operational basis for a complete, parsimonious explanation of phenomena that some theorists, operating in other conceptual frames, might attempt to explain in terms of presumed cognitive, intrapsychic mediating activities. The conditioning concepts I have found sufficient for my explanatory purposes include response classes, their controlling cue and reinforcing stimuli, and S-R chains acquired and maintained under intermittent, extrinsic reinforcement from some environmental agency.

Let me note that the approach outlined is open to the operation of determinants of behavior systems that are (often residually) termed maturational (i.e., not simple or obvious outcomes of experience-learning). Thus, at any point in the child's history, relevant receptor-effector capacities (one connotation of "developmental level") will surely determine the impact of stimulation on his behavior. At the same time, I have emphasized (Gewirtz, 1969a, 1969b) that chronological age is but a poor, and often misleading, index of process (i.e., of the sequential effects through time of stimulation on behavior). Hence, wherever possible, I would emphasize process variables in their sequential (hence, developmental) contexts, and I would assess directly the receptor and/or effector capacities assumed pertinent to those process variables under investigation (Gewirtz, 1969b, pp. 105-119).

Of the theoretical statements in this volume, however, my own explicit molar-behavior emphasis (in E. C. Tolman's sense) may seem to be the most discrepant with respect to assumed biological contributions to maturation. I have conceived that a theory must remain complete at its own level of analysis, although it should be sensitive to the potential relevance of data from other analytic levels. But notwithstanding my assumption that theory and research about biological determinants of behavior have their place, I have considered speculation about such factors to be orthogonal to, and thus essentially irrelevant for, molar-behavioral approaches like those of this volume. Thus, the posture I have outlined here does not depend on the fact that so little is as yet known about the biological substrate or its correlations with molar-behavior systems far simpler than those characterizing attachment and dependence. It depends rather on the self-contained requirements of an abiological molar-behavior analysis, in the context of questions about the relative efficiency of theories whose concepts cross explanatory levels, such as the molar behavioral, the biological, or the chemical (Gewirtz, 1969a). Finally, I have conceived that it can be a most inefficient tactic to implicate biological, genetic, emotional, or similar factors in an analysis unless, at the very same time, explicit directional assumptions are made on how these factors determine the behavioral outcomes that are of interest.

I shall try to illustrate this issue with the conception of "emotional state." Regardless of how they are defined, phenomena taken to reflect emotional states may be involved, perhaps differentially, in the social relationship patterns termed attachment or dependence. However, there is little apparent heuristic utility in conceiving of such states in the abstract, when no operational basis is proposed for them. A further consideration applies when emotional-state phenomena are not themselves the primary focus of study. Even if such conceptions were operationalized in approaches to predicting the patterns of social control over behavior that are at issue, their use would be justified tactically only if they could provide substantially more predictive leverage than would a straightforward molar emphasis simply on stimuli, responses, and the functional relations into which they enter. I have raised precisely this practical issue in analyses of the matching-behavior patterns that characterize observational-learning and imitation (Gewirtz, 1971a, pp. 295-297). I there considered the level of analytic detail required, and questioned the predictive utility in such analyses of phenomena taken to reflect presumed cognitive, intrapsychic acts. My question there applied not only to stimulus-response approaches, but to other theoretical approaches as well.

ASSUMPTIONS ABOUT SOME PSYCHOLOGICAL ISSUES

As with other abstract concepts, such as intelligence, certain concerns involved in the study of attachment and dependence have also had relevance independently for broader, traditional conceptual issues in molar psychology. These have included issues of theory and of research tactics or style such as: the role of stimuli (including those denoting contexts) that acquire control over responses on which criterion indices are based, and the nature of theoretical explanations of the phenomena under scrutiny; identifying the determinants of, and behaviors comprising, early attentional processes; identifying behaviors which seem to occur "naturally" in the early life of an organism, and that could be species-specific; identifying unconditioned stimuli (including "releasers") and determining their roles in conditioning at successive developmental points; identifying originally neutral events that acquire control over behaviors (e.g., via conditioning procedures); attending to systematic changes in response topography at different developmental points, including those that can be attributed to conditioning factors; detailing how S-R chains and more complex patterns develop; describing the conditions under which responses of (assumed) lesser strength supersede responses of greater strength and, more generally, the stimulus contexts of conflicting response tendencies; specifying short-term contextual-setting (including "drive") factors that determine the momentary efficacy of stimuli for behavior; and detailing the role of experience with stimuli in coming to "appreciate" their dimensions (as through discrimination learning), in the acquisition of fear responses (as in a fear of strange situations or persons), and in conflict (as in approach-avoidance patterns).

A class of similar issues deals broadly with short-term factors like curiosity-exploration, satiation, or habituation—in one sense, the issue of determining the evocative efficacy of familiar versus novel stimuli (e.g., Gewirtz, 1967, 1969a, 1972b). Finally, some standard systematic considerations come to the fore under the terms attachment and dependence, such as how conditioning, cognitive, and/or motivational terms can be applied to properties of the behavior systems implied by the terms attachment or dependence.

Every one of the issues I have listed here has validity within diverse comparative and developmental theoretical orientations. Yet many of these are often approached efficiently only when they are considered independently of such abstract headings as attachment or dependence.

Recapitulation

The aim of my chapter has been to examine the concepts dependence and attachment, and to suggest a heuristic distinction between them in terms of their modes of acquisition and operation. My aim has also been to illustrate the utility of the distinction made. As a framework for this distinction, I considered the different, often overlapping ways those terms have been used and some issues involved in each usage. In this frame, I thought it gratuitous to use dependence and attachment as anything more than metaphoric labels for the stimulus-response functions grouped under them.

Commensurate with a functional analysis, dependence and attachment seemed reasonably conceptualized as classes of functional relationships involving the (mostly positive) control over a wide variety of an individual's responses by the discriminative and reinforcing stimuli provided by some common physical and behavioral characteristics of a *class* of persons (dependence) or those of a *particular* "object-person" (attachment). The analysis has focused on only one side (the child's) of the reciprocal learning process between children and adults (caretakers or mothers). Even so, I have conceived of the attachment and dependence terms and the processes they signify as applicable to any age range or interaction partner.

I considered several implications of this heuristic distinction between dependence and attachment. One was that the conditions in the caretaking environment (such as the discriminability of the unique cues provided by a single caretaker on the one hand, or by any one of a group of caretakers on the other) determine whether the initially acquired pattern of behavior systems is best summarized by the concept of attachment or by the concept of dependence. Another implication was that these processes for the acquisition and maintenance of attachment and dependence are similar to but independent of one another, and that dependence is *not* the generalization of attachment. Furthermore, I assumed that situational or ecological factors, some of which were enumerated, often will determine whether an individual (whatever his reinforcement history) exhibits a behavior pattern that connotes attachment or one that connotes dependence.

I assumed also that the seeming suddenness with which attachment behavior systems can be acquired, as well as the initially persistent, and the subsequently perseverative and/or emotional, response patterns resulting from interference with them, may combine to give attachment behaviors, more than dependence behaviors, the appearance of great intensity ("passion," "affect") and pervasiveness. When the implications of a functional distinction between the concepts of attachment and dependence are not used to explain such phenomena, the difference between them can appear to some theorists to be a qualitative one with the two systems operating according to entirely different principles. Yet, my analysis has suggested that the acquisition, maintenance, and extinction of behaviors connoting both attachment and dependence can be ordered efficiently by common principles of acquired stimulus control over behaviors (operating upon the child's biogenic makeup and developmental changes in effector and receptor systems). In this heuristic frame, therefore, a conclusion that the two systems differ qualitatively would not be warranted.

In the context of the possible operation of unconditioned stimuli or unlearned behavior patterns, I sketched heuristically how basic conditioning processes might be involved in the acquisition and maintenance of the behavior systems that connote attachment or dependence. I conceived the acquisition context to involve two intimately correlated facets of the same process which can begin when an infant is helpless and relatively immobile: (a) the conditioning of the physical and behavioral characteristics of a particular person (attachment) or those common to a class of persons (dependence) as discriminative and/or reinforcing stimuli for the child's behaviors; and (b) the reinforcement and maintenance of various of the child's behavior systems by the diverse stimuli provided by that person or by members of a class of persons. The complexity of these behaviors would increase with the child's developing capacities. I assumed that diverse distal and proximal events provided by that person or by members of a class of persons, in addition to those directly related to organismic survival, come to function as cue and reinforcing stimuli for numerous child behaviors and behavior sequences (e.g., those involving approaching, tracking, smiling, and vocalizing).

I assumed also that changes occur in both the stimuli and the responses involved in the interactions, and that behaviors of the interacting object-person or persons come under the control of stimuli provided by the behavior and appearance of the child or class of children, at various points in the sequence of the child's (physical and social) development. Thus, child and adult could be said to become mutually "attached" or "dependent" (the label for the relationship depending only on whether the controlling stimuli are provided by an object-person who has acquired unique value *or* by members of a class of object-persons who share certain stimulus characteristics and from each of whom a stimulus is equally effective).

Thus, a learning approach such as the one I have presented emphasizes the sequential and contingent stimulus and response features of the interaction between an individual and his environment. Gross concepts like attachment or dependence were thought useful in labeling an area of broad scientific interest or for occasional summary purposes. Apart from this utility, however, there is often little need to employ such gross concepts, particularly when their use is not supported by articulate theories.

Acknowledgements

The author appreciates the editorial suggestions he received at various stages in the preparation of this and the succeeding chapter from Sharon Houck, Laura Rosenthal, Betsy Rubinstein, Danielle Spiegler, and Elizabeth Wigler.

REFERENCES

Ainsworth, M. D. The development of infant-mother interaction among the Ganda. In B. M. Foss (Ed.), *Determinants of infant behavior II.* London: Methuen (New York: Wiley), 1963. Pp. 67-112.

Ainsworth, M. D. Patterns of attachment behavior shown by the infant in interaction with his mother. *Merrill-Palmer Quarterly*, 1964, **10**, 51-58.

Ainsworth, M. D. S. *Infancy in Uganda: Infant care and the growth of love.* Baltimore: Johns Hopkins Press, 1967.

Ainsworth, M. D. S. Object relations, dependency, and attachment: A theoretical review of the infant-mother relationship. *Child Development*, 1969, **40**, 969-1025.

Ainsworth, M. D. S., & Wittig, B. A. Attachment and exploratory behavior of one-year-olds in a strange situation. In B. M. Foss (Ed.), *Determinants of infant behaviour IV.* London: Methuen, 1969. Pp. 111-136.

Bandura, A., & Walters, R. H. *Social learning and personality development.* New York: Holt, Rinehart, & Winston, 1963.

Beller, E. K. Dependency and independence in young children. *Journal of Genetic Psychology*, 1955, **87**, 25-35.

Beller, E. K. Dependency and autonomous achievement striving related to orality and anality in early childhood. *Child Development*, 1957, **28**, 287-315.

Beller, E. K. Exploratory studies of dependency. *Transactions of the New York Academy of Sciences*, 1959, **21**, 414-426.

Beller, E. K. Adult-child interaction and personalized day care. In E. H. Grotberg (Ed.), *Day care: Resources for decisions.* (OEO Pamphlet 6106-1), Washington, D. C.: U. S. Office of Economic Opportunity, June 1971. Pp. 229-264.

Bowlby, J. Critical phases in the development of social responses in man and other animals. *New Biology*, 14. London: Penguin Books, 1953. Pp. 25-32.

Bowlby, J. The nature of the child's tie to his mother. *International Journal of Psychoanalysis*, 1958, 39, 1-34.

Bowlby, J. Ethology and the development of object relations. *International Journal of Psychoanalysis*, 1960, 41, 313-317.(a)

Bowlby, J. Separation anxiety. *International Journal of Psychoanalysis*, 1960, 41, 89-113.(b)

Bowlby, J. Comment on paper by Dr. Gewirtz. In B. M. Foss (Ed.), *Determinants of infant behaviour*. London: Methuen (New York: Wiley), 1961. Pp. 301-303.

Bowlby, J. Effects on behaviour of disruption of an affectional bond. In J. M. Thoday & A. S. Parkes (Eds.), *Genetic and environmental influences on behaviour*. Edinburgh: Oliver & Boyd, 1968. Pp. 94-108.

Bowlby, J. *Attachment and loss*. Vol. 1. *Attachment*. London: Hogarth (New York: Basic Books), 1969.

Bronfenbrenner, U. Freudian theories of identification and their derivatives. *Child Development*, 1960, 31, 15-40.

Cairns, R. B. The influence of dependency inhibition on the effectiveness of social reinforcement. *Journal of Personality*, 1961, 29, 466-488.

Cairns, R. B. Attachment behavior of mammals. *Psychological Review*, 1966, 73, 409-426.

Cairns, R. B., & Lewis, M. Dependency and the reinforcement value of a verbal stimulus. *Journal of Consulting Psychology*, 1962, 26, 1-8.

Caldwell, B. M., Wright, C. M., Honig, A. S., & Tannenbaum, J. Infant day care and attachment. *American Journal of Orthopsychiatry*, 1970, 40, 397-412.

Dollard, J., & Miller, N. E. *Personality and psychotherapy*. New York: McGraw-Hill, 1950.

Fenichel, O. *The psychoanalytic theory of neurosis*. New York: W. W. Norton, 1945.

Freud, A. Psychoanalysis and education. *Psychoanalytic Study of the Child*, 1954, 9, 9-15.

Freud, S. Three contributions to the theory of sex. In A. A. Brill (Trans.), *The basic writings of Sigmund Freud*. New York: Modern Library, 1938. Pp. 553-629. (Originally published: 1905.)

Freud, S. On narcissism: An introduction. *The standard edition of the complete psychological works of Sigmund Freud*. Vol. XIV. London: Hogarth, 1957. Pp. 73-102. (Originally published: 1914.)

Freud, S. Inhibitions, symptoms and anxiety. *The standard edition of the complete psychological works of Sigmund Freud*. Vol. XX. London: Hogarth, 1959. Pp. 87-172. (Originally published: 1926.)

Freud, S. Female sexuality. *The standard edition of the complete psychological works of Sigmund Freud*. Vol. XXI. London: Hogarth, 1961. Pp. 225-243. (Originally published: 1931.)

Freud, S. *An outline of psychoanalysis*. London: Hogarth, 1938.

Gewirtz, J. L. Three determinants of attention-seeking in young children. *Monographs of the Society for Research in Child Development*, 1954, 19 (2, Serial No. 59).

Gewirtz, J. L. A factor analysis of some attention-seeking behaviors of young children. *Child Development*, 1956, 27, 17-37.(a)

Gewirtz, J. L. A program of research on the dimensions and antecedents of emotional dependence. *Child Development*, 1956, 27, 205-221.(b)

Gewirtz, J. L. A learning analysis of the effects of affective privation in childhood. *Acta Psychologica*, 1961, 19, 404-405.(a)

Gewirtz, J. L. A learning analysis of the effects of normal stimulation, privation and deprivation on the acquisition of social motivation and attachment. In B. M. Foss (Ed.), *Determinants of infant behaviour*. London: Methuen (New York: Wiley), 1961. Pp. 213-299.(b)

Gewirtz, J. L. Deprivation and satiation of social stimuli as determinants of their reinforcing efficacy. In J. P. Hill (Ed.), *Minnesota symposia on child psychology.* Vol. 1. Minneapolis: University of Minnesota Press, 1967. Pp. 3-56.

Gewirtz, J. L. On designing the functional environment of the child to facilitate behavioral development. In L. L. Dittmann (Ed.), *Early child care: The new perspectives.* New York: Atherton, 1968. Pp. 169-213.(a)

Gewirtz, J. L. The role of stimulation in models for child development. In L. L. Dittmann (Ed.), *Early child care: The new perspectives.* New York: Atherton, 1968. Pp. 139-168.(b)

Gewirtz, J. L. Levels of conceptual analysis in environment-infant interaction research. *Merrill-Palmer Quarterly,* 1969, 15, 7-47.(a)

Gewirtz, J. L. Mechanisms of social learning: Some roles of stimulation and behavior in early human development. In D. A. Goslin (Ed.), *Handbook of socialization theory and research.* Chicago: Rand McNally, 1969. Pp. 57-212.(b)

Gewirtz, J. L. Potency of a social reinforcer as a function of satiation and recovery. *Developmental Psychology,* 1969, 1, 2-13.(c)

Gewirtz, J. L. Conditional responding as a paradigm for observational, imitative learning and vicarious-reinforcement. In H. W. Reese (Ed.), *Advances in child development and behavior.* Vol. 6. New York: Academic Press, 1971. Pp. 273-304.(a)

Gewirtz, J. L. The roles of overt responding and extrinsic reinforcement in "self-" and "vicarious-reinforcement" phenomena and in "observational learning" and imitation. In R. Glaser (Ed.), *The nature of reinforcement.* New York: Academic Press, 1971, Pp. 279-309.(b)

Gewirtz, J. L. Stimulation, learning, and motivation principles for day-care settings. In E. H. Grotberg (Ed.), *Day Care: Resources for decisions.* (OEO Pamphlet 6106-1), Washington, D. C.: U. S. Office of Economic Opportunity, June 1971. Pp. 173-226.(c)

Gewirtz, J. L. Deficiency conditions of stimulation and the reversal of their effects via enrichment. In F. J. Mönks, W. W. Hartup, & J. deWit (Eds.), *Determinants of Behavioral Development.* New York: Academic Press, 1972, in press.(a)

Gewirtz, J. L. Some contextual determinants of stimulus potency. In R. D. Parke (Ed.), *Recent trends in social learning theory.* New York: Academic Press, 1972. Pp. 7-33.(b)

Gewirtz, J. L., & Baer, D. M. Deprivation and satiation of social reinforcers as drive conditions. *Journal of Abnormal and Social Psychology,* 1958, 57, 165-172.(a)

Gewirtz, J. L., & Baer, D. M. The effect of brief social deprivation on behaviors for a social reinforcer. *Journal of Abnormal and Social Psychology,* 1958, 56, 49-56.(b)

Gewirtz, J. L., & Stingle, K. G. Learning of generalized imitation as the basis for identification. *Psychological Review,* 1968, 75, 374-397.

Harlow, H. F. The nature of love. *American Psychologist,* 1958, 13, 673-685.

Harlow, H. F. The primate socialization motives. *Transactions and Studies of the College of Physicians of Philadelphia,* 1966, 33, 224-237.

Harlow, H. F., & Harlow, M. K. The affectional systems. In A. M. Schrier, H. F. Harlow, & F. Stollnitz (Eds.), *Behavior of nonhuman primates.* Vol. 2. New York: Academic Press, 1965. Pp. 287-334.

Harlow, H. F., & Harlow, M. K. Learning to love. *American Scientist,* 1966, 54, 244-272.

Harlow, H. F., & Zimmermann, R. R. Affectional responses in the infant monkey. *Science,* 1959, 130, 421-432.

Hartup, W. W. Dependence and independence. In H. W. Stevenson (Ed.), *Child psychology: The sixty-second yearbook of the National Society for Study of Education. Part I.* Chicago: University of Chicago Press, 1963. Pp. 333-363.

Heathers, G. Acquiring dependence and independence: A theoretical orientation. *Journal of Genetic Psychology,* 1955, 87, 277-291.(a)

Heathers, G. Emotional dependence and independence in nursery school play. *Journal of Genetic Psychology,* 1955, 87, 37-57.(b)

Kagan, J., & Moss, H. A. *Birth to maturity: A study in psychological development*. New York: Wiley, 1962.

Kantor, J. R. *Interbehavioral psychology*. (2nd ed., rev.) Bloomington, Ind.: Principia Press, 1959.

Levy, D. M. Primary affect hunger. *American Journal of Psychiatry*, 1937, 94, 643-652.

Lorenz, K. Companionship in bird life. In C. H. Schiller (Ed.), *Instinctive behavior*. New York: International Universities Press, 1957. Pp. 83-128. (Originally published: 1935.)

Maccoby, E. E., & Masters, J. C. Attachment and dependency. In P. H. Mussen (Ed.), *Carmichael's manual of child psychology*. (3rd ed.) Vol. 2. New York: Wiley, 1970. Pp. 73-157.

Mason, W. A. Motivational factors in psychosocial development. *Nebraska Symposium on Motivation*, 1970, 18, 35-67.

McDougall, W. *An introduction to social psychology*. (30th ed.) London: Methuen, 1950. (Originally published: 1908.)

McDougall, W. *Outline of psychology*. New York: Scribner's, 1923.

Miller, G. A., Galanter, E., & Pribram, K. H. *Plans and the structure of behavior*. New York: Holt, Rinehart, & Winston, 1960.

Miller, N. E., & Dollard, J. *Social learning and imitation*. New Haven: Yale University Press, 1941.

Mowrer, O. H., & Kluckhohn, C. Dynamic theory of personality. In J. McV. Hunt (Ed.), *Personality and the behavior disorders*. Vol. 1. New York: Ronald Press, 1944. Pp. 69-135.

Piaget, J. *The origins of intelligence in children*. New York: International Universities Press, 1952. (Originally published: 1936.)

Piaget, J. *The construction of reality in the child*. New York: Basic Books, 1954. (Originally published: 1937.)

Rheingold, H. L., & Eckerman, C. O. The infant separates himself from his mother. *Science*, 1970, 168, 78-83.

Rosenthal, M. K. Effects of a novel situation and of anxiety on two groups of dependency behaviours. *British Journal of Psychology*, 1967, 58, 357-364.(a)

Rosenthal, M. K. The generalization of dependency behaviour from mother to stranger. *Journal of Child Psychology and Psychiatry*, 1967, 8, 117-133.(b)

Salzen, E. A. Imprinting in birds and primates. *Behaviour*, 1967, 28 (3-4), 232-254.

Schaffer, H. R. Some issues for research in the study of attachment behaviour. In B. M. Foss (Ed.), *Determinants of infant behaviour II*. London: Methuen (New York: Wiley), 1963. Pp. 179-196.

Schaffer, H. R., & Emerson, P. E. The development of social attachments in infancy. *Monographs of the Society for Research in Child Development*, 1964, 29 (3, Serial No. 94).

Scott, J. P. Comparative social psychology. In R. H. Waters, D. A. Rethlingshafer, & W. E. Caldwell (Eds.), *Principles of comparative psychology*. New York: McGraw-Hill, 1960. Pp. 250-288.

Scott, J. P. The process of primary socialization in canine and human infants. In J. Hellmuth (Ed.), *Exceptional infant: The normal infant*. Vol. 1. Seattle, Wash.: Special Child Publications, 1967. Pp. 469-514.

Sears, R. R. A theoretical framework for personality and social behavior. *American Psychologist*, 1951, 6, 476-483.

Sears, R. R. Dependency motivation. *Nebraska Symposium on Motivation*, 1963, 11, 25-65.

Sears, R. R., Maccoby, E. E., & Levin, H. *Patterns of child rearing*. Evanston, Ill.: Row, Peterson, 1957.

Sears, R. R., Rau, L., & Alpert, R. *Identification and child rearing*. Stanford, Calif.: Stanford University Press, 1965.

Sears, R. R., Whiting, J. W. M., Nowlis, V., & Sears, P. S., in collaboration with E. K. Beller, J. C. Cohen, E. H. Chasdi, H. Faigin, J. L. Gewirtz, M. S. Lawrence, & J. P. McKee. Some child-rearing antecedents of aggression and dependency in young children. *Genetic Psychology Monographs*, 1953, 47, 135-234.

Shaffer, L. F. *The psychology of adjustment.* Boston: Houghton Mifflin, 1936.

Sluckin, W. *Imprinting and early learning.* Chicago: Aldine, 1965.

Spalding, D. A. Instinct, with original observations on young animals. *Macmillan's Magazine*, 1873, 27, 282-293. (Reprinted: *British Journal of Animal Behaviour*, 1954, 2, 2-11.)

Spitz, R. A. The role of ecological factors in emotional development in infancy. *Child Development*, 1949, 20, 145-156.

Whiting, J. W. M. The frustration complex in Kwoma society. *Man*, 1944, 115, 140-144.

Whiting, J. W. M., & Child, I. L. *Child training and personality.* New Haven: Yale University Press, 1953.

Yarrow, L. J. The development of object relationships during infancy and the effects of a disruption of early mother-child relationships. *American Psychologist*, 1956, 11, 423. (Abstract)

Yarrow, L. J. Separation from parents during early childhood. In M. L. Hoffman & L. W. Hoffman (Eds.), *Review of child development research.* Vol. 1. New York: Russell Sage Foundation, 1964. Pp. 89-136.

Yarrow, L. J. The development of focused relationships during infancy. In J. Hellmuth (Ed.), *Exceptional infant: The normal infant.* Vol. 1. Seattle, Wash.: Special Child Publications, 1967. Pp. 429-442.

ON THE SELECTION AND USE OF ATTACHMENT AND DEPENDENCE INDICES

Jacob L. Gewirtz
National Institute of Mental Health

Introduction

In this chapter, I discuss some strategic and tactical considerations that might be taken into account in the selection and use of attachment or dependence indices (indicators, criteria) and measures.[1] My presentation here is intended to be independent of both the theoretical posture and the conceptual distinction I advanced in the preceding chapter. It may therefore be read independently of that chapter. Nevertheless, my theoretical analysis there is compatible with the considerations I discuss in this chapter.

The conceptual metaphors of attachment and dependence have ordinarily been used with limited specificity. Considering the typical absence of close coordination between those abstract terms and either empirical operations or theoretical assumptions, it is not surprising that attachment and dependence have each rarely been indexed in a systematic manner. Occasionally, phenomena that may be fundamentally different have been grouped under each concept. At other times, attachment and dependence have been defined identically and used interchangeably. Moreover, the patterns of sequential behavior that comprise the interaction chains thought characteristic of each of the concepts have not yet been pictured in sufficient detail under the relevant theoretical approaches. Such analyses have occasionally emphasized only behaviors, specifying neither the stimuli that control them nor the stimulus contexts in which they are observed. These environmental features would be important determinants of the meanings of those behaviors. Thus, under many approaches diverse behaviors have connoted attachment or dependence and may serve as reasonable indices of one or the other of the concepts, or even of both.

In the preceding chapter and elsewhere (Gewirtz, 1961, 1969a, 1969b), I outlined a functional approach to the concepts of attachment and dependence. I also suggested the utility of a heuristic distinction between them, based upon whether an individual's behaviors are under the control of (a) stimuli from a particular person (attachment) or (b) shared stimuli from a specific class of persons (dependence). In common with the previous discussion and most analyses in the field, the present chapter focuses on interchanges between a child and an adult. But I stress again that my analysis in both chapters is not limited to a specific age range, to particular interaction partners, or indeed even to the child as the focus of analysis. In accordance with my earlier analysis, I will emphasize the need to determine the patterns of relations between antecedent, concurrent, and consequent stimuli from interacting object-persons on the one hand, and child behaviors on the other. Within this perspective, my main focus is on the relationship of each such stimulus from interactors to its response in the child. [A reciprocal and equally important focus, which is not stressed here, is on the impact of stimuli from the child for the responses of interactors (Gewirtz, 1961).] These S-R sequences comprise the reciprocal learning process that is often summarized or labeled by the attachment or dependence concepts. In this

---

[1] The writer's treatment of this issue was begun in earlier papers (Gewirtz, 1969a, 1969b, 1972a). Here it is expanded further to encompass a larger number of indicator types and the tactics of their use under various research strategies, as well as the conceptual artifacts to which certain such tactics may lead.

frame, when I use the term *index* (or criterion) of attachment or of dependence, it will stand for a child's response to a stimulus (or in a stimulus context) provided by an interactor—the indexed unit being that of stimulus-response (S-R). For convenience, I will refer occasionally only to a response class and merely imply the stimulus context.

For many purposes, one could study behavior systems (i.e., S-R units) that touch on a conception of attachment or of dependence *without* invoking either term. At the same time, the stimulus-response phenomena considered in this chapter could be relevant to several (even contradictory) theoretical conceptions of attachment or dependence. Moreover, the considerations in the selection of indices of attachment or dependence are generic and can therefore proceed independently of any particular theoretical approach or distinction. Finally, the discussion here would qualify the heuristic distinction I have proposed between attachment and dependence only insofar as any indices employed happen to identify an individual's behaviors as being under the control of stimuli from a particular person or of stimuli from any one of a class of persons.

Some Frequently Employed Indices of Attachment or Dependence

RESPONSE CLASSES USED AS BASES FOR INDICES

As abstract concepts not often closely related either to empirical constructs or to theoretical postulates, attachment and dependence have each been denoted by diverse groups of response classes. These responses are for the most part inflected by their situational contexts. In turn, each such response class could provide the basis for *measures* of different response attributes (e.g., latency, amplitude, probability). Also, overall *summary* statements may be devised for the combinations or patterns of behaviors grouped under each construct. (For instance, these could be used to characterize the "strength" or "intensity" of attachment or dependence.) In this paper, I consider only in passing the issues of response measures, of the overall summary characterization of response groups, and of the patterns of developmental change through which responses go. Instead, I emphasize, in their stimulus contexts, the identities (contents) of response classes that have been used to denote attachment, dependence, or both concepts. These behavior classes have included:

1. Responses reflecting the *direct positive control* of stimuli provided by an "object" organism, as used by Sears, Whiting, Nowlis, Sears, and collaborators (1953), by Sears, Rau, and Alpert (1965), by Ainsworth (1967 and this volume), by Rosenthal (1967), and by Mason (1970), and as emphasized by Gewirtz (1954, 1956a, 1961). These responses include orienting and visual tracking, greeting, approaching, and responses that maintain nearness; touching, holding, hugging, clinging, scrambling over, and kissing; and such other responses as

crying that are maintained by attention or approval [the latter as used, for example, by Cairns and Lewis (1962), by Gewirtz and Baer (1958), and by Gewirtz (1967, 1969c); this usage was summarized by Eisenberger (1970)].

2. Responses indicating *differential recognition* of, or *preference* for, the stimuli provided by an object-person relative to the stimuli some other person(s) provides—for instance differential clinging, crying, smiling, visual tracking, or vocalizing (Harlow & Zimmermann, 1959; Cairns, 1966, 1968; Ainsworth, 1967 and this volume; Yarrow, 1967 and this volume; Sackett, 1968, 1970; Mason, 1970).

3. The *absence* of *exploratory and similar responses* in a novel context, in the presence of an object-person, where those responses would be *incompatible with responses reflecting the positive control of stimuli from the object-person.* (These responses would be incompatible in the sense of only one stimulus being in predominant control at any one time.) Hence, instead of displaying exploratory responses (e.g., toward new toys), the child orients his behavior toward the object person (Ainsworth & Wittig, 1969). Another set of responses that may be included in this class is investigatory responses oriented to the object person (Bowlby, 1969).

4. Responses assumed to indicate *direct positive stimulus control, but only in particular stimulus-control contexts*; for instance, the index mother-as-a-secure-base-for-exploration as used by Harlow and Zimmermann (1959) and by Ainsworth (1963, 1967; Ainsworth & Wittig, 1969), or the avoidance of seemingly aversive events. [These behaviors might be termed "security-getting" responses and have been emphasized by Bowlby (1960b), by Ainsworth (1967), and possibly also by Sears and his associates (1953, insofar as the latter's "seeking reassurance" index of dependence is involved).]

5. *Avoidance responses* (including facial sobering or interruption of an ongoing act) at the approach, or in the presence, of strange persons or places, in a context where, if an object-person is present, no approach is made to him or her to avoid the stranger (e.g., Yarrow, 1967; Ainsworth & Wittig, 1969).

6. *Emotional responses* such as crying, whimpering, temper tantrums, or other behaviors that connote "distress" or "apathy," or that may have been brought about by interference with a response sequence reflecting positive stimulus control. In the case of interference effected by separation from a mother-figure, such responses have been taken to represent "protests" or "discriminative vocalizations" that are sometimes said to connote "separation anxiety." Insofar as the occurrence of these emotional responses are incompatible with the occurrence of responses reflecting positive stimulus control or other responses (e.g., exploration), they are here termed "disorganization behaviors" (for the lack of a better label). Such indices have been used by Ainsworth (1964, 1967; Ainsworth & Wittig, 1969), by Schaffer and Emerson (1964), by Yarrow (1967), and by Cairns (1966; Fleener & Cairns, 1970).[2]

---

[2] The qualities of attachment or dependence, or the distinctions between them, have been discussed occasionally in terms of such behavior attributes as "intensity." I noted in

The listed response classes have sometimes been grouped informally within assumed developmental phases to reflect differential responsiveness to the object-person (e.g., see Ainsworth, 1967; Yarrow, 1967). However, several writers have noted that whichever indices happen to be chosen to define a "relationship" will determine the developmental point at which that relationship is said to be established (e.g., Ainsworth, 1967; Yarrow, 1967). Furthermore, some of the responses involved would seem species- or phylum-specific (e.g., clinging). Other responses (such as smiles, laughter, and displays of what are termed "positive affect") have often been assumed by fiat to reflect such states as "pleasure," "happiness," or "joy," that have sometimes also been postulated to be relevant attachment qualities or indices (e.g., see Caldwell, Wright, Honig, & Tannenbaum, 1970; Sears, this volume). [I have discussed the role of such terms, and their translation into observable stimulus-response events, in an analysis of the smile response (Gewirtz, 1965) and elsewhere (Gewirtz, 1968, 1971).]

There has been no consensus of opinion among theorists and researchers about the particular response classes to use as indices of attachment and those to use as indices of dependence. Indeed, to date there has been no consensus even about the headings under which given responses should be classified. Researchers on dependence (e.g., Sears et al., 1953; Gewirtz, 1954, 1956a, 1956b; Beller, 1955, 1959; Sears, 1963; Sears, Rau, & Alpert, 1965) have emphasized criteria that fall mainly under the heading of responses indicating direct positive control (1), including such control under limiting conditions (4) as in "seeking reassurance." On the other hand, researchers on attachment (e.g., Bowlby, 1958, 1960a, 1960b; Ainsworth, 1964, 1967) have emphasized indices that fall under several of the aforementioned headings. For instance, an infant's crying or protest upon the departure of his mother or others [used as the basis for the index of attachment by Schaffer and Emerson (1964)] and his crying upon the approach of "strangers" in different contexts [conceived as attachment behaviors by Ainsworth (1964, 1967) and by Yarrow (1967), among others], may be classed as "avoidance" responses (5) or "emotional" responses (6), or even as responses indicating direct positive control (1) insofar as such protests may have been extrinsically reinforced in those stimulus contexts).

Theorists have also used indices from each of the classes, but typically without indicating the basis for their choice of index combinations. Thus,

the preceding chapter that Sears (this volume) has distinguished between these two classes of phenomena on the basis that attachment is, and dependence is not, characterized by "passion," a term he has not yet operationalized. As discussed in the preceding chapter, the two behavior systems can be ordered efficiently by a single conditioning paradigm. Further, in this case one has the option of attributing such affective qualities to either system. Such qualities as intensity or passion could be used to characterize cued responses (of any content) under any one of the earlier-listed index classes. Therefore, for many conceptual and research purposes, establishing separate categories for those characteristics could be redundant with the index classes themselves. That is, one's working assumption can be (as mine is in the present analysis) that it is likely that the performance implications of the acquired stimulus-control features are already being reflected in the indices.

Ainsworth (1967) employed 16 indices [several more than she had used in earlier years (Ainsworth 1963, 1964)], of which roughly half reflected positive stimulus control (approach) (1), three differential recognition (preference) (2), one exploratory behavior (3), two or three positive control but in particular stimulus contexts (4), one avoidance (5), and one emotional response upon mother's departure (6). Her work which culminated in the 1967 study was carried out under the general conception that "attachment behavior is behavior through which a discriminatory, differential affectional relationship is established with a person or object... [Ainsworth, 1964, p. 51]." More recently, she and a colleague have stressed behaviors that maintain proximity to, or interaction with, the particular object of attachment (Ainsworth & Bell, 1970). In the present volume, Ainsworth also stresses the utility of multiple, differentially manifested indices of attachment. In a similar vein, Bowlby (1969) has emphasized recently that the patterns of attachment might best be described in terms of several "forms of behaviour." These include: behaviors that initiate interaction (e.g., greeting, approaching, touching, embracing, scrambling over mother-figure, burying face in her lap, calling, talking, hands-up gesture, smiling); behaviors in response to initiatives that maintain interaction (e.g., the aforementioned behaviors as well as watching); behaviors aimed at avoiding separation (e.g., following, crying, clinging); exploratory behaviors, especially those oriented to the attachment-object; and withdrawal (fear) behaviors, especially those in the context of orientation to the attachment-object (Bowlby, 1969, p. 334). These behavior systems represent essentially the entire range covered by the six classes of criteria listed previously.

I noted in earlier sections and in the preceding chapter that the indices used in studies of attachment or of dependence are generic, and that they had been and could be used to characterize diverse behavior systems under many theoretical models. Thus, the behaviors involved in attachment or dependence contexts—whether orienting, touching, talking or smiling, remaining near, or crying, being angry, fearful, or anxious—are not unique to the attachment or dependence case. Even so, the earlier list shows there are classes of index variables that have often been used by researchers on attachment or dependence.

Occasionally, some of these indices have been dropped or added in a research report without indication being given of how the set of indices selected was considered representative or uniquely appropriate under the theory employed. While this practice presents obvious difficulties, it is perhaps inevitable, given that many researches of recent years have used inexplicit conceptions of dependence or of attachment whose relationships to empirical operations have not been well formulated. Under such conceptions, diverse responses could serve as plausible criteria under each concept, whether or not one takes account of the stimuli controlling them. In addition, various indices or sets of indices involving any or all such response classes could be emphasized, depending upon the strategy and tactics of a particular theoretical approach.

ON THE USE OF SUMMARY STATEMENTS FOR
ATTACHMENT OR DEPENDENCE

In a context where the selection of the number and combination of indices as criteria of attachment or dependence has often seemed arbitrary, it may be worthwile to consider briefly the matter of generating a summary characterization for either concept. Specifically, when a number of criterion behaviors or situations have been grouped under either concept, an overall summary statement of the "strength," or "intensity," or other feature of an attachment or dependence pattern may be desired. Various parameters might be used for such overall description, singly or in combination, irrespective of the number or type of criterion indices employed. As noted in the preceding chapter, these parameters may include:

1. The range and/or number of behaviors under the control of stimuli from a class of persons or from a particular person.

2. That range and/or number relative to the range/number of behaviors under the control of stimuli from others.

3. The degree of positive stimulus control over each behavior system (for instance, as indicated by response probability).

4. The number of stimulus settings in which the control process operates.

5. The degree of disorganization and/or the intensity of emotional behaviors that ensues from interference with the interaction (though, as I suggest later on, such disorganization measures will necessarily be indices of confounded, partly irrelevant, conditions).

For particular summary purposes, one could emphasize parameters based only on selected indices, patterns, or stimulus-control conditions. Alternatively, if responses implying attachment (or dependence) are each under a different form of stimulus-control function, an overall summary statement may obscure these differentiated patterns and thus may be of limited utility.

DIRECT VERSUS INDIRECT INDICES

Because of their comparative tactical utility, in the previous chapter and elsewhere (Gewirtz, 1961) I have emphasized the use, wherever possible, of *direct* rather than *indirect* criteria of positive stimulus control over behaviors. Thus, I have called for indices comprised of positive, approach responses to discriminative stimuli from object-persons over indices based on disorganization responses. At the same time, as members of the same general behavior class, approach responses can be assumed to be under the control of rather similar stimuli. On this basis, one could expect a positive correlation between approach responses to a person in the absence of aversive stimulation and similar approach responses that simultaneously constitute the avoidance of some other person or situation. Compared to simple approach responses, however, the latter behaviors are conceived to represent only a more complex instance of the process of direct stimulus control over behaviors that connotes "attachment" or "dependence."

Let me now consider the nature and relative utility of some indirect indices of positive stimulus control. Recall that in the preceding chapter I listed diverse reaction patterns to interference with S-R sequences (the interference conditions being those often termed "frustration"). Indirect indices can be provided by various reactions to interference conditions, including behaviors that can be termed "emotional." Because they would reflect interference with organized behavior systems that involve positive stimulus control, these reaction patterns can reflect "disorganization." For example, the interference may be brought on via physical blocking of an ongoing S-R (interaction) sequence, or via physical separation from an object-person (in which case it may lead to "separation protests"). In the many varieties of separation, stimulus-response chains are conceived to become blocked or terminated due to a stoppage in the provision of relevant discriminative or reinforcing stimuli from the separated person that would ordinarily maintain the chain behaviors.

When "emotional" responses result from such interference conditions, they will necessarily provide the bases for indirect indices of such intercorrelated factors as:

1. The strength of the response sequence blocked.

2. The value for the individual of the terminal reinforcing consequence involved.

3. The degree to which a stimulus condition actually interferes with a response sequence.

4. Individual thresholds for emotional responding, and particularly for the emotional responses evoked by that interference.

5. The availability of potential alternative responses in the individual's repertory, and their relative strengths.

Given the nature of these factors, "disorganization" responses will constitute less direct and therefore less efficient indices of the positive control acquired by the stimuli provided by an object-person.

One might assume, then, that "disorganization" responses will occur as a function of the strength of the response sequence interfered with or blocked, the value of the reinforcer, and the other listed factors (holding constant the magnitude of the interference condition). But it is conceivable that thresholds of the responses in the blocked sequence, or of the registration of interference with it, are also involved. Thus, if the degree of interference were held constant, it might be found that "disorganization" responses are emitted only for higher "response-strength" values of the sequence blocked. Or, alternatively, if response strength were held constant, such "disorganization" responses might result only from higher degrees of (i.e., more complete) interference with the attachment or dependence behavior sequence. Moreover, the emotional responses that often result from interference with approach response sequences connoting attachment or dependence may themselves come under the control of the very same discriminative and reinforcing stimuli that control the approach behavior patterns those concepts imply (e.g., operant crying). In the latter case, these responses need not be termed "emotional," and would be functioning as direct rather than as indirect indices of acquired stimulus control.

Under nearly all theoretical approaches, therefore, one would need to identify both the response and the contextual-setting condition controlling its occurrence to make the appropriate functional classification of the behavior and the determination of its relevance. Thus, approach responses that occur in the context of avoidance and disorganization or security responses can each constitute reasonable and potentially useful attachment or dependence indices, particularly in contexts where the earlier-mentioned limitations in their use are recognized. For instance, this could be the case when the purpose of an approach is not to deal directly with issues of positive stimulus control over attachment or dependence behaviors as such, but is specifically to understand in natural settings: (a) aversive stimulus control, (b) the disorganization brought on by interference with attachment or dependence behaviors, and/or (c) disorganization generally.

Before I leave this matter of criteria, let me return to my earlier suggestion that, for most purposes, direct indices are likely to be more efficient than indirect indices of the sort I have labeled "disorganization" responses. Insofar as their approach has emphasized indices based on separation protests that I have termed "indirect," the view of such authors as Schaffer and Emerson (1964) seems discrepant from the considerations I stress here. Those authors have proposed that the most suitable index of an "attachment" is the degree of the infant's reactions and efforts to restore the status quo ". . . when he is frustrated in his attempts to remain attached by the withdrawal of the object . . . [p. 8]," in particular, his separation protests. One difficulty with the Schaffer and Emerson (1964) view is their notion that the child's separation protest only denotes that an "attachment exists" but is not itself an "attachment behavior." However, insofar as their conception of "attachment behaviors" as responses oriented to attaining proximity reflects direct positive stimulus control factors, it may not diverge from the tactical emphasis I outline here.

INFLUENCE OF METHODOLOGICAL CONTEXT ON INDICES

Before discussing in greater detail some tactical issues relevant to the determination of appropriate indices of attachment or dependence under different approaches, I should note some general points about this topic as well as about sampling and methods of measurement. It is commonly accepted that such factors play major roles in determining the results of a study. A survey of the researches under the headings of attachment and dependence reveals an unusual paucity of data replications among investigations. This appears to be due in part to differences in criteria, in methods of measurement and whether cross-sectional or longitudinal sampling procedures are employed, and/or in samples studied (Maccoby & Masters, 1970). For example, Ainsworth (1963) and Schaffer and Emerson (1964) have both studied the age of onset of "specific attachments." However, Schaffer and Emerson concluded that "specific attachments" develop at a later age (in months) than that reported by Ainsworth. This disparity may simply be an outcome of sampling from different subject populations, or of using chronological age as the key independent variable. [I have noted elsewhere that the tactic of using the age variable is questionable in psychological research on developmental processes (Gewirtz, 1969b, particularly pp. 105-119).] However, there is a possible basis for this discrepancy in findings that may be more pertinent for the case here. It is the fact that different criteria were used by Ainsworth and by Schaffer and Emerson (Maccoby & Masters, 1970). Whereas Schaffer and Emerson indexed attachment mainly in terms of separation-protest reactions, Ainsworth employed a wider range of indices. Other things equal, these two sets of indices may simply have shown different relationships to chronological age.

Reviewers of attachment and dependence studies have also noted that discrepant findings can be traced to differences in the methods of measurement. For instance, with nursery-school-age subjects, when teacher ratings were employed as the method of generating data, five dependency measures were found to yield a pattern of reliable intercorrelations (Beller, 1959). But when similarly labeled frequency-count measures were based on direct observation, they showed almost no intercorrelations (Sears, 1963). After reviewing the literature and evaluating research instruments, Maccoby and Masters (1970) concluded that dependency emerges as a "coherent dimension" having a fairly high degree of "trait consistency" when rating scores are employed, but that a much more differentiated picture of dependency is obtained when observation-count scores are used.

It has been common in this area of study to search for relations between earlier parental socialization practices with reference to the child, and the attachment or dependence behavior patterns the child later manifests. However, here too there are arbitrary factors in the measurement of socialization practices that can influence research findings and can account for discrepancies among investigations. Thus, such factors as the information source, the way the data are extracted, the dimensions and number of child-rearing practices studied, and the way they are measured can each determine the findings of an investigation. For instance, a widely used method for assessing parental practices (and sometimes child responses) is the retrospective interview or questionnaire report. Yet such reports are of dubious validity and thus have come increasingly into question as research devices. [On this issue, see Hartup (1963), Maccoby and Masters (1970), and particularly M. R. Yarrow, Campbell, and Burton (1968).] Further, the scores these methods generate may be attenuated when measures have different reliabilities. Finally, built-in interrelationships among the various socialization practices and the manner of reporting them can make it extremely difficult to separate the effects of a given parental practice from other characteristics of parental behavior or of the child's environment (e.g., see Sears et al., 1953). In principle, difficulties like these can be overcome. However, there have been researchers in the area of dependence or attachment who have employed such criteria or methods of measurement, and who have not seemed to recognize fully the role arbitrarily chosen methods can play in determining a pattern of results.

Some Issues Underlying the Roles of Indices in Diverse Attachment and Dependence Conceptions

A number of strategic and tactical issues have become involved with the conception of attachment or of dependence. The procedure of index selection has seemed to reflect the postures of the various conceptual approaches to some of these issues. At the same time, when an approach is not guided by an articulate theory, there is (as I have already noted) the possibility that terms like those of attachment or dependence could be replaced by terms that are more routine as the relations among indices organized under them come to a more general conceptual focus in one of the more basic, traditional problem areas of psychology (e.g., perceptual or cognitive development). In this section, I illustrate but a few of the strategic and/or tactical considerations that can be involved with either the attachment or the dependence concept.

INFLUENCE OF THEORIES ON INDEX SELECTION AND LABELING

The first issue I consider bears on how a theoretical approach will inevitably impose interpretive constraints upon indices, even when in early phases it might only suggest gross ways of packaging or labeling results. Approaching this matter neutrally, I shall illustrate the point with the report of Schaffer and Emerson (1964). Those authors conceived that the core of attachment is "... the tendency of the young to seek the proximity of certain other members of the species [p. 6]." They indexed attachment by an infant's "protest" behaviors (crying, fussing, moaning, and whimpering) directed at a specific (object) person upon separation from (i.e., being left alone by) that person. Those authors found that the number of different persons from whom separation would evoke "protests" (denoting "breadth of attachment") correlated positively with both: (*a*) the intensity of "protests" upon separation from the principal object (in the first month after the first recording of protest behavior directed at a particular individual—their index for "attachment intensity to principal object"); and (*b*) the intensity of similar responses (as well as of sobering, withdrawing, turning away, etc.) evoked by strangers, denoting "proximity avoidance" and hence a "fear-of-strangers." Although Schaffer and Emerson seemed to consider this latter variable to be akin to some unspecified process other than attachment, they related the three measures to each other (and to chronological age) under a conception of attachment.

Theorists who operate outside an attachment framework might conceive of the relationships Schaffer and Emerson have detected among the three listed behavior indices as connoting not an "attachment," but only something akin to a generalized "anxiety" or "fear of the strange" (i.e., resulting from the child being left alone or being left in the presence of a stranger). Or those relationships may connote yet some other conception—one orthogonal to attachment that in some reference frames might be thought more efficient than this concept. In particular, such an alternative conception might be emphasized where there are no demonstrated relations that anchor separation-protest scores to any direct attachment behaviors (which to Schaffer and Emerson were those that insure proximity). Indeed, Schaffer and Emerson (1964) have themselves noted that the common element in their three indices might be only the "threshold" or "degree of general responsiveness in social situations [p. 65]." However, after having (very commendably) raised the issue of the meaning of their own indices, those authors did not directly confront its corollary—whether the attachment term was conceptually necessary (or even economical) for organizing the empirical findings among their three indices.

Still, there is an important sense in which use of the attachment concept to organize or label their results flowed directly from their theoretical orientation, and in this frame, their course in "accentuating the positive" is not difficult to understand. Even so, the Schaffer and Emerson report can provide us with an interesting didactic example of how the empirical relations among a small set of attachment (and ancillary) indices could conceivably be organized in an alternative manner. In principle, the alternative need not involve the concept of attachment at all, but rather some more traditional (though not necessarily superior) psychological conception, such as one akin to a "generalized fear of the strange," "degree of general responsiveness in social situations," or simply "social behaviors" [as Gesell and Thompson (1934) termed them].

MOTIVATIONAL OR COGNITIVE TERMS AND INDEX USAGE

Another strategic issue related to the use of criteria stems from the fact that various conceptual treatments of object relations have attributed certain inexplicit motivational or cognitive properties to behavior systems connoting attachment or dependence. I can begin my treatment of this issue with some illustrative cases in which *motivational* assumptions are used.

Schaffer and Emerson (1964) have written of an "attachment need as the motivational force behind proximity seeking." It is "... a directional force within the organism, of an enduring character and evoked by certain specific conditions [p. 63]." In a similar vein, "dependency motivation" has sometimes been thought to provide the drive basis for diverse dependent responses such as help-, attention-, and approval-seeking [e.g., by Sears (1963), who in the cited reference has himself questioned this usage of the motive construct]. One apparent consequence in such cases is that the stimulus contexts that acquire control over the relevant responses are often underemphasized, while the response classes themselves serve as the main focus of concern. In such cases, there may also be a tendency to use variables that summarize the incidence of diverse indices grouped under the concept (e.g., a "total dependency" score).

However, there are theorists (myself included) for whom differential, acquired stimulus control can provide a plausible basis for the acquisition and maintenance of behaviors thought to reflect dependence and attachment (as was detailed in the preceding chapter). For these theorists, the positing of a motive force to account for behaviors under direct stimulus control is unnecessary and, indeed, could only amplify the ambiguities inherent in the dependence or attachment terms.

Another consequence of this questionable usage of drive terms appears to be an emphasis on limited "response-response" relations. I can illustrate this by taking note of the occasional practice in the literature of placing much value on a simple functional relation between two (or more) response measures. The assumption underlying this practice often seems to be that one of the two response measures more directly (than the other) reflects the essential nature of a theoretical construct, and is therefore more "basic." By the same token, that measure approximates the role of an independent variable. Examples of this are the "learned social need" for approval (Crowne & Strickland, 1961; Crowne & Marlowe, 1964) and the "learned motivational system" of dependency (e.g., Cairns & Lewis, 1962). At the same time, the second, "less-basic" response measure is implicitly assumed to constitute the outcome and, by that token, to approximate a dependent variable. For instance, a social-desirability questionnaire, which is assumed to assess "approval need" directly, has been used to predict the reinforcing efficacy of approval stimuli on a conditioning task. And, in a parallel fashion, dependency status (high or low), as assessed by a Personal Preference Schedule, has been used to predict the differential social reinforcing efficacy (as well as the subjective evaluations) of assent-approval stimuli.

But such research reports appear to provide merely a straightforward response-response, or part-whole, relationship between response data from two (or more) alternative empirical operations that each denote, for the individual subject, the importance of a set of stimuli constituting assent-approval. Some of the theorists involved have noted this themselves (e.g., Crowne & Marlowe, 1964). However, even when this limitation is recognized, researchers may still give insufficient attention to the earlier-listed possibility: that while one of the two response variables is conceived to be more fundamental than the other—a cause for the effect, as it were—as parts of the same process both variables may simply represent joint outcomes of the very same antecedents. In these conceptual contexts, therefore, there has seemed to be a tendency to disregard the utility of close analyses of acquired stimulus control and reinforcer efficacy. Instead, there has seemed to be a concentration on the problem of relating responses as a means of validating a system's constructs. The result has often been a neglect of the search for antecedent or concurrent environmental causal factors.

In a similar though more differentiated vein, some approaches to attachment as focused relationships have noted that sequential levels of object relationship parallel closely the developmental sequence of basic *perceptual* and *cognitive functions* (e.g., see Yarrow, 1967). One implication in some of these approaches to the origins of socio-emotional response systems connoting attachment has seemed to be that: a particular developmental level of perceptual and/or cognitive functioning denoted by one set of discriminative responses (in both nonsocial and social contexts, or in nonsocial contexts alone) is a precondition for a particular level of attachment that is denoted by another set of discriminative responses (in a social context).

Before applying the same line of reasoning I used in the preceding section on motivational determinants, let me for the moment assume that the terms "discrimination," "perception," and "cognition" are mutually exclusive—which, of course, they are not. For conceptions employing those more traditional headings, therefore, what may be conceived to be involved in each such case is merely a part-whole, or a response-response, correlation in which both sets of response variables are involved in the same process. As conventionally defined, many perceptual-cognitive and attachment behaviors either are members of the same larger response class, or they are joint outcomes of the same determinants. On this basis, therefore, one would expect the two sets of indices to be highly correlated. The analysis here is in keeping with Yarrow's (this volume) observation that it is difficult to distinguish between perceptual-cognitive and socio-emotional development. It also meshes with the conclusion of various others from the available evidence, that the onset of specific attachments is likely to be but one manifestation of a general development (e.g., Bell, 1970; Schaffer & Emerson, 1964).

In a very different way from the preceding examples, the issue of indices appears to be involved in theoretical treatments of attachment that have emphasized a conception of stimulus control (such as that advanced in the preceding chapter). In what appears to be a limiting case of such a conception, Wahler (1967) has written that: ". . . one could argue that the infant has become socially attached when it can be demonstrated that his behavior is subject to social reinforcement control" from an adult, in that the social-reinforcement and the social-attachment concepts both imply that the child is influenced by the social behavior of others (p. 1080). Thus, Wahler has conceived of a "social reinforcement criterion of attachment." In the process, he seems to have made attachment synonymous with the first demonstrated instance of social-reinforcer control. In this frame, myriad behaviors can come under social-reinforcer control and would thus provide attachment indices. Therefore, the utility of the term attachment, even as a label, would become virtually nil at any level of analysis. The conceptual tactic of continuing use of the attachment term in such a framework can lead to confusion and also raises the question of parsimony.

INDICES AND UNDERLYING "ENTITIES"

There is one last issue to consider in this section on the relation of selected indices to conceptions of dependence or attachment. It concerns instances of terms that have evolved to characterize differentially, and to label, a set of behaviors. In some approaches in which this usage has developed, terms like attachment have also seemed to come to stand for an underlying intraorganismic structure (e.g., "inner representation," "inner structural basis") "inside" the organism, that is assumed independent of the overt behaviors which "mediate" it (e.g., Ainsworth, 1963, 1964, 1967, 1969; Ainsworth & Bell, 1970). Another view that seems to imply an attachment-as-entity position is that of Schaffer and Emerson (1964), who have held that the child's separation protest is an index only that "an attachment exists," but is not in itself an "attachment behavior." In the position underlying these views, there is the implication (possibly unintended) that what is involved "inside the organism" is an "under the skin" entity that will require physiological or similar operations for its investigation. The position implied in these views would seem to be irrelevant for a behavioral approach, which I would judge every approach in this volume to be.

Apart from this implication of an underlying biological basis for behavior systems, however, the writings singled out above have also seemed to imply an underlying entity with a status that is independent of the overt behaviors it would explain. This implication follows from the assumption in those writings that there are occasions on which particular attachment behaviors do not reflect the strength of the underlying attachment bond. This latter assumption may be similar to a notion one occasionally finds in the field of intelligence testing, when the tested individual has not performed as well as the tester has assumed he should: It is that performance on a particular testing occasion might not reflect an individual's "true" intelligence.

To put the matter generally, in these apparently parallel cases an individual is said to show attachment behaviors because of his underlying attachment bond and to behave intelligently because of his underlying intelligence. In both instances, however, a single set of facts—behaviors labeled attachment or intelligent—would appear to provide the basis for two statements. These statements are spoken of as independent, but are actually dependent—one, attachment or intelligent behaviors, and the other, an underlying attachment bond or intelligence. And one of these statements appears to have evolved to become the basis for the other—viz., intelligent behavior is due to an underlying intelligence; attachment behavior is due to an underlying attachment bond. This practice can imply that the underlying "cause" of the behaviors has been uncovered and that further search may be unnecessary. However, the statements are entirely dependent. Therefore, to use a semantic metaphor, these seeming transformations of descriptive behavior properties (adjectives) into underlying structural bases (nouns) add nothing to an explanation of the nature of the process underlying attachment (or dependence) behaviors—that is, the network of functional relations between those behaviors and controlling stimuli (see Skinner, 1953). Indeed, these transformations may detract from the explanation required, inasmuch as the theorists and researchers following such usage seem to be operating in terms of an entity that has no status independent of the overt behavior it purports to explain. Therefore, they may not be prepared to accept the properties of the process that are eventually discovered by systematic operational analysis.

Even so, this apparent notion of attachment as an entity sometimes may be merely a preliminary metaphor for organizing attachment behaviors in the absence of, and prior to, determination of much of the network of differential stimulus-control functions involved. In this connection, Ainsworth has taken steps in this volume to clarify her earlier (e.g., Ainsworth, 1969) emphasis on the "attachment [that] resides in the inner structure . . . which affects behavior [p. 1016]." She has indicated that terms like "inner representation" or "inner structure" serve as theoretical constructs in her approach.

Technical Assumptions Often Underlying the Use of Attachment and Dependence Indices

In the preceding section, I noted some strategic considerations often involved in the choice of indices in research conducted under abstract conceptions like those of dependence or attachment. There are also a number of tactical considerations bearing on the way those criteria are used. In this section, I examine several of these.

SOME TACTICAL CONSIDERATIONS IN INDEX SELECTION AND USE

One relevant tactical consideration is that there is likely to be some overlap among the criteria used under either the attachment or the dependence concept. This may be due in part to the necessarily arbitrary selection of criteria by early investigators [for example, in the case of dependence, those chosen by Beller (1948) or Gewirtz (1948)]. This overlap may thus be inbuilt, even definitional, particularly when behaviors are grouped in abstract categories. For instance, it is difficult to conceive of a case when a child is held by an adult and is not simultaneously caressed or provided with behaviors that connote "positive attention," if not also "approval" or "affection." The overlap among criterion indices may have been fostered by the number used and by the scarcity of statistical attempts to reduce that number. The artifactual patterns due to criterion overlap could be accentuated by rater biases that enter when index scores are derived from ratings. Hence, if substantial intercorrelations among indices were found, they could be due to these artifactual bases alone. Holding these considerations constant, in the remainder of this section I discuss some reasons for expecting either low or zero-order relationships among indices.

There are a number of grounds that have been put forth for expecting indices of attachment or of dependence to intercorrelate. These assumptions also warrant close examination. I commented earlier that there are numerous potential indices that can be used under the various conventional conceptions of dependence or of attachment, and that this fact has rarely been given explicit recognition. As a result, diverse behaviors might appear to provide the basis for reasonable criteria of attachment or of dependence, singly or in various combinations. In addition, I noted that the theoretical terms used have rarely been well coordinated with empirical index operations. Further, those indices may differ in such features as their consistency or observer reliability. It would be well for such considerations to be taken into account when inferences are made from any set of criteria, however relevant they might seem for a researcher's theory.

At the very least, these considerations can stand as caveats against a set of implicit assumptions that I think has been widely, though uncritically, held: (*a*) that the various indices used under either the concept of attachment or the concept of dependence are interchangeable measures of a unitary process (e.g., in the case of dependence, the indices would include touching and holding, being near, and positive attention-seeking); (*b*) that, therefore, they should yield high (in principle, perfect), mostly positive, intercorrelations; and (*c*) that the coefficients comprising a single intercorrelation matrix should characterize all subjects in all situations.

This set of implicit assumptions is unwarranted, whether the responses generating the indices under either concept are in fact alternatives to each other or mutually exclusive, and whether they are observed in a given situation or across settings-contexts. In either case, the variegated indices need not intercorrelate in a simple way, or with the same sign, or even at all [as has been demonstrated for dependency by Sears et al. (1953), Heathers (1955), Gewirtz (1956a), Emmerich (1964), and Sears et al. (1965)]. I think it may be an oversimplification to expect that one set of intercorrelation matrix values will characterize the interrelationships among indices for some group of randomly selected subjects. In the sections that follow, I attempt to give some of the reasoning behind the technical concerns I am raising here.

THE INFLUENCE OF CONDITIONING HISTORY ON INDICES

By the very nature of the life setting, it seems reasonable to suppose that the histories of individual children would differ with regard to each of the response systems upon which dependence or attachment indices are based. One might expect to find something like a standard S-R interaction chain pattern that would characterize closely the sequential attachment or dependence behaviors for subgroups of children, each identified as homogeneous in conditioning history (or operating within a particular restrictive setting that homogenizes the group experience and behavior options). However, the characteristic mode of sampling in this research area has been to select individual children for sample groups without regard either to their conditioning histories or to their behavior patterns. Because of their different reinforcement histories, it is plausible to assume that the behaviors of such individuals will be organized according to quite different interaction-chain patterns. As a consequence, the index intercorrelation matrix values obtained for such an otherwise unselected group of subjects would be nothing more than an average or mode that reflects random-sampling factors, specifically the number from each homogeneous reinforcement-history subgroup that happened to be selected for the sample group.

Let me detail for the individual case (or subgroup homogeneous in conditioning history) how such factors might play roles in determining the intercorrelation values among criterion indices. Some responses typically providing the bases for indices may have a certain relation to other responses in each S-R chain pattern. For instance, one response may be a precondition, or an alternative, for another response. Thus, in a standard (and perhaps artificial) setting in which assessments are made, Child (or Subgroup) A might be (misleadingly) scored higher than Child (or Subgroup) B on nearness behaviors and lower on behaviors connoting deviations for attention, simply because Child A's response to stimuli early in an attention-seeking chain pattern was moving near, while Child B's was making loud noises or crying. Further, such patterns may be obscured or qualified by the possibility that, at later phases in the learning process, there may be a "short-circuiting" as a chain becomes more efficient. Fewer behavior steps may come to be required for a stimulus consequence connoting attention, approval, or the like, to occur following a child's behaviors. Finally, if a response to a stimulus close to the end point of a chain is prevented from occurring, it is conceivable that a child would then more frequently use a response which originally would occur (only) earlier in the organization of an S-R sequence.

THE INFLUENCE OF SITUATIONAL CONTEXT ON INDICES

The assumption that a particular behavior occurs independent of the situations sampled often seems to have lain behind the implicit expectation that a set of indices should intercorrelate in a homogeneous way. A similar assumption appears to have underlain much early trait-concept usage, that averaged the responding of either the child *or* the environmental agency across situations and setting conditions (Gewirtz, 1969a). However, there is considerable evidence from diverse sources that situational contexts acquire differential discriminative control over child behaviors (e.g., see Gewirtz, 1972b). Hence, an assumption of independence between behavior and situational contexts is seldom if ever tenable. In this frame, the sample of situations that happens to be selected for study will bias the behavioral data obtained, the intercorrelation matrices they form, and the conclusions drawn from them. This bias would constitute no problem when the situations sampled are those specified by a researcher's theoretical model. However, when a sampling condition does not conform to that model, the attempt to generalize from the intercorrelation matrix that happened to be found would be impeached.

The particular situations in which behaviors occur may dramatically affect the operation of a chain. For example, when a child is ill in bed, one stimulus-response pattern could characteristically occur; while, when a child is in a peer group, a quite different organization of stimuli and responses could occur. Moreover, some response patterns could on occasion cancel others, or lead to the same end result. Finally, the momentary setting conditions involved (such as when a child is hungry or tired) could differentially determine the efficacy of stimuli and hence the behaviors for which they are discriminative or reinforcing. In this frame, the stimulus context in which a response is exhibited will determine its meaning and theoretical relevance. Therefore, both response content and the environmental situation (as well as contextual-setting conditions) must be specified and taken into account. However, analyses have often seemed unaware of the possible importance, for their criteria of attachment or dependence, of such contextual factors and of such factors as social and physical ecological constraints and the definitional overlap of those presumably independent criteria. This limitation can make some researches on dependence or attachment artifactually complex as well as arbitrary, and can insure that their reported findings will be difficult to evaluate.

REINFORCEMENT HISTORY, SITUATIONAL CONTEXT, AND INDICES

I have discussed separately the possible influences on criterion indices of conditioning history and of situational context. In this frame, it seems reasonable to suppose that the occurrence of a behavior could often depend upon the relative response strengths determined by the reinforcement histories of the subjects in addition to the constraints in the situations represented, or possibly upon the interaction of those two factors. For instance, a child who ordinarily exhibits consensually valued behaviors that are maintained by positive attention might exhibit undesired behavior deviations for attention when those around him are quite busy and otherwise unresponsive to him. Similarly, after exposure to a brief period of social isolation, children for whose behaviors social approval had acquired strong positive reinforcing value (as determined by a questionnaire) emitted relatively more "*in*correct" responses that were (positively) reinforced by contingent disapproval connoting "negative attention" (hearing the visible experimenter say "You're wrong") than they emitted "correct" responses that were followed by a contingent flash of light (Gallimore, Tharp, & Kemp, 1969).

SOME CLOSING POINTS ABOUT INDEX INTERCORRELATIONS

Criterion indices (subcategories) of dependence or of attachment often seem to have been selected for research more for traditional than for systematic reasons. In this frame, I used the basic conditioning conception that the S-R chain represents to suggest some reasons why such indices need *not* relate to each other highly, in a particular homogeneous way, or necessarily even at all. My reasoning held especially for children studied without regard to their S-R chain histories—to date, the characteristic mode of sampling. I have noted that generalizations about the relationships among the indices, or between them and environmental settings, could be limited because these sampling factors would tend to determine (bias) a particular intercorrelation matrix. A matrix of index intercorrelations summarizing (e.g., averaging) the diverse relations considered could fail to reflect, and could even obscure, the differentiated natures of the underlying S-R chain patterns. That is, if only certain responses are observed in selected settings while the entire functioning S-R chain and its conditioning history are overlooked, an incomplete, even misleading, impression of the child's differentiated behavior patterns may be obtained. (I noted earlier that these patterns represent but one focus of a functional analysis of the sequential relations between stimuli and responses. The reciprocal focus is that of the behaviors manifested by the caretaking environment which are here considered to be the bases of the stimuli affecting the child's behaviors.) Knowing the different conditioning-history patterns of the individuals comprising a group of subjects, the stimulus and setting conditions operating in the situation, and how those factors interact, would therefore provide a reasonable basis for understanding and predicting the pattern in which the dependence or attachment responses are organized.

I shall close this section by noting that researchers have occasionally sought intercorrelations between indices, or between gross summary statements (based on groups of indices) like total attachment (or dependence), and a term or terms at similar levels of analysis from another conceptual area, for instance, some global "identification" score. Under a functional analysis like that of the preceding chapter, such intercorrelations could prove to be of little theoretical consequence when the two abstract terms (in our example, attachment and identification) are reduced to their component functional relations between stimuli and responses. These relations would involve the discriminative and reinforcing value, for particular child responses, of stimuli from the attachment object and from the identification model (Gewirtz & Stingle, 1968; Gewirtz,

1969b). Use of such a differentiated functional analysis can avoid what are difficulties at more abstract analytic levels. For instance, it would be focused at the level of detail appropriate for describing and explaining instances where individual children display different or opposite patterns of behaviors; or where some children do, and others do not, display behaviors which fall under the attachment or dependence criteria used.

Considerations Regarding the Number and Types of Indices to Employ

ON THE USE OF A SINGLE INDEX

I have indicated that there are in use many and varied criteria of dependence and of attachment. The employment of several presumed indices of a process is not in itself detrimental. However, I have noted some limitations of using a large number of such indices uncritically. A convenient and fruitful tactic often employed in conditioning and other experimental analyses has been the use of a single index (and measure). This tactic has seldom been considered in the dependence-attachment research area. Even so, the use of one response class as the basis for a single index may be sufficient for a researcher's purposes if it is:

1. reliable and generates a sufficient range of empirically consistent scores (a criterion for any measure);

2. representative of the stimulus-control process under the researcher's theoretical conception; and

3. functionally related to important independent variables under the researcher's theoretical expectations.

A single index can be convenient when it seems effectively to focus the stimulus control functions under investigation on one response. In this way, it can preclude the need to use numerous indices that require complicated analysis by multivariate statistical procedures, if their number is not reduced on some basis.

Much has been made of investigations that have explored the differential reinforcing efficacy of stimuli like the spoken word *good* for discriminative child responding following short-term deprivation and satiation pretreatments (e.g., Gewirtz, 1967, 1969c, 1972b; Landau & Gewirtz, 1967). Laboratory studies of social discriminative and reinforcing stimuli connoting "attention" or "approval" and the responses they control have not ordinarily been considered related to attachment or dependence behaviors in life situations [though studies like that of Cairns and Lewis (1962) have been exceptions]. But such stimuli are often very similar to those maintaining behaviors classified under the two concepts. It should therefore be instructive for researchers of attachment and dependence to examine the functional relations into which the social stimuli labeled attention and approval enter [as Maccoby and Masters (1970) have done so well]. At the very least, these functions can illustrate the advantages (and perhaps some disadvantages as well) of using a single criterion index in research.

I have noted that an index based on a single cued response (or a very small number of responses) can serve efficiently and usefully in attachment or dependence research when it is representative of the broader set of stimulus-control functions that characterize the individual's behaviors in connection with an object-person(s). However, I should note some reservations about the use of small numbers of indices, particularly under an approach that is not far advanced and hence is inevitably inexplicit or unfocused. An important caveat here is that a single attachment or dependence index might be extremely unrepresentative. That is, children displaying high scores on that index might show low scores on other indices (that reflect either positive or negative stimulus control over responses). For instance, it is possible that an index of attachment or dependence in life settings based on a single response (or on a small number of responses) may only reflect the conditioning history of an isolated response system that is actually under some special form of social stimulus control independent of, and unrepresentative of, that implied by the attachment or dependence conception used. Thus, the utility of a single index may be limited in some contexts by the difficulty of insuring that it does not simply reflect uncharacteristic conditions in a child's conditioning history.

In an earlier section, I noted that Etzel and Gewirtz (1967) have shown that infant crying can be readily maintained (i.e., reinforced) by caretaker attention (such as is provided by hovering around the child, talking, picking him up), even in the early weeks of life.[3] Various investigators have demonstrated similarly how diverse other responses, which some have used as bases for attachment indices, can be instrumentally conditioned in the early weeks of life. This is also

---

[3] In this volume, Ainsworth has described some cases of infant crying which, at first glance, might seem anomalous for an instrumental-learning conception. To determine definitively how that conditioning paradigm might apply to such problematic cases as those where caretakers respond to infant crying, information would be required about actual response and contingent event definitions, the role in the situations of unconditioned noxious events that can evoke crying, information about the consistency of the contingency across trials, and similar data. For example, as Ainsworth suggests in this volume, when caretakers characteristically respond rapidly and discriminably to pre-intense crying responses (signals), their infants may subsequently cry less. That is, it may be pre-crying signal responses and not intense, lengthy crying responses that are conditioned in that set of situations. In a context where the response and the contingent, reinforcing event are codetermined, it is only when the provision of a contingent event systematically changes the rate of a defined response that it is termed a reinforcing stimulus or reinforcer for that response. In this frame, a contingent event that can reinforce one response need not serve as a reinforcer for that response under all contextual-setting conditions, nor for another response (Gewirtz, 1972b). It should be noted also that there is no obvious relation in such an operant-conditioning approach between a reinforcing stimulus and either an event that could serve as an unconditioned stimulus to "activate" a response or an event that could "terminate" a response. However, if an unconditioned aversive stimulus ("activator") for a response like crying is removed and hence terminates that response, that stimulus might be functioning in a reinforcing role for whatever response brought about its removal.

well before the time many would conceive that an "attachment" could have been acquired. Among others, these responses include eye contact, smiling, vocalizing, and crying (e.g., Brackbill, 1958; Rheingold, Gewirtz, & Ross, 1959; Weisberg, 1963; Etzel & Gewirtz, 1967). Also, the ages of onset and of the acquisition of selective stimulus control may vary with the differences in experience implied by diverse child-rearing settings (Ambrose, 1961; Gewirtz, 1965; H. B. & J. L. Gewirtz, 1969). Therefore, if a single attachment or dependence index is used, the researcher must take account of the possibility that the attributes of the cued response upon which it is based might reflect only a history in which the child had been routinely reinforced for displaying that behavior in the same situation, for instance, crying whenever his mother was about to leave his vicinity. This should constitute no problem for the researcher under whose model the particular conditioned stimulus-control function governing a response is representative of functions that connote attachment or dependence. However, a researcher might attempt to employ another response or set of responses (perhaps one less likely to be under this type of acquired stimulus control) if he would consider that stimulus-control function to be either unrepresentative under his model or irrelevant to his conception of attachment or dependence.

Instrumentally conditioned behaviors could conceivably provide the bases for indices that are assumed representative of the stimulus-control process connoting attachment or dependence in a functional analysis. But this may not be so under some theoretical conceptions that do not emphasize a conditioning model. Under some such conceptions, a conditioned basis for a discriminative response that generates an attachment (or a dependence) index might imply artifacts that impeach the results from an investigation of attachment. Alternatively, such a conditioning basis might only imply confounded rather than direct attachment criteria under the researcher's model. A nonlearning approach would therefore do well to address directly the issue of possibly-conditioned behavior systems serving as its criterion indices.

The issue might be illustrated didactically with the Schaffer and Emerson (1964) report that I considered earlier in another context. By citing their most interesting report, I do not imply criticism of it or of its authors. However, it has been an influential document in the attachment (-dependence) literature and, as such, can serve as a useful vehicle for considering an important aspect of the selection of indices. Schaffer and Emerson employed several measures derived from what was essentially a single cued-response-based index of attachment. Those measures summarized the occurrence, intensity, and direction of infant protests (comprised of whimpers, fusses, and cries) after seven different types of separations from their mothers and others.[4] On the basis of mothers' reports,

---

[4] It is interesting to note that Ainsworth (1963), who employed 13 behavior criteria in her study of attachment, found that the use of the single protest index was insufficient and (in terms of her findings) possibly even misleading. (Considerations in the use of a large number of indices were discussed earlier.)

Schaffer and Emerson (1964, p. 50) found that the "intensity of attachment-to-mother at 18 months" (measured in terms of the characteristic intensity of protests at separation) was a positive function of (scale scores for) the frequency and speed with which a mother responds to her infant's crying (initiations).

Under a routine instrumental-learning conception, one possible basis for these results might have been that the infants who protested (cried) most strongly at separation were those whose mothers consistently and rapidly reacted to their protest and crying behaviors. In this way, the mothers could have reinforced aspects of those behaviors, and cues provided by a mother's preparations for departure from her infant would have become discriminative for his crying and fussing protest responses. Schaffer and Emerson (1964, p. 51) have themselves noted this possibility in their discussion of the relationship between attachment intensity and the frequency and speed of maternal responsiveness to infant crying. However, those investigators chose to discount this conditioning explanation of their attachment-measure results, feeling that cause and effect could not be disentangled in this context. They conceived that the result could just as likely have reflected a mother's having learned to "give in" to her infant's persistent crying.

But there remains an issue for researchers like Schaffer and Emerson to resolve. The composite of the various measures of protests-in-separation situations used in their investigation to index the child's attachment to his mother alternatively might have reflected what their theory could conceivably consider to be only a limited fact. Such a limited fact for them might be that, in the sample studied, mothers had systematically reinforced the crying-protest behaviors of their children, particularly when about to leave their children's vicinities. Those authors could find that possibly conditioned mother-infant pattern to be a limited fact under their theory if they did *not* conceive it to be representative of the wider infant-mother interaction process, or if they thought it irrelevant to attachment on some other ground. In either event, it would be necessary for them to develop what would be considered a more adequate set of indices under their theoretical model.

Another facet of this conditioning issue also has implications for the Schaffer and Emerson findings. Those authors found pronounced individual differences in the age of onset of a "specific attachment." Differences in specific protest-training conditions (particularly in the discriminability of the unique cues provided by the object-mother when she prepared her departures) might have accounted, at least in part, for this result. Whether single or multiple criteria of attachment are used, an analysis of the stimulus conditions that have acquired control over relevant responses of the individual could help to hold constant these conditioning factors when they are thought to confound the indices selected under a particular theoretical conception.

ON SEQUENTIAL INTERACTION DETAILS AND
SUMMARY VARIABLES

There is yet another dimension to the issue of the choice of indices of attachment or of dependence. The tactics of different theoretical approaches to the phenomena grouped under these terms will often differ. Nevertheless, at the core of nearly every approach is a concern with process and, therefore, with the sequential details of caretaker-child interchanges (Gewirtz, 1969a). However, researchers have occasionally used summarizing variables (e.g., "total dependency") to characterize the child's behavior systems that were of interest. Also, they have sometimes used terms at similar levels of abstraction for summarizing the controlling details of the environment that are assumed to be relevant.[5] This usage has sometimes been justified on practical grounds in preliminary investigations and by near-term tactical considerations (as a research short cut) in research on more differentiated issues.

In the frame outlined, as well as under an instrumental-learning model, the potentially profitable approach is to determine which stimuli provided by the object-person(s) are, or become, effective in controlling the child's responses, and which of the child's responses are cued and maintained (reinforced) by those stimuli (and vice versa for the object-person). A functional approach to the reciprocal-control conditioning process therefore emphasizes the details of the sequential patterning of the contingencies between environmental and behavioral events occurring in the interchanges between the child and his (caretaking) environment (Gewirtz, 1961, 1969a). This emphasis is not dissimilar to that advocated by Cairns in this volume. Nor is it unlike Ainsworth's concern in this volume or Bowlby's (1969) recent stress upon the sequential details of interaction and upon the settings and conditions in which the observed behaviors occur. In this volume, Sears has also recognized the importance of an emphasis like this, agreeing that such "global attitudinal qualities" as warmth and permissiveness ". . . do not accurately reflect the really relevant variables, i.e., the contingencies of reinforcement and the precise behavior being reinforced [p. 8]." He therefore also stresses the relevance of an interaction analysis which details the specific stimulus conditions associated with a particular response as well as the reinforcement schedule for each action.

Variables that summarize behaviors or stimulus events across contexts, or that are almost demographic in character (e.g., time a mother spends interacting with her child in a given setting or merely being near him there), can be reduced readily to patterns of environmental stimuli in contingent relations with child behaviors, in a developmental framework. [This can be illustrated by some research in which I have been engaged (J. L. & H. B. Gewirtz, 1965; H. B. & J. L.

[5]The role of such one-sided variables in research on the two-sided parent-child interaction process has been considered in detail elsewhere (e.g., Gewirtz, 1969a, 1969b; J. L. & H. B. Gewirtz, 1965; H. B. & J. L. Gewirtz, 1969).

Gewirtz, 1969).] A functional learning approach emphasizes the sequential features of stimulus control for both the acquisition and the maintenance of behavior, as well as the situational and setting-condition context of interaction (Gewirtz, 1967, 1972b). Under such an approach, there tends to be little need for gross terms like attachment or dependence, except possibly to point to the particular literature for which a set of findings are considered relevant. Even so, once the sequential details of the interchanges between stimuli and responses are identified, there are many ways in which those data could be grouped (e.g., by content or control function) and summarized for different analytic purposes. These purposes might include: (a) detailing successive behavior patterns (including those connoting attachment or dependence) during the first year of life for particular infant subgroups; (b) comparing widely different child-rearing groups; or (c) devising strategies for fostering desired outcomes in interpersonal behavior.

For research problems such as these, there could be some utility in attempting to identify: (a) the types of social-response patterns that occur at successive points in a child's history; and (b) the sequences in time that they constitute. At the same time, there are in principle problem definitions for which these response-pattern types and sequences need not differ markedly from those detected under quite different conceptual approaches. Thus, patterns collected under our conditioning approach for children in the first year of life (under a and b above) may resemble the five phases Ainsworth (1967) has concluded characterize the development of attachment of Ganda infants or the five somewhat different social response patterns Yarrow (1967) has concluded correspond to "levels of object relationship" in infants prior to and following their separation from foster mothers. Alternatively, the naturally occurring behaviors might be grouped according to principles under a quite different problem definition, such as that of identifying ordered phases in a single-response-based index. Hence, phases, levels, or patterns may be used to represent a more abstract order of response definition under any approach, including one like ours that is oriented toward detailing the functional relations denoting stimulus control over responses. The basic point is that there are purposes for which these or other pattern-summary variables could have utility, for instance when they can organize efficiently the already-identified sequential details of interactions.

Diverse research approaches have tended to rely on the method of studying generalized patterns of environmental stimulation, such as those termed nurturance, consistency, or frustration, and of relating them to general behavior traits in children, like those termed dependency, attention-seeking, or insecurity (Gewirtz, 1969a). Even approaches that emphasize learning conceptions have done this, often for tactical reasons. At the same time, even when stimulus conditions that control and maintain attachment or dependence behaviors have provided the basis for summary variables that have proved useful, the interchange data have frequently been obscured. (Those data are made up of the moment-to-moment behavior changes effected by moment-to-moment changes in the controlling stimuli.) In this context, there have been too few attempts, using either summary variables or those representing the details, to tie closely dependence or attachment behaviors as outcomes to antecedents comprised of extreme aberrant conditions (e.g., those connoting "maternal deprivation").

On occasions when global variables do not function effectively in a summarizing role, their use can simply obscure the fundamental characteristics of the processes loosely grouped under the dependence or attachment headings. By their nature, therefore, such gross summary variables have limited the analyses of both the stimulus conditions and the behaviors of the child. This is because they have tended to index only some average characteristics of the behaviors and/or stimulus conditions through extended time spans. And they have tended to preclude the necessity of focusing upon the sequential and contingent aspects of the interchanges between the discrete stimuli provided by (behaviors of persons in) the environment and the discrete behaviors of the child. As an apparent result, use of such summary variables has been accompanied by the de-emphasis, even neglect, of the details of parent-child interchanges. Therefore, such methods cannot help but miss the subtleties of the underlying process(es) that various extant theoretical approaches would consider relevant and important.

Relevance of the Empirical Normative Literature to Attachment and Dependence Indices

I now move to a consideration of the empirical child development literature and its relevance for attachment or dependence criteria. This literature contains findings that have been reported in the form of chronological-age norms for behavior systems which are defined similarly to those used as criterion indices of attachment or dependence. Moreover, attachment (and to a lesser extent, dependence) behavior-based indices have often been plotted in terms of chronological age (e.g., see Schaffer & Emerson, 1964; Yarrow, 1967). Nevertheless, there have been remarkably few attempts, not to mention systematic ones, by such investigators of attachment or dependence to compare the age course of their criterion indices with extant norms in this child development literature. I here explore this noteworthy phenomenon and some of its consequences.

The child development literature is replete with normative studies of age-related differences for a variety of behaviors oriented (differentially) to mothers and others, or evoked by "strangers" (e.g., Bühler, 1933; Shirley, 1933; Gesell & Thompson, 1934; Gesell, Halverson, Thompson, Ilg, Castner, Ames, & Amatruda, 1940). Studied at monthly or bimonthly intervals during the first year of life, these social behaviors include differential regard, recognition, or knowing of mothers, and the acceptance of "strangers" or sobering at, fearing, or withdrawing from them. The literature also contains diverse reports of investigations of particular chronological age-related social behaviors, for instance, infant smiling to a human face (e.g., Washburn, 1929; Spitz & Wolf, 1946; Ambrose, 1961; Gewirtz, 1965), crying at psychological (Bayley, 1932) and medical (Levy, 1960) examinations, and similar behaviors.

Moreover, almost all infant developmental or "intelligence" tests contain items that are similar to some of the social responses studied in normative researches (e.g., Gesell, 1925, 1928; Bühler, 1930; Bayley, 1933, 1969; Cattell, 1960; Gesell & Amatruda, 1962; Gilliland, 1949, 1951; Griffiths, 1954). These test items are derived from the response norms of standardization samples. Hence, the chronological age placement of each item could indicate at what monthly age children from the test standardization groups characteristically exhibited the item response in the standard stimulus context used (holding constant the criterion of item placement used).

THE LACK OF COORDINATION BETWEEN SOME CONTEMPORARY AND EARLIER STUDIES

The age norms of a variety of such studies have been available for many years. However, investigators of the age-course of often very similar responses, which have been used as indices of an "attachment" ("relationship") or of "dependence," have rarely even attempted either to compare their results to those of studies that did not use the same labels, or to explain similarities or differences in result patterns (e.g., see Ainsworth, 1963, 1964, 1967; Schaffer & Emerson, 1964; Yarrow, 1967). Furthermore, it has often seemed that the age norms found in investigations carried out under the aegis of conceptions like attachment or dependence are somehow considered to be more conceptually relevant or important than the age norms identified in studies to which such labels were not applied.

Investigators who have operated under the headings of attachment or dependence have tried in various ways to emphasize a patterning of their response-based indices in relation to their concepts. Nevertheless, it is remarkable that the age functions for their heavily stressed indices have typically been reported only in isolation, without being in any way related to what appear to be earlier, well-known studies that have tabled age functions for very similar and sometimes apparently identical response indices (e.g., based on patterns of smiling, crying at separation, or withdrawing from strangers).[6] Nor have those reports indicated how such operations as stimulus and response definitions, methods of measurement, and samples differ (if indeed they do) from those of the earlier, apparently similar studies, how the age-related results differ (as they often do), and how these discrepancies may be explained (e.g., by sampling

---

[6] In his contribution to this volume, Yarrow has embarked upon a comparative listing of the age course of similar behaviors from diverse investigations. His is a most timely survey.

considerations). As a result, it has been difficult, if not impossible, for a reader to place the reported findings of each of these later studies of human attachment or dependence in proper perspective, to permit evaluating their relevance, not to mention their reliability.

Some examples can help us to appreciate the critical importance of this failure to coordinate the results of later investigations with the findings of earlier ones. Yarrow (1967), Schaffer and Emerson (1964), and Ainsworth (1967) have each reported the age course of social behaviors that seem to be similar to some of those for which age norms have been reported by Gesell and Thompson (1934). Thus, Yarrow investigated "active recognition of mother" at 1, 3, and 5 months of age, and Gesell and Thompson studied "knows mother" at comparable age points. Similarly, Schaffer and Emerson reported the number of children at successive age points who showed the onset of a "fear-of-strangers" (by crying, withdrawing, turning away, etc.); and Yarrow reported the percentage of subjects showing "stranger anxiety" [involving "active protest or withdrawal in the presence of a stranger (p. 436)"] ; while Gesell and Thompson employed the apparently similar indices of "withdraws from strangers" (and of "sobers at strangers") as well as the reciprocal index of "accepts strangers." Yet neither Yarrow nor Schaffer and Emerson have anywhere coordinated their studies or findings to those of Gesell and Thompson (or of others). Nor, what may be equally important, have they indicated their reasons for not thus "anchoring" their studies in the literature.

A comparison of some age-related results of the above investigations, however, reveals both apparent similarities and differences. For instance, Yarrow's (1967) criterion of "active recognition of mother" yielded similar results to the Gesell and Thompson index of "knows mother"; whereas Yarrow's index of "stranger anxiety" showed poor agreement with the Gesell and Thompson index of "withdraws from strangers" but reasonable agreement with their index of "accepts strangers." If such similarities and differences had at least been noted by Schaffer and Emerson or by Yarrow, and if an attempt had been made to explain them (where necessary), it would be easier for a reader to put their reported findings into proper perspective. That is, the reliability of the age-related results of the responses upon which their indices were based could be better appraised; and a sounder foundation would be provided for appreciating the conceptual implications of the social response patterns emphasized by those authors [for instance, in Yarrow's case, the five types of social-response patterns that he has posited correspond to different levels in the development of a focused object relationship (Yarrow, 1967)] .

Moreover, several of the researchers cited and others, doing work on attachment-dependence but also outside that conceptual frame, have related the response patterns studied to developmental levels as denoted by the chronological age course of behaviors. Yet there has seldom appeared to be an adequate empirical basis for their statements. The percentage or number of subjects showing a given response (e.g., sobering at the appearance of a stranger) or passing a given test item are often charted by chronological age in such normative studies. However, investigators of child behaviors have rarely even attempted to relate an individual's performance on an item at one age point to his performance on that same item at an earlier age point, or to his performance on some other item at the same or at an earlier age point. Thus, almost no one has even tried to describe the sequencing of the appearance of responses in the same individual, even in longitudinal studies.

EMPIRICAL FINDINGS AND CONCEPT LABELS

Although many researchers of age-related social behaviors have referred their indices to a conception of "attachment" ("focused relationship") or of "dependence," such labeling does not necessarily make their investigations or findings more relevant or useful than those that involve the very same indices but do not employ such labels. For instance, Yarrow (1967) and Gesell and Thompson (1934) employed similar indices; but Yarrow referred his findings to a conception of "focused object relationship" (attachment), while Gesell and Thompson seemed to conceive they were studying only "social behaviors." In this connection also, Ainsworth (1967) employed differential smiling as an attachment behavior under her research strategy, while a colleague and I (Gewirtz, 1965; J. L. & H. B. Gewirtz, 1965; H. B. & J. L. Gewirtz, 1969) did not so label the differential smiling behaviors we investigated. We reported the age course and environmental-group differences for such seemingly key social behaviors as smiling, vocalizing, watching, and crying, in sequential interchange with several key behaviors of the caretaking environment. In the process of studying those consensually meaningful child behavior systems, we found no compelling conceptual reason or tactical necessity for grouping these behavior results under, or referring them to, a superordinate concept like attachment or dependence. Although such a tactic has remained open to us, we thought such a focus might obscure some differential features of the response patterns detected that seem theoretically important.

In the same vein, Ainsworth and Wittig (1969) and Rheingold (1969) each investigated the effects of a strange environment on the behaviors of infants in the presence and absence of their mothers. In both studies, similar environmental conditions were implemented experimentally and similar infant behaviors served as dependent variables. Vocalizations and emotional distress responses (denoted by crying) as well as locomotor responses (denoting exploration or approach) were investigated (though Ainsworth and Wittig scored several other behaviors as well). In this frame, Ainsworth and Wittig did, and Rheingold did not, refer the functional relations detected between the behavior outcomes and the manipulated stimulus situations to a concept of attachment.

Thus, the decision to refer a set of functional relations to a superordinate concept like "attachment" or "dependence" has often been one of strategy (more than of tactics). Nevertheless, an all-too-frequent consequence of such an entirely legitimate conceptual decision has been the de-emphasis of the functional S-R relations detected. As a result, such findings have been contributing far less than they should have been to the literatures of the behavior systems involved. This is regrettable in a conceptual context where those approaches that have been thought to give detailed and specialized developmental accounts of attachment or dependence are only now beginning to detail the conceptual bases for the selection of some types of the indices they employ, though not yet for all their number. We must keep in mind that the addition of a conceptual label to the results of a study neither changes them nor accounts for differences between studies, nor necessarily makes one study more relevant than another. At the level of S-R criterion indices, empirical findings remain just that, regardless of the concept label to which they are referred.

Recapitulation

In the chapter preceding this one, I considered the functional relations connoting attachment or dependence and the various ways use has been made of those abstract terms, which have been closely related neither to empirical constructs nor to theoretical postulates. In this chapter, my discussion has focused upon the great variety of cued response classes that have provided bases for indices of attachment and/or dependence. These criterion indices, which often seem to have been chosen on arbitrary bases, have included combinations of approach behaviors (such as those reflecting differential preference or recognition, and approach behaviors in the context of avoidance) as well as emotional-disorganization behaviors [including those following interference with (approach) behavior sequences]. Noting the diversity of indices that have been used, I detailed considerations for index selection under different research strategies and tactics. These may be applied regardless of the particular theoretical orientation involved.

I emphasized the importance of employing variables that attend to (or at least that do not obscure) the sequential stimulus and response details in the interchanges between environment and child. In addition, I reasoned that the use of positive responses, cued by stimuli from object-persons or classes of persons, would serve as the most direct indices of the control process connoted by the term "attachment" or the term "dependence." At the same time, I noted some conditions in which one may also find it potentially useful and meaningful to employ indirect rather than direct attachment or dependence indices. Such indirect indices might be provided by responses reflecting approach in the context of avoidance or emotional-disorganization responses following interference with approach behavior sequences. Indeed, even single cued responses thought to be representative under a given theoretical approach could provide useful indices.

I emphasized that the measures employed by theorists to characterize the "strength" (or some other attribute) of dependence or attachment could be used for almost any behavior system, whatever its label; and that for many purposes one could study behavior systems that touch on a conception of attachment or dependence *without* invoking either concept. Progress in the direction of accumulating functional relations to characterize the processes at issue could proceed most efficiently in terms of operational concepts closely linked to observational data. However, the individual's responses can also be grouped in terms of such criteria as content or control function, depending upon a researcher's theoretical purpose. On this basis, one may identify phases, levels, or patterns that represent a more abstract order of response definition. This can also occur under a conditioning approach oriented toward detailing the functional relations denoting stimulus control over responses.

Several assumptions that often underlie the use of indices, and that qualify their validity, were noted and critically examined. A frequently implied but unwarranted assumption is that the various (often arbitrarily chosen) criteria of attachment—or the various dependence criteria—are each alternative indices of the same unitary attachment or dependence process and that, therefore, a homogeneous set of coefficients of a single intercorrelation matrix should characterize all subjects in all situations. In this frame, the conception of a common or standard S-R chain was used to illustrate some reasons why the different indices (subcategories) of dependence or of attachment should not be expected to relate to each other in a homogeneous way, or necessarily even at all. Furthermore, information about the different conditioning-history patterns of the individuals comprising a group of subjects and the stimulus conditions making up the situation sampled were assumed important for the comprehension and prediction of the intercorrelation pattern in which their dependence or attachment responses are organized.

Some tactical and strategic considerations regarding the number of indices to employ were also discussed. I noted that the uncritical use of a large number of such criteria could have detrimental consequences. But the use of several presumed indices of a process is not in itself detrimental, when the complexities involved and the possible consequences of this practice are taken into consideration. Moreover, as most recent approaches to attachment or dependence have not been maximally explicit, the potentially useful practice of employing a single behavior-based index and measure may have several limitations. For example, the cued response involved might be extremely unrepresentative of the individual's social repertoire and could actually be under some special form of social stimulus control independent of, and irrelevant to, that implied by a researcher's conception of attachment or dependence. Finally, I suggested that an instrumental-learning analysis of how stimulus conditions have acquired control over relevant responses of the individual can be one way of controlling factors that confound the inferences that may be drawn from indices.

Researchers have frequently used variables that summarize (often through time) the child's behaviors and/or the environmental details assumed relevant to those behaviors. This is related to the issues of the choice of attachment or dependence indices and the level of analysis. The tactic of using summary variables is occasionally warranted under strategies focused on process (which effectively include nearly every contemporary approach). However, an alternative emphasis outlined in this chapter urges increasing attention to the sequential and contingent stimulus and response details in the interaction between the child and his environment, for both the acquisition and the maintenance of (systems of) behavior. Under such a conceptual approach, there are a large number of practical ways in which the identified sequential details of the interchanges could be organized. For most conceptual purposes, a functional learning approach would minimize the need for gross summary variables for concepts like attachment or dependence. Such an emphasis would therefore avoid some of the difficulties encountered when attachment or dependence, as abstract terms, are indexed by criteria that may involve confounding factors, that may not be representative, or that may preclude considering the necessary interrelationships between stimuli provided by the environment and the relevant behaviors of the individual.

REFERENCES

Ainsworth, M. D. The development of infant-mother interaction among the Ganda. In B. M. Foss (Ed.), *Determinants of infant behaviour II*. London: Methuen (New York: Wiley), 1963. Pp. 67-112.

Ainsworth, M. D. Patterns of attachment behavior shown by the infant in interaction with his mother. *Merrill-Palmer Quarterly*, 1964, **10**, 51-58.

Ainsworth, M. D. S. *Infancy in Uganda: Infant care and the growth of love*. Baltimore: Johns Hopkins Press, 1967.

Ainsworth, M. D. S. Object relations, dependency, and attachment: A theoretical review of the infant-mother relationship. *Child Development*, 1969, **40**, 969-1025.

Ainsworth, M. D. S., & Bell, S. M. Attachment, exploration, and separation: Illustrated by the behavior of one-year-olds in a strange situation. *Child Development*, 1970, **41**, 49-67.

Ainsworth, M. D. S., & Wittig, B. A. Attachment and exploratory behavior of one-year-olds in a strange situation. In B. M. Foss (Ed.), *Determinants of infant behaviour IV*. London: Methuen, 1969. Pp. 111-136.

Ambrose, J. A. The development of the smiling response in early infancy. In B. M. Foss (Ed.), *Determinants of infant behaviour*. London: Methuen (New York: Wiley), 1961. Pp. 179-201.

Bayley, N. A study of the crying of infants during mental and physical tests. *Journal of Genetic Psychology*, 1932, **40**, 306-329.

Bayley, N. *The California first-year mental scale*. Syllabus Series, No. 243. Berkeley: University of California Press, 1933.

Bayley, N. *The Bayley scales of infant development*. New York: Psychological Corp., 1969.

Bell, S. M. The development of the concept of object as related to infant-mother attachment. *Child Development*, 1970, **41**, 291-311.

Beller, E. K. Dependency and independence in young children. Unpublished doctoral dissertation, State University of Iowa, 1948.

Beller, E. K. Dependency and independence in young children. *Journal of Genetic Psychology*, 1955, **87**, 25-35.

Beller, E. K. Exploratory studies of dependency. *Transactions of the New York Academy of*

Sciences, 1959, **21**, 414-426.

Bowlby, J. The nature of the child's tie to his mother. *International Journal of Psychoanalysis*, 1958, **39**, 1-34.

Bowlby, J. Ethology and the development of object relations. *International Journal of Psychoanalysis*, 1960, **41**, 313-317.(a)

Bowlby, J. Separation anxiety. *International Journal of Psychoanalysis*, 1960, **41**, 80-113.(b)

Bowlby, J. *Attachment and loss*. Vol. 1. *Attachment*. London: Hogarth (New York: Basic Books), 1969.

Brackbill, Y. Extinction of the smiling response in infants as a function of reinforcement schedule. *Child Development*, 1958, **29**, 115-124.

Bühler, C. *The first year of life*. New York: John Day, 1930.

Bühler, C. The social behaviour of children. In C. A. Murchison (Ed.), *Handbook of child psychology*. (2nd ed., rev.) Worcester, Mass.: Clark University Press, 1933. Pp. 347-417.

Cairns, R. B. Attachment behavior of mammals. *Psychological Review*, 1966, **73**, 409-426.

Cairns, R. B. Modification of social preferences in children and young animals. Paper presented at the meeting of the American Psychological Association, San Francisco, September 1968.

Cairns, R. B., & Lewis, M. Dependency and the reinforcement value of a verbal stimulus. *Journal of Consulting Psychology*, 1962, **26**, 1-8.

Caldwell, B. M., Wright, C. M., Honig, A. S., & Tannenbaum, J. Infant day care and attachment. *American Journal of Orthopsychiatry*, 1970, **40**, 397-412.

Cattell, P. *The measurement of intelligence of infants and young children*. New York: Psychological Corp., 1960.

Crowne, D. P., & Marlowe, D. *The motive for approval: Studies in evaluative dependence*. New York: Wiley, 1964.

Crowne, D. P., & Strickland, B. R. The conditioning of verbal behavior as a function of the need for social approval. *Journal of Abnormal and Social Psychology*, 1961, **63**, 395-401.

Eisenberger, R. Is there a deprivation-satiation function for social approval? *Psychological Bulletin*, 1970, **74**, 255-275.

Emmerich, W. Continuity and stability in early social development. *Child Development*, 1964, **35**, 311-332.

Etzel, B. C., & Gewirtz, J. L. Experimental modification of caretaker-maintained high-rate operant crying in a 6- and a 20-week-old infant (*Infans tyrannotearus*): Extinction of crying with reinforcement of eye contact and smiling. *Journal of Experimental Child Psychology*, 1967, **5**, 303-317.

Fleener, D. E., & Cairns, R. B. Attachment behaviors in human infants: Discriminative vocalization on maternal separation. *Developmental Psychology*, 1970, **2**, 215-223.

Gallimore, R., Tharp, R. G., & Kemp, B. Positive reinforcing function of "negative attention." *Journal of Experimental Child Psychology*, 1969, **8**, 140-146.

Gesell, A. *The mental growth of the preschool child*. New York: Macmillan, 1925.

Gesell, A. *Infancy and human growth*. New York: Macmillan, 1928.

Gesell, A., & Amatruda, C. S. *Developmental diagnosis: Normal and abnormal child development, clinical methods and practical applications*. (3rd ed.) New York: Harper, 1962.

Gesell, A., Halverson, H. M., Thompson, H., Ilg, F. L., Castner, B. M., Ames, L. B., & Amatruda, C. S. *The first five years of life: A guide to the study of the preschool child*. New York: Harper, 1940.

Gesell, A., & Thompson, H. *Infant behavior: Its genesis and growth*. New York: McGraw-Hill, 1934.

Gewirtz, H. B., & Gewirtz, J. L. Caretaking settings, background events, and behavior differences in four Israeli child-rearing environments: Some preliminary trends. In B. M.

Foss (Ed.), *Determinants of infant behaviour IV*. London: Methuen, 1969. Pp. 229-252.

Gewirtz, J. L. Succorance in young children. Unpublished doctoral dissertation, State University of Iowa, 1948.

Gewirtz, J. L. Three determinants of attention-seeking in young children. *Monographs of the Society for Research in Child Development*, 1954, **19** (2, Serial No. 59).

Gewirtz, J. L. A factor analysis of some attention-seeking behaviors of young children. *Child Development*, 1956, **27**, 17-37.(a)

Gewirtz, J. L. A program of research on the dimensions and antecedents of emotional dependence. *Child Development*, 1956, **27**, 205-221.(b)

Gewirtz, J. L. A learning analysis of the effects of normal stimulation, privation and deprivation on the acquisition of social motivation and attachment. In B. M. Foss (Ed.), *Determinants of infant behaviour*. London: Methuen (New York: Wiley), 1961. Pp. 213-299.

Gewirtz, J. L. The course of infant smiling in four child-rearing environments in Israel. In B. M. Foss (Ed.), *Determinants of infant behaviour III*. London: Methuen (New York: Wiley), 1965. Pp. 205-260.

Gewirtz, J. L. Deprivation and satiation of social stimuli as determinants of their reinforcing efficacy. In J. P. Hill (Ed.), *Minnesota symposia on child psychology*. Vol. 1. Minneapolis: University of Minnesota Press, 1967. Pp. 3-56.

Gewirtz, J. L. The role of stimulation in models for child development. In L. L. Dittmann (Ed.), *Early child care: The new perspectives*. New York: Atherton, 1968. Pp. 139-168.

Gewirtz, J. L. Levels of conceptual analysis in environment-infant interaction research. *Merrill-Palmer Quarterly*, 1969, **15**, 7-47.(a)

Gewirtz, J. L. Mechanisms of social learning: Some roles of stimulation and behavior in early human development. In D. A. Goslin (Ed.), *Handbook of socialization theory and research*. Chicago: Rand McNally, 1969. Pp. 57-212.(b)

Gewirtz, J. L. Potency of a social reinforcer as a function of satiation and recovery. *Developmental Psychology*, 1969, **1**, 2-13.(c)

Gewirtz, J. L. Stimulation, learning, and motivation principles for day-care settings. In E. H. Grotberg (Ed.), *Day care: Resources for decisions*. (OEO Pamphlet 6106-1) Washington, D. C.: U. S. Office of Economic Opportunity, June 1971. Pp. 173-226.

Gewirtz, J. L. Attachment and dependence: Some strategies and tactics in the selection and use of indices for those concepts. In T. M. Alloway, L. Krames, & P. Pliner (Eds.), *Communication and affect*. New York: Academic Press, 1972. Pp. 19-49. (a)

Gewirtz, J. L. Some contextual determinants of stimulus potency. In R. D. Parke (Ed.), *Recent trends in social learning theory*. New York: Academic Press, 1972. Pp. 7-33.(b)

Gewirtz, J. L., & Baer, D. M. The effect of brief social deprivation on behaviors for a social reinforcer. *Journal of Abnormal and Social Psychology*, 1958, **56**, 49-56.

Gewirtz, J. L., & Gewirtz, H. B. Stimulus conditions, infant behaviors, and social learning in four Israeli child-rearing environments: A preliminary report illustrating differences in environment and behavior between the "Only" and the "Youngest" child. In B. M. Foss (Ed.), *Determinants of infant behaviour III*. London: Methuen (New York: Wiley), 1965. Pp. 161-184.

Gewirtz, J. L., & Stingle, K. G. Learning of generalized imitation as the basis for identification. *Psychological Review*, 1968, **75**, 374-397.

Gilliland, A. R. *The Northwestern Intelligence Tests. Examiner's manual. Test A: Test for infants 4-12 weeks old*. Boston: Houghton Mifflin, 1949.

Gilliland, A. R. *The Northwestern Intelligence Tests. Examiner's manual. Test B: Test for infants 13-36 weeks old*. Boston: Houghton Mifflin, 1951.

Griffiths, R. *The abilities of babies: A study in mental measurement*. New York: McGraw-Hill, 1954.

Harlow, H. F., & Zimmermann, R. R. Affectional responses in the infant monkey. *Science*, 1959, **130**, 421-432.

Hartup, W. W. Dependence and independence. In H. W. Stevenson (Ed.), *Child psychology: The sixty-second yearbook of the National Society for Study of Education. Part I.* Chicago: University of Chicago Press, 1963. Pp. 333-363.

Heathers, G. Emotional dependence and independence in nursery school play. *Journal of Genetic Psychology,* 1955, **87**, 37-57.

Landau, R., & Gewirtz, J. L. Differential satiation for a social reinforcing stimulus as a determinant of its efficacy in conditioning. *Journal of Experimental Child Psychology,* 1967, **5**, 391-405.

Levy, D. M. The infant's memory of inoculations: A contribution to public health procedures. *Journal of Genetic Psychology,* 1960, **96**, 3-46.

Maccoby, E. E., & Masters, J. C. Attachment and dependency. In P. H. Mussen (Ed.), *Carmichael's manual of child psychology.* (3rd ed.) Vol. 2. New York: Wiley, 1970. Pp. 73-158.

Mason, W. A. Motivational factors in psychosocial development. *Nebraska Symposium on Motivation,* 1970, **18**, 35-67.

Rheingold, H. L. The effect of a strange environment on the behavior of infants. In B. M. Foss (Ed.), *Determinants of infant behaviour IV.* London: Methuen, 1969. Pp. 137-166.

Rheingold, H. L., Gewirtz, J. L., & Ross, H. W. Social conditioning of vocalizations in the infant. *Journal of Comparative and Physiological Psychology,* 1959, **52**, 68-73.

Rosenthal, M. K. Effects of a novel situation and of anxiety on two groups of dependency behaviours. *British Journal of Psychology,* 1967, **58**, 357-364.

Sackett, G. P. Innate mechanisms, differential rearing experiences, and the development of social attachments by rhesus monkeys. Paper presented at the meeting of the American Psychological Association, San Francisco, September 1968.

Sackett, G. P. Unlearned responses, differential rearing experiences, and the development of social attachments by rhesus monkeys. In L. A. Rosenblum (Ed.), *Primate behavior: Developments in field and laboratory research.* Vol. 1. New York: Academic Press, 1970. Pp. 111-140.

Schaffer, H. R., & Emerson, P. E. The development of social attachments in infancy. *Monographs of the Society for Research in Child Development,* 1964, **29** (3, Serial No. 94).

Sears, R. R. Dependency motivation. *Nebraska Symposium on Motivation,* 1963, **11**, 25-65.

Sears, R. R., Rau, L., & Alpert, R. *Identification and child rearing.* Stanford, Calif.: Stanford University Press, 1965.

Sears, R. R., Whiting, J. W. M., Nowlis, V., & Sears, P. S., in collaboration with E. K. Beller, J. C. Cohen, E. H. Chasdi, H. Faigin, J. L. Gewirtz, M. S. Lawrence, & J. P. McKee. Some child-rearing antecedents of aggression and dependency in young children. *Genetic Psychology Monographs,* 1953, **47**, 135-234.

Shirley, M. M. *The first two years: A study of twenty-five babies.* Vol. 3. *Personality manifestations.* Minneapolis: University of Minnesota Press, 1933.

Skinner, B. F. *Science and human behavior.* New York: Macmillan, 1953.

Spitz, R. A., & Wolf, K. M. The smiling response: A contribution to the ontogenesis of social relations. *Genetic Psychology Monographs,* 1946, **34**, 57-125.

Wahler, R. G. Infant social attachments: A reinforcement theory interpretation and investigation. *Child Development,* 1967, **38**, 1079-1088.

Washburn, R. W. A study of the smiling and laughing of infants in the first year of life. *Genetic Psychology Monographs,* 1929, **6**, 397-535.

Weisberg, P. Social and non-social conditioning of infant vocalizations. *Child Development,* 1963, **34**, 377-388.

Yarrow, L. J. The development of focused relationships during infancy. In J. Hellmuth (Ed.), *Exceptional infant: The normal infant.* Vol. 1. Seattle, Wash.: Special Child Publications, 1967. Pp. 429-442.

Yarrow, M. R., Campbell, J. D., & Burton R. V. *Child-rearing: An inquiry into research and methods.* San Francisco: Jossey-Bass, 1968.

SUMMARY OF ISSUES IN THE ATTACHMENT-DEPENDENCY AREA[1]

Overview

The chapters of this volume indicate that the theoretical and empirical work on the origins of interpersonal relationships carried out under the aegis of the dual concepts of *attachment* and *dependency* involve a number of issues of theory and method. Some of these issues are continuing ones for which only arbitrary solutions can be given at present. For other issues, there may be a consensus on positions that can be put forth as working solutions. The purpose of this summary chapter (and, indeed, of each of the preceding chapters) is thus not to resolve the points at issue. It is rather to enumerate them and to highlight their relevance in the conceptualization of object relations that is under discussion. The preceding chapters illustrate that, in this area of study, a wide range of positions can be, and have been, entertained with respect to these theoretical and methodological issues. At the same time, the various views expressed by the contributing authors are not necessarily inconsistent with one another. In fact, the approaches often seem to differ more in style or emphasis than in substantive matters or predicted outcomes.

In a discussion of any concept, the first concern is the way in which that concept (and the phenomena ordered by it) is to be approached. This book contains a wide range of conceptualizations of attachment and dependency. These include the following:

1. A conception of an underlying attachment structure that is distinct from attachment behaviors, with the utility of a dependency concept seen as minimal (Ainsworth).

[1]This summary chapter was prepared by the Editor and R. B. Cairns. M. D. S. Ainsworth, R. R. Sears, and L. J. Yarrow have each contributed suggestions to improve this chapter.

2. A postulation of a cluster of actions representative of the help- and attention-seeking higher level construct of dependency, with attachment seen as involving a different process and an emotional concomitant termed "passion" (Sears).

3. A proposal that both the attachment and dependency terms are useful in pointing toward differences among children in interpersonal orientation, but that each term refers to multiple mechanisms which account for these behavioral differences (Cairns).

4. The conception that both attachment and dependency are mere abstractions which, for most purposes, might better be reduced to a delineation of the functional relations between stimuli and responses that they summarize (Gewirtz).

5. The similar conception that the two terms may represent only specific aspects of social development and relationships whose meanings change at different levels of development (Yarrow).

A second issue raised is the manner of *distinguishing* the attachment term from the dependency term. This has been done in various ways and on diverse bases. Specifically, one position is that the phenomena organized by the two concepts may be conceived as operating under the same set of principles (Gewirtz). A second position is that the phenomena subsumed by the two concepts may differ qualitatively and operate according to different principles (Ainsworth, Sears). And a third position conceives that there may be considerable overlap in the mechanisms involved. This position (and all the others) emphasizes that the processes governing social interactions would change with the developmental age of the individual (Cairns, Yarrow). Thus, the theorists differ in their conceptions of the processes underlying attachment and dependency, and seemingly even on the definitions of those terms.

The contributors also differ in their approaches to the *level or mode of analysis* selected to investigate the two concepts of attachment and dependency. Of particular concern here is the level and type of summarizing concept used. There is a consensus that these should be closely related to an investigator's theoretical conceptualization. All contributors to this volume also agree that the level of analysis must be made explicit, and that the sequential flow of events comprising the dyadic interaction of caretaker and child must be the focus of examination. However, the contributors tend to disagree on both the proper level of detail of this examination and the types of indices and summarizing terms that should be used. Thus, Cairns and Gewirtz emphasize the tactical importance of specifying interaction in terms of functional relationships between stimuli and responses; and Gewirtz would introduce summarizing concepts only to organize the already specified details of the sequential flow of the interaction. In contrast, Ainsworth and Sears conceive that such analyses may be too detailed for many reasonable questions. They therefore suggest that interaction details should be indexed and examined in terms of larger analytic units, including global summarizing concepts.

How closely the theoretical concepts must be *tied to operational definitions* is related to this concern with the level or mode of analysis and the use of summarizing concepts. Also related is the question of the utility of concepts that are not closely tied to operations. In this connection, the contributors present varying positions regarding the relevance of postulations that emphasize: genotypic factors, underlying biological structural bases, and the evolutionary role of behaviors (especially with regard to attachment). In this same context, Ainsworth and Cairns imply concepts at this level in their treatments, whereas Gewirtz takes exception to the use of such concepts when they serve neither an independent operational nor a differential role in a theoretical approach. The contributors also vary in the heuristic preferences exemplified in their theoretical approaches to attachment and dependency. In particular, they differ on whether they prefer concepts with a clinical, intrapsychic flavor (especially Ainsworth) or concepts with a behavioral flavor (especially Cairns and Gewirtz). But all contributors call for the use of clearly specified definitions.

Best discussed concomitantly with these issues is the *level of abstraction* of the behaviors selected to index attachment or dependence. The theorists take positions on this issue that tie in with their views about the appropriate level of concept to use. Even so, all contributors agree that the relevance and meaning of a behavior will depend on the given stimulus context in which it occurs. Therefore, response content and environmental context must both be specified. As a corollary, Cairns and Gewirtz also conceive that the identification of the environmental conditions that precede, accompany, and/or follow a behavioral indicator can be more important than the choice of particular indices. In this connection, Gewirtz also notes that, no matter how one sees environment-behavior functions, such functions may be generic and, therefore, at the same time relevant to various other psychological issues or concepts. In a parallel vein, Yarrow in particular emphasizes a continuity between, and interdependence of, the child's cognitive behavior capacities and attachment-dependency behavior patterns.

Several contributors have raised the issue of how concomitant *emotional states* ("affect," "love," "passion") may be involved with the behavior systems connoting attachment or dependency. Ainsworth and Sears conceive that an intense emotional involvement is a fundamental feature of attachment and a critical basis for distinguishing attachment from dependency. Gewirtz, on the other hand, sees no utility in conceiving of emotional states in the abstract, if they are not operationalized (e.g., in terms of stimuli and responses). Despite these differences, however, all five theoretical approaches remain open to the possibility that emotional-state variables may be involved in the social-relationship patterns termed attachment or dependency. However, this possibility raises certain tactical questions (for Gerwirtz in particular). For instance, is it useful to emphasize emotional states like these at this point in our knowledge of the phenomena ordered by the attachment and dependency concepts? More important still, is it useful to emphasize such states at all if their postulation does not provide increased leverage on the relevant patterns of social stimulus control over behavior?

The theoretical approaches to attachment and dependency indicate or imply that the behavioral phenomena those terms encompass can be organized *throughout the life span* of the individual. However, research carried out under those headings has often seemed limited to particular groups or to particular time segments of development. For example, infants and children in the nursery-school years have been the typical research subjects. The contributors therefore think it important to include an explicit statement of the age range, as well as of the gender and other sampling bases, of the organisms whose behaviors are described or indexed. They do not limit this requirement to descriptions of the developmental course of attachment or dependency in children (such as Ainsworth, Sears, and Yarrow provide).

In psychological research, the implications of *chronological age* per se are recognized to be vague. By its nature, chronological age is a crude measure that can only imply grossly some as-yet-not-well-defined concept of overall developmental level. Nevertheless, most of the contributors to this volume think chronological age may conceivably be useful as a qualifying factor for conclusions that can be drawn from developmental studies of particular behavior systems. In this context, all the theoretical approaches either emphasize or are open to the requirement that one take explicit account of changes in levels of functioning of sensory-effector systems, discriminative abilities, and behavior-system topography at sequential points and in widely separated phases of the life cycle.

The issues discussed so far also involve determining the necessary conditions for, and the processes involved in, the *acquisition* of attachment and of dependence. The theorists who approach this topic in detail from a learning orientation are Cairns, Gewirtz, and Sears. All three would agree that a learning analysis must take account of changes in the learner's sensory-effector capacities and capabilities, in which context learning occurs. That is, they conceive that the type and form of social behavior patterns change with development. However, in their view the principles governing the acquisition of interaction patterns connoting attachment and dependency remain constant. Moreover, while these theorists might differ on some assumptions about the learning process, in the paradigms they use, or in the language they prefer for describing learning, they would agree that such distinctions are not the critical ones for distinguishing among their approaches to attachment and dependency.

The contributors to this volume would agree that the key to understanding the acquisition of attachment or dependency lies in the interaction between the factors termed *learning* and those termed *maturation*. In the most general sense, learning is conceived to involve orderly changes in behavior brought about by recurring, systematic experience with environmental stimuli (with behavioral capacity development held constant); and maturation is conceived to involve orderly, sequential changes in the behavioral capacities of the organism (with systematic experience held constant). The emphasis on the interaction between maturation and learning may seem obvious. However, discussions of attachment and dependency often pose the problem of how to combine behavior theory with biological theory. In part, this may be because theorists who have approached the topic mainly from one orientation have often failed to discuss the other in any detail, even when they would recognize the relevance of both approaches.

Let us now turn to more detailed comparisons of the five conceptual treatments of attachment and dependency.

Specific Positions

DEVELOPMENTAL-BIOPHYSICAL FACTORS

It has been noted that none of the statements deny the importance of developmental and biophysical factors in attachment and dependency behavior systems. However, the features of organismic control attributed to these factors by the theorists differ.

Ainsworth's theoretical statement appeals to an underlying biogenic system to account for the timing of the onset of attachment phenomena and for the activation and cessation of the response system once it has become established in ontogeny. She also conceives that evolutionary-genetic biases heighten the probability that preferences will form with respect to particular environmental objects. Ainsworth assigns considerable weight to these factors in the control of object-choice. The locus of these biasing factors (for example, the sensory-receptor network or the central nervous system) and the means by which they enter to determine behavior remain to be specified by Ainsworth.

Sears, Yarrow, and Cairns are also concerned with behavior changes associated with age. (Cairns emphasizes biophysical factors in addition.) These three theorists differ, however, in the features to which they give primary attention. Because such functions have not heretofore played prominent roles in social-learning theories, Sears' focus on them may be particularly noteworthy. It is not that social-learning analyses have disregarded the biology of the organism. Rather, social-learning theorists have typically assumed that they might proceed most fruitfully by focusing on those experiential variables that are susceptible to immediate observation and/or control. In his statement on attachment, Sears sees the maturational level of the individual child (as indexed by chronological age) as a primary factor in the timing of stages of social development and of object-choice. He views intermediate- or between-stage attachment behavior that occurs intermittently as preparation for the subsequent establishment of a primary attachment.

Emphasizing behavior changes with age, Yarrow provides an account of the course and nature of the child's social development. He is concerned with behaviors that are typically assigned to the construct of attachment or object relationship. Yarrow conceives of an interdependence between the development of social behaviors and cognitive capacities, such that social development is paced by the development of the child's discriminative and cognitive abilities. In this volume, Yarrow limits his statements to a consideration of the early social processes and the events that control those processes.

Cairns' statement about attachment behavior deals principally with the young animal and child, and with the varied contributions to it of the biology of the organisms involved in the interaction. His distinctive focus is a concern with the specific ways in which biophysical influences elicit and maintain social relationships. This is in contrast with a focus on biophysical factors as simply preparatory for the interaction. Cairns' emphasis is in harmony with the basic theme proposed by Sears and Ainsworth. The latter two emphasize that developmental events pace the nature and type of interactions that evolve, by indicating the ways in which the changes in the biophysical status of both members of the relationship are involved in the pacing operation. Cairns' concern with specifying how sensory-effector changes determine the kinds of social responses that occur in animals is parallel to Yarrow's emphasis on the role of cognitive development in the child. It is compatible as well with Gewirtz' account of receptor-effector capacities as qualifiers of behavior and learning. In Cairns' view, social-learning models have failed to give explicit attention to psychobiological events. This is a major basis for his judgment that they are deficient in accounting for long-term stability and change.

Of the statements in this volume concerning biological contributions to maturation, that of Gewirtz is perhaps the most discrepant. His emphasis is (in E. C. Tolman's sense) entirely on molar behavior and environmental stimulation. Gewirtz is receptively open to the operation of child behavior system determinants that are residually termed "maturational" (i.e., not simple or obvious outcomes of experience-learning), and thus assumes that relevant receptor-effector capacities will qualify the impact of stimulation on behavior. This assumption would not differ markedly from the other contributors' emphases on "developmental level." At the same time, however, he conceives that chronological age is but a poor and often misleading index of process (that is, of the opportunities for systematic environmental stimulation to have a monotonic impact on behavior outcomes). Gewirtz assumes further that theory and research about biological-substrate factors have their place. But he considers that speculation about such factors is clearly orthogonal to, and thus essentially irrelevant for, molar-behavior approaches like all of those in this volume. Further, he questions the relative efficiency of theories whose concepts cross levels of conceptual analysis. Finally, Gewirtz argues that it can be most inefficient and confusing to implicate biological, genetic, emotional, or cognitive factors in an analysis unless one makes explicit directional assumptions about how these factors determine the behavioral outcomes that are of interest.

EXPERIENTIAL DETERMINANTS OF
DYADIC INTERACTIONS

The five theoretical statements also differ in the attention each gives to the explication of learning-experiential factors in the development of attachment behaviors. Once again, the theorists differ in emphasis, but none deny the relevance of experiential factors.   Gewirtz and Cairns both assume that attachment and dependency patterns are appropriately denoted by their component interaction sequences. Each tries in his way to provide a detailed heuristic account of the events that underlie the formation and dissolution of particular dyadic sequence patterns. They concentrate their analyses on reciprocal interaction sequences in which mother and child each provide cue and/or reinforcing stimuli for the other's behaviors.

To some degree, each chapter is concerned with an analysis of the ways in which experience can modify dyadic interaction patterns. (On this matter, several of the papers owe a debt to Sears' 1951 statement of the need for a detailed dyadic focus in analyses of social development.) Though they have disparate origins, the conceptual emphases and research strategies of the contributors have evoled from converging trends in behavioral analysis. These trends include the sequential chaining features of operant conditioning analyses, the naturalistic-descriptive techniques of child ecological research and of comparative psychology, and the detailed accounts by ethologists of behaviors in dyads.

The statements in this volume also recognize the potential gains that can be made by detailed analysis of the events that control specific interaction sequences. There is appropriate recognition of the fact that experiential factors play a prominent role in object choice. However, in contrast to some contributors' concern with individual dyadic sequences, Sears indicates that one should not too readily ignore the coherence of attachment responses, or denigrate the utility of larger units of analysis. He conceives that losses in the specificity of the analysis may be compensated for by gains in its generality.

In summarizing the role of learning-experientail factors, the theorists generally agree that an adequate account of attachment behaviors must be concerned with the specific issues of (a) how object preferences are acquired and (b) how dyadic sequences develop and are maintained. The contributors appear about evenly divided on the actual or potential merits of possible analytic strategies. Three contributors propose that a direct analysis of the stimuli and responses comprising interaction sequences and of the conditions of their formation could be sufficient. In contrast, Sears and Ainsworth believe that experiential factors can be studied with at least equal success at more complex levels of conceptual organization. The concepts favored by Sears are behavioral; those favored by Ainsworth are cognitive and evolutionary. As noted earlier, there is an emphasis in the papers which emphasize learning that may represent a broadening of the conception of learning in social development: any analysis of what is learned must take into account changes in the capacities of the learner.

ATTACHMENT AND DEPENDENCY: DISTINCT OR INTERDEPENDENT RESPONSE SYSTEMS

A principal question raised in the discussion is about the relationship between the phenomena of attachment and the phenomena subsumed by dependency, a more "traditional" concept of developmental psychology. Sears emphasizes that distinct behavior systems are involved. A primary basis for his differentiating the two behavior systems is the intensity of affective emotional involvement that he assumes accompanies attachment behaviors but not dependency behaviors. However, Sears assumes that there are other dimensions, besides affective involvement, along which attachment behaviors can be differentiated from dependency behaviors: (*a*) the extent to which the behaviors are linked to a genetic substrate; (*b*) the manner in which the behaviors are paced directly by the individual's maturational level; and (*c*) the behavioral effects of frustration and deprivation.

Sears sees ample grounds for retaining both the attachment and dependency concepts. On the other hand, Ainsworth implies that the primary explanatory functions of the dependency concept have been replaced by the attachment concept. Therefore, she does not see the continuing utility of a dependency concept. From very different vantages, Gerwirtz and Yarrow question whether, for many conceptual purposes, the attachment and dependency terms are necessary at all. This is in a context where each sees the reference behavior systems of attachment and dependency as better reduced to component dyadic sequences. These two theorists assume that the form and type of social behavior patterns clearly change over time. But they conceive that the principles which govern the development of dyadic sequences do not change. Hence, they believe it could prove inefficient and even misleading to use the two concepts for other than limited descriptive purposes, and they would limit the use of the terms to the labeling of groupings of funcitonal relations. In a very similar vein, Cairns tolerates the attachment and dependency concepts for descriptive and organizational purposes, but not for the strategy of explanation. He notes that these concepts have traditionally referred to distinct behavior patterns. They have evolved from different orientations, assessment devices, and types of observations. The basic developmental issue for Cairns is whether or not attachment behaviors are precursors of subsequent dependency behaviors of the child. He questions how a dyadic response that is acquired at one age-maturational level can provide the substrate for a social response pattern that appears later. Finally, he holds that detailed analysis of the multiple determinants of the component behavior sequences and their concomitant emotional states can be productive, regardless of the ultimate fate of the attachment and dependency constructs.

A dominant theme throughout this volume is the concern with how developmental factors (and, for some, biophysical events also) contribute to, and direct, systematic changes in social behavior. In this frame, every contributor places the essential focus for analysis on the interaction between experimental and developmental determinants of caretaker-child interchanges.

Recapitulation

This summary chapter has only touched on the most salient issues raised by the treatments of attachment and dependency in this volume. Each of the five contributing theorists has tried to clarify his position on these issues in his paper. However, none conceived of presenting a definitive solution to any of the issues raised. Rather, each has presented what he considers to be the most plausible and efficient heuristic interpretation of the available evidence on attachment and dependency, in terms of the theoretical concepts that he favors. At the same time, each theorist has recognized that there are alternative conceptualizations of the phenomena. Indeed, the contributors have recognized that their positions, although diverse, are not incompatible in principle, and that each position will surely have to be modified further to reconcile evidence from future research. Each theoretical position could therefore be viewed as open, receptive, and potentially responsive to new developments in theory and research—perhaps even as catalytic for such developments.

ATTACHMENT
AND
DEPENDENCY

AUTHOR INDEX

Numbers in italics refer to the pages on which the complete references are listed.

SUBJECT INDEX

A

Acquired drive, *See* Secondary drive
Action theory, 1
Active differentiation, 162
    ambivalent approach/withdrawal to/from
      strangers, with negative affect, as pre-
      cursors of stranger anxiety, 89-90
    See also Stranger anxiety
Active recognition, 162
Activity-passivity, 121
Admiration, seeking of, 12,13
    and achievement motivation, 13
    and availability of a love object, 21
    as a higher level construct, 12
    See also Indices of dependency
Affect, 163-166,
    and attachment, 101-102, 143, 224
    and dependency, 143
    See also Emotional state, Passion
"Affectionate" behaviors, as attachment in-
    dices
    embracing, 113, 181
    hugging, 113, 181
    kissing, 113, 181
    See also Indices of attachment
Age, chronological, 220
    and attachment indices, 115
    and attachment onset, 14, 18, 113

Age, chronological, *(Cont'd.)*
    and dependency, 23-24
    differences, 11-12
    and maturational level, 221-222
    and reinforcement, 11
    and separation anxiety, 14
    and stimulation, 11
    as a poor variable in developmental anal-
      ysis, 169-188
    norms for diverse attachment/dependen-
      cy response indices, 205-209
Age-related,
    behavior changes, 11, 14, 18, 23-24,
      64-65
    reinforcement, 11
    stimulation, 11
Age, developmental,
    and behavioral capacities, 220
    and changes in receptor-effector appara-
      tus, 58-60, 218, 220, 222
Ambivalence, 119-121
    proximity-avoiding behavior and, 120-
      121
    returning home following separations,
      119
    See also Conflict
Analysis, levels of, 218, 223
    and higher-level concepts, 8
    See also Behavioral analysis

235